Lecture Notes in Computer Science 9055

Commenced Publication in 1973
Founding and Former Series Editors:
Gerhard Goos, Juris Hartmanis, and Jan van Leeuwen

More information about this series at http://www.springer.com/series/7409

Jan Hodicky (Ed.)

Modelling and Simulation for Autonomous Systems

Second International Workshop, MESAS 2015
Prague, Czech Republic, April 29–30, 2015
Revised Selected Papers

 Springer

Editor
Jan Hodicky
NATO Modelling and Simulation Centre
   of Excellence
Rome
Italy

ISSN 0302-9743   ISSN 1611-3349   (electronic)
Lecture Notes in Computer Science
ISBN 978-3-319-22382-7   ISBN 978-3-319-22383-4   (eBook)
DOI 10.1007/978-3-319-22383-4

Library of Congress Control Number: 2015945131

LNCS Sublibrary: SL3 – Information Systems and Applications, incl. Internet/Web, and HCI

Springer Cham Heidelberg New York Dordrecht London

Printed on acid-free paper

Springer International Publishing AG Switzerland is part of Springer Science+Business Media
(www.springer.com)

Preface

This volume contains the papers presented at the MESAS Workshop 2015: Modelling and Simulation for Autonomous Systems, held during April 29–30, 2015, in Prague. MESAS 2015 was a two-day workshop organized by the NATO Modelling and Simulation Centre of Excellence. The event gathered together — in opening, regular, and way ahead sessions — fully recognized experts from different technical communities in military, academia, and industry. The aim of the conference was to explore the role of modelling and simulation in the development of systems with autonomous capabilities and in its operationalization to support coalition interoperability. The community of interest submitted 33 papers for consideration. Each submission was reviewed by two Program Committee members. The committee decided to accept 22 papers to be presented during the workshop. The plenary session and way ahead panel discussions included an extra six invited presentations. Following a thorough review process, only 18 papers were accepted to be included in the proceedings.

June 2015

Jan Hodicky

MESAS 2015 Program Committee

Technical Chair

Vaclav Hlavac   Czech Technical University in Prague, Czech Republic

Members

Gianluca Antonelli   University of Cassino and Southern Lazio, Italy
Agostino Bruzzone   DIME University of Genoa, Italy
Andrea Caiti   University of Pisa, Italy
Alessandro Cignoni   Centre for Maritime and Technology Organization, Italy
Andrea D'Ambrogio   University of Rome Tor Vergata, Italy
Jan Hodicky   NATO Modelling and Simulation Centre of Excellence, Italy
Jan Mazal   University of Defence in Brno, Czech Republic
Lucia Pallottino   Università di Pisa, Italy
Libor Preucil   Czech Technical University in Prague, Czech Republic
Petr Novak   Technical University of Ostrava, Czech Republic
Stefan Pickl   Universität der Bundeswehr, Munich, Germany
Andreas Tolk   SimIS Inc. / Old Dominion University in Norfolk, USA
Alexandr Stefek   University of Defence in Brno, Czech Republic
Richard Stansbury   Embry-Riddle Aeronautical University in Daytona Beach,
                         USA

Logo

MESAS 2015 Organizer

NATO MODELLING AND SIMULATION CENTRE OF EXCELLENCE (NATO M&S COE)

The NATO M&S COE is a recognized international military organization activated by the North Atlantic Council in 2012, and does not fall under the NATO Command Structure. Partnering Nations provide funding and personnel for the Centre through a memorandum of understanding the Czech Republic, Italy, and the USA are the contributing nations, as of this publication.

The NATO M&S COE supports NATO Transformation by improving the networking of NATO and nationally owned M&S systems, promoting cooperation between Nations and organisations through the sharing of M&S information and serving as an international source of expertise.

The NATO M&S COE seeks to be a leading world-class organization, providing the best military expertise in modelling and simulation technology, methodologies, and the development of M&S professionals. Its state of the art facilities can support a wide range of M&S activities including but not limited to: Education and Training of NATO M&S professionals on M&S concepts and technology with hands-on courses that expose students to the latest simulation software currently used across the alliance; Concept Development and Experimentation using a wide array of software capability and network connections to test and evaluate military doctrinal concepts as well as new simulation interoperability verification; and the same network connectivity will enable the COE to become the focal point for NATO's future Distributed Simulation environment.

https://www.mscoe.org/

MESAS 2015 Event Director

Stefano Nicolo', NATO M&S COE Director

MESAS 2015 Deputy Event Director

John Ferrell, NATO M&S COE Deputy Director

MESAS 2015 Event Manager

Jan Hodicky, Doctrine Education and Training Branch Chief in the NATO M&S COE

MESAS 2015 Organizing Committee

Corrado Cacciatori – NATO M&S COE
Tiziana Cartechini – NATO M&S COE
Carmine Di Blasi – NATO M&S COE
Paolo Proietti – MIMOS

MESAS 2015 Technical Sponsors

MESAS 2015 Commercial Sponsors

Contents

Methods and Algorithms for AS

State of the Art and Future of AS

Developing an Ontology for Autonomous Entities in a Virtual Reality: The PRESTO Experience

Paolo Busetta[1]([✉]), Mauro Fruet[1], Piero Consolati[1],
Mauro Dragoni[2], and Chiara Ghidini[2]

[1] Delta Informatica, Trento, Italy
{paolo.busetta,mauro.fruet,piero.consolati}@deltainformatica.eu
[2] FBK–IRST, Trento, Italy
{dragoni,ghidini}@fbk.eu

Abstract. The PRESTO project focuses on modeling the behaviour of humans and rational entities in general (e.g. animals, vehicles with a human driver), specifically to represent decision making driven by norms or doctrine as well as culture and emotional factors. PRESTO's models are used to drive NPCs (Non-Player Characters) in serious games, currently applied to emergency management and training in health environments (hospitals and such) even if the technology is not domain- nor game-specific.

A number of requirements have led to the adoption of ontologies as the main classification and annotation mechanism of both the external world and the internal states of an NPC. Structuring and building these ontologies have been done by adopting a mixed top-down and bottom-up approach. The main results are (1) a top-level ontology inspired by the well-known DOLCE; (2) the structuring of the ontologies in composable domain-specific and individual sections; (3) a tool for the semi-automatic extraction of categories from the available virtual reality assets.

This paper focuses on the ontology design, illustrated with a few practical examples.

Keywords: Virtual reality · Serious games · Ontologies

1 Introduction

Serious games with 3D interfaces are a branch of VR systems often used for the training of military personnel and, more recently, for the training of civilian professionals (firefighters, medical personnel, etc.) in emergency situations. Commonly used systems include VBS3 by Bohemia Interactive[1] and XVR by E-semble[2].

---

[1] https://www.bisimulations.com/.

[2] http://www.xvrsim.com.

© Springer International Publishing Switzerland 2015
J. Hodicky (Ed.): MESAS 2015, LNCS 9055, pp. 3–16, 2015.
DOI: 10.1007/978-3-319-22383-4_1

A crucial step towards the adoption of VR for training is the ability to configure scenarios for a specific training session at reduced costs and complexity. State of the art technologies typically enable the user to specify physical landscapes, physical phenomena, and crowds (including their behaviours). Trainers and system integrators can assemble and customize serious game products for a specific scenario using commercial products and libraries that need to be (easily) adapted to the specific landscapes and needs of the clients.

Not so advanced is the technology for enriching the scenarios with non-player characters (NPCs), that is, those characters (people, animals, vehicles, small teams, and so on) directly involved in game playing in collaboration with (or in opposition to) human players, but whose behaviour is entirely animated in an artificial manner. Here the problem is (at least) twofold. A first problem is the lack of configuration environments for trainers and system integrators to complement the "physical landscape" with descriptions of the non-player characters at a high-level, ideally in a way suitable to a non-programmer. As an example, such an environment would allow the configuration of a scenario for fire emergency training in a hospital ward that contains, in addition to the physical reconstruction of the ward building and of the fire, a set of non-player characters composed of three nurses, of which one expert and two novices, one doctor from another ward who is not familiar with the safety procedures of the ward, and eight patients among which a child and a blind patient; the configuration should specify the physiological and psychological characteristics of these NPCs and what is expected from them while a game session unfolds. A second problem is the lack of algorithms for the generation / selection of realistic and plausible behaviours for non-player characters, able to adapt themselves to the evolution of the game. Currently, the programming of NPCs mostly relies on ad hoc specifications / implementations of their behaviours done by game developers. Thus, a specific behaviour (e.g., a function emulating a panicking reaction) is hardwired to a specific item (e.g., the element "Caucasian_boy_17" in XVR) directly in the code. This generates a number of problems typical of ad hoc, low level solutions: the solution is scarcely reusable, it often depends on the specific knowledge of the code of a specific developer, and is cumbersome to modify, since every change required by the trainer has to be communicated to the developers and directly implemented in the code in a case by case manner. While this is not perceived as a major issue in entertainment games (but economics and a push for better game experiences are changing this, too), in serious gaming the cost and complexity of ad-hoc development is only partially covered by available budgets. Thus, typical solutions to this problem include, in multi-player games, the recruitment of experts to impersonate characters (such as team mates, enemies, victims, injured people, and so on) or, as in XVR, letting the trainer changing the scenario in real-time by hand.

In this paper, we focus on the experience of using Semantic Web techniques, and in particular lightweight ontologies, for the high level description of the artificial entities (including characters) and their behaviours in gaming in order to uncouple the description of scenarios performed by training specialists by means of end-user tools from the implementation of behavioural models, in charge to software developers. Differently from a number of works in literature that often uses ontologies for a detailed description of the geometrical properties of space and objects, the focus of our work is on the description of the entities of a VR scenario from the cognitive point of views of the trainers and the developers alike, in a way that is semantically well founded and independent of a specific game or scenario [13], and with the goal of fostering clarity, reuse, and mutual understanding [14].

PRESTO is briefly introduced in the next section. Section 3 sketches the approach adopted to build its main ontology. Its result is the shared vocabulary presented in Sect. 4, grounded in the foundational ontology DOLCE, that helps in identifying the basic entities of a VR scenario, together with their mappings to items of a specific VR implementation (such as XVR). Section 5 briefly discusses a part of the ontology that is strictly related to decision-making and coordination, independently of the VR.

2   Overview of PRESTO

PRESTO (Plausible Representation of Emergency Scenarios for Training Operations) [5,6] aims at adding semantics to a virtual environment and modularising the artificial intelligence controlling the behaviours of NPCs. Its main goal is to support a productive end-user development environment directed to trainers building scenarios for serious games (in particular to simulate emergency situations such as road and industrial accidents, fires and so on) and in general to game masters wanting to customize and enrich the human player's experience. The framework for behavioural modeling in PRESTO, called DICE, was inspired by a BDI (Belief-Desire-Intention) [4,15] multi-agent system with cognitive extensions, CoJACK [9,16]. PRESTO offers powerful end-user development tools for defining the parts played by virtual actors (as end user-written behaviours) and the overall session script of a game. PRESTO supports a specific virtual reality, XVR from E-Semble, a well known tool in use for Emergency Management and Training (EMT) in a number of schools and organisations around the world, as well as Unity 3D and, at least in principle, is agnostic with respect to the game engine in use.

PRESTO provides three main mechanisms that enable the reuse and adaptation of behavioural models to different scenarios, games or even game engines: semantic facilities, an interpreter of scripts in DICE, and facilities for game session control.

The semantization of the game environment and of part of the cognitive states of an NPC supports decision-making based on game- and scenario-independent properties. To this end, ontologies are used for the classification of objects and locations, for annotating them with properties and states (called "qualities") that allow abstract reasoning and for the (agent-specific) appraisals of perceptions, in particular to deal with potentially dangerous situations. The use of ontologies in PRESTO has been partially discussed in [8] and will be the focus of the following sections.

The flow of perceptions, the properties of entities, the appraisal values of DICE behavioural models are classified by means of the PRESTO ontologies, thus enabling the development of generic BDI logic (goals, plans and beliefs) independent of the scenario of use. Additionally, DICE provides an interpreter for high-level scripts, called "DICE Parts", written by means of a graphical editor by the end-user (typically a trainer during the preparation of a specific scenario). A DICE Part can invoke multiple goals concurrently, terminate them when specific events happen (including timeouts and perceptions), define reactions to perceptions or to modifications of the internal state of the agent (including appraisals and moderators), change the state of the agents itself, and so on. While the DICE Part language is limited in its expressivity, the cost of producing a part is minuscule with respect to directly programming the underlying BDI logic. An effort is required on developers of behavioural models in BDI logic to provide goal-directed behaviours that are suitable for composition within user-written parts and adaptable to different scenarios thanks to semantic-based reasoning; the PRESTO pilot project and other demonstrators are helping in accumulating experience and defining guidelines.

Finally, PRESTO has an end-user facility to edit and control session-level scripts inspired by interactive books. A session script is composed of a set of scenes connected as a graph. At each scene, goals can be given to NPCs (which may trigger user-written parts), their internal state changed (including emotions) and objects manipulated. The trainer starts a script at the beginning of a training session and advances it by manually navigating the graph of scenes or letting PRESTO choose the next one e.g. when certain events happen or when a timer expires. This allows a large, potentially unlimited number of different sessions to unfold from a single script with no need to reprogram the NPCs once equipped with all required behavioural models and DICE Parts. In the hospital ward example presented earlier, the initial scene would command visitors, patients and nurses to accomplish their routine goals; the script may continue with alternative scenes such as "fire breaking in a patient room" or "fire breaking in a surgical facility", each with different people involved, and then with sequences that may lead e.g. to smoke filling the area and visitors fleeing or an orderly managed situation with the intervention of fire fighters, chosen according to the decisions of the trainer and the events occurring during a session.

3   PRESTO Ontology Design

The development of programming environment for the high level description of artificial entities (including characters) and their behaviours in scenarios of serious games requires the ability to represent a wide range of entities that *exist* in the (artificial) world. The approach taken in PRESTO is to use ontologies to represent this knowledge, in a way that is semantically well specified and independent of a specific game or scenario [13].

The construction of the PRESTO ontology therefore is driven by typical questions that arise when building ontological representations of a domain, that is:

- "What are the entities that exist, or can be said to exist, in a Virtual Reality scenario?"
- "How can such entities be grouped, related within a hierarchy, and subdivided according to similarities and differences?"

Differently from Ontology in philosophy, where these questions are motivated from the need to investigate the nature and essence of being, we have looked at these questions from the pragmatic point of view of computer science, where ontologies and taxonomic representations have been widely proposed and used to provide important conceptual modeling tools for a range of technologies, such as database schemas, knowledge-based systems, and semantic lexicons [14] with the aim of fostering clarity, reuse, and mutual understanding.

A serious problem we had to face in PRESTO was the lack-of/limited-availability of training experts and software developers, and the broad scope of items and behaviours that can occur in an arbitrary scenario of VR, that can range from terrorist attacks in a war zone, to road accidents in a motorway, to a fire alarm in a nuclear plant or hospital and so on. Because of that reason, building everything from the ground up by relying on domain experts and using one of the state of the art ontology engineering methodologies such as METHONTOLOGY [11] was deemed unfeasible. Thus the process followed in PRESTO has been driven by an attempt to: (1) maximize the reuse of already existing knowledge and (2) revise and select this knowledge with the help of experts by means of more traditional ontology engineering approaches such as the one mentioned above. The choice of already existing knowledge has led us to consider the following two sources:

- State of the art foundational ontologies which provide a first ontological characterization of the entities that exist in the (VR) world; and
- The concrete items (such as people, tools, vehicles, and so on) that come with virtual reality environments and can be used to populate scenarios.

Our choices for the PRESTO project were the upper level ontology DOLCE (Descriptive Ontology for Linguistic and Cognitive Engineering) [12], and the classification of elements provided by XVR. DOLCE was chosen as this ontology since, in addition to providing one of the most known upper level ontologies in literature, it is built with a strong cognitive bias, as it takes into account the ontological categories that underlie natural language and human common sense. This cognitive perspective was considered appropriate for the description of an artificial world that needs to be plausible from a human perspective. The decision to use the classification of elements provided by XVR was due to the extensive range of items available in their libraries (approximately one thousand elements describing mainly human characters, vehicles, road related elements, and artifacts like parts of buildings) and the popularity of XVR as virtual reality platform.

The construction of the first version of the ontology of PRESTO was therefore performed by following a middle-out approach, which combined the reuse and adaptation of the conceptual characterization of top-level entities provided by DOLCE and the description of extremely concrete entities provided by the XVR environment. In more detail,

- We performed an analysis and review of the conceptual entities contained in DOLCE-lite [12] together with the Virtual Reality experts (both trainers and developers) and selected the ones referring to concepts than needed to be described in a VR scenario; this analysis has originated the top part of the PRESTO ontology described in Sect. 4.1.
- We performed a similar analysis and review of the XVR items, together with their classifications, in order to select general concepts (e.g., vehicle, building, and so on) that refer to general VR scenarios; this analysis has originated the middle part of the PRESTO ontology described in Sect. 4.2.
- As a third step we have injected (mapped) the specific XVR items into the ontology, thus linking the domain independent, virtual reality platform independent ontology to the specific libraries of a specific platform, as described in Sect. 4.3.

A reader could ask now why we didn't simply/mainly rely on the XVR classification in order to produce the, so called, PRESTO ontology. The reason is twofold: first of all, the XVR classification mainly concerns with objects. It provides therefore a good source of knowledge for entities "that are" (in DOLCE called Endurants), but a more limited source of knowledge on entities "that happen" (in DOLCE called Perdurants). Second, the XVR libraries contain objects described at an extremely detailed level whose encoding and classification resembles more to a directory structure built to facilitate the selection of libraries rather than a well thought is-a hierarchy and therefore presents a number of problems that prevent its usage 'as such'. In the following, we review the most common problems we found in the categorization of the XVR items:

- Concepts names are used to encode different types of information. For instance the concept name "Caucasian_male_in_suit_34" is used to identify a person of Caucasian race, dressed in suit and of 34 years of age. Encoding the information on race, age, and so on via e.g., appropriate roles enables the definition of classes such as e.g., "Caucasian_person", "young adult", "male" and so on and the automatic classification (and retrieval) of XVR items via reasoning.
- The terminology used to describe concepts is not always informative enough: for instance, it is difficult to understand the meaning of the entity "HLO_assistant" from its label and description and to understand whether this item may suggest a type of "assistant" that may be useful in several scenarios and could therefore be worth adding to the ontology.
- The level of abstraction at which elements are described varies greatly. For instance the library containing police personnel items classifies the general concept of "Police_Officer" and the rather specific concept of "Sniper_green_camouflage" at the same hierarchical level.
- The criteria for the classification are not always clear: for instance, the "BTP_officer" (British Transport Police) concept is not a subclass of "Police_Officer".
- Certain general criteria of classification are not present in all the libraries. As an example, the general concept "Adult_Male" should be a general concept used for the classification of male characters. Nonetheless, it is present in

e.g., the library of "Environment_humans" (that is, the library that describes generic characters) and is not present in e.g., the libraries of "Rescue_humans" and "Victims" (that is, the libraries of characters impersonating rescuers and victims, respectively).

- Unclear classification: for instance, in the XVR original classification a "sign" is a "road_object", and a "danger_sign" is an "incident_object". By considering that no relations are defined between the entities "sign" and "danger_sign", it is not possible to infer any relation between "danger_sign" and "road_object".
- Duplication of concept names: for instance, the label "police_services" is used to describe both human police characters in the library "environment_human", and police vehicles, in the library "rescue_vehicle".

In the next section we provide an overview of the PRESTO ontology and of its top-level, middle level and XVR specific components in detail.

4   The PRESTO Ontology

As introduced in Sect. 3, the PRESTO ontology[3] is composed of three parts: (i) a top level part constructed with the help of DOLCE; (ii) a middle level describing general entities that can occur in a VR scenario, and (iii) a specific set of entities representing objects and "behaviours" available in a concrete VR.

4.1   The Top-Level Ontology: DOLCE Entities

Figure 1 shows the taxonomy of DOLCE entities taken from [12] revised and customised to the needs of PRESTO.

Entities in gray where not included in the PRESTO ontology, while entities in boldface where added specifically for PRESTO.

Among the first level of entities we selected **Endurants** and **Perdurants**: endurants are indeed useful to describe the big number of physical and non-physical objects that can occur in a serious game, including avatars, vehicles, tools, animals, roles and so on; perdurants are instead useful to describe what happens in a scenario. Concerning endurants the diagram in Fig. 1 shows the ones we selected to be included in PRESTO; note that we did not include the distinction between agentive and non-agentive physical objects because of an explicit requirement by the PRESTO developers. In fact, they require the possibility to treat every object in a VR as an agentive one for the sake of simplicity[4]. While perdurants can be useful in a VR to describe a broad set of "things that

---

[3] The current version of the PRESTO ontology cannot be published due to copyrights constraints. A preliminary version, from which it is possible to observe the rational used for modeling it, may be found here: https://shell-static.fbk.eu/resources/ ontologies/CorePresto.owl.

[4] A typical example is vehicle, which the developers prefer to treat as an agentive object, rather than a non agentive object driven by an agent, for the sake of simplicity of the code.

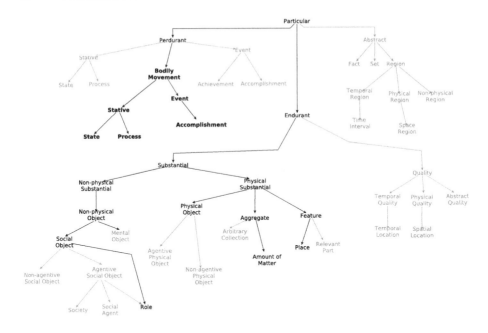

Fig. 1. The top-level PRESTO ontology

happen", in the current version of the ontology they were mainly used to describe animations (that is, "bodily_movements") of avatars. From an ontological point of view we felt it was appropriate to classify them according to the categories of stative and eventful perdurants included in DOLCE. In fact, we can have *state* bodily movements (e.g., being sitting), *process* bodily movements (e.g., running), and *accomplishment* bodily movement (e.g., open a door). The investigation of animations did not show examples of *achievement* bodily movements, which were therefore not included in the ontology.

We will discuss **Qualities** in Sect. 5. Instead **Abstracts** do not seem to play a role in the PRESTO ontology.

4.2   The Middle-Level Domain Ontology

This part augments the top level ontology described above with concrete, but still abstract, entities that may appear in a broad range of virtual reality scenarios for serious games. The current version of the ontology is composed of 311 concepts, 5 object properties and 3 annotations properties. Concerning the Endurant part the main entities modeled in the middle-level ontology pertain classifications of persons (avatars), buildings, locations, tools / devices, vehicles, and roles. Concerning perdurants the ontology contains concepts describing *state*, *process* and *accomplishment* bodily movement. An excerpt of the middle-level ontology can be seen in Fig. 2.

Fig. 2. The middle-level PRESTO ontology

4.3   Injecting the Bottom-Level Ontology

The linking of the bottom-level ontology, representing the classification scheme used for organizing the items contained in the 3D-library, is not a trivial task. Indeed, the correct alignment of these levels enables the transparency of the system with respect to the actual content of the 3D-library.

While the creation of the top and middle-level of the PRESTO ontology is meant to create a stable knowledge source, the definition of the alignments with the bottom-level elements is an activity that has to be done every time a new 3D-library is plugged into the system.

To ease this injection we decided to accomplish it in two separate steps: (i) an automatic definition of alignments by using an ontology alignment tool and (ii) a manual refinement of the alignments before using the complete ontology in the production stage.

The output of the alignment task is the linking between the abstract concepts contained in the middle PRESTO ontology and the concrete items contained in the underlying 3D-library implemented in the system. Indeed, such alignments allow the access to the entire set of items defined in the 3D-library and that are physically used for building the virtual reality scenario.

By considering the XVR use case, the automatic alignment procedure allowed a time-effort reduction, with respect of doing everything manually, of around 65 % in the definition of the alignment between the middle-level and the bottom-level ontologies, thus showing the potential of using ontology mapping technologies in the concrete scenario of virtual reality libraries. More details on the alignment procedure, including cases in which the automatic step fails, can be found in [8].

5   Enriching the VR for Decision-Making and Coordination

The previous section illustrated a classification of the VR world in which NPCs act. However, there are a number of aspects required for decision-making and coordination of activities that cannot be fully captured via static taxonomies and aggregations but are worth describing in an ontology not only for its inherent representational and deductive power, which helps in structuring abstract reasoning, but for the ability built into PRESTO of dynamically and arbitrarily add and remove tags to any item within the VR. These tags are generically called "qualities" since they are mostly described as **Qualities** entities in the PRESTO ontology. They form a layer of knowledge shared by all PRESTO components (including configurator systems, DICE agents, monitor and control GUIs, and end-user development tools) without the need of modifying the game engine or hardcoding relationships among categories and properties into software. Note that this layer could have been built into the ontology itself (technically, by representing all items in the VR as individuals stored in a triple store) but this would have created issues with distribution, deployment and performance, so it is managed differently. Further, DICE supports the tagging of BDI plans and intentions by software developers; these tags can be used for introspection and monitoring of the activity of an agent.

Qualities are still work in progress, since they reflect the progressive development of behavioural models. At the moment, they are used for two main reasons: to represent an item's characteristics and dynamic state; and, to enable recognition (of activities and intentions) and coordination.

Examples of characteristics and states represented as qualities include:

- The characteristic of being a "gate", which indicates something that can be crossed but only after performing some enabling actions if required and coordinating with others, thus it is relevant to the models of navigation. A gate may be the revolving door at the entrance of a room, the sliding door of a lift, a driveway gate, a railroad crossing, and so on, all of which may have been classified very differently in the VR. Note that a permanently sealed door is not a gate in this definition;

- The dynamic state of being "open", which may be associated to gates (as above) as well as to entities not relevant to navigation (e.g. windows). Stative qualities are represented as a is-a hierarchy, whose root is a generic name (such as "openness") and whose children are the possible values of the quality (in this example, open, close, semi-open, semi-close, etc.). Items are tagged with the leaves (e.g., open or close) but the PRESTO API allows querying the current state by using the root, thus implicitly checking if the item does have that quality in the first place. Other examples of wide applicability include "liveliness" (which includes "alive", "dead", "impaired") and "functioning" (specialized in "running" and "stopped");

- Dynamic states such as "body posture" and "facial expression", also organized in hierarchies as mentioned above. While posture and expression apparently are properties of humans only, they can be also applied to animals and even to non-living entities; for instance, in shooting ranges (and their VR reconstructions), puppets used as targets may have different postures;

- Dynamically changing values of various nature. PRESTO allows the association of an arbitrary content together with a tag to an item, thus this mechanism is essentially a way to add data fields to an object without impacting the general PRESTO API. For instance, the reward mechanism in a Unity game built for instructional purposes has been implemented as a "money"-tagged accumulator on a specific item.

As mentioned earlier, the PRESTO ontology classifies also the animations that can be applied by a game engine to entities. While this classification is used at the moment as a configuration tool, essentially to make DICE models agnostic with respect to the underlying technology, it is the first step towards a solution to the problem of intention recognition, which in turn is the base for the simulation of coordinated behaviour (no matter whether amicable, e.g. teamwork as fire fighters in the fire example presented earlier, hostile, e.g. opposition in a security scenario, or simply observation to anticipate future moves and take decisions, e.g. avoiding a safety exit door when too many people are engaging it during an alarm). Intention recognition is something that is innate in humans and cognitively complex animals (e.g. dogs) but computationally very hard if taken by principle; machine learning may come to the rescue in certain situations, but in a VR scenario where nuances of body and expressions are hard to capture and represent, let alone the limited number of training cases, this is not an option. In PRESTO, qualities are exploited to allow entities to make their recognizable activities publicly visible; thus, intention and action recognition is reduced to reading certain qualities automatically set by DICE when starting animations or appropriately tagged plans.

To do a further step ahead, work is in progress on game-theoretical descriptions of coordinated behaviour, including queuing and other crowding behaviours, accessing shared resources, and so on, in order to enable the definition of policies at a very abstract (meta-) level. This work exploits, in addition to PRESTO's tagging of items, the equivalent in DICE for goals and plans as well as its support for introspection of intentions and motivations. In a nutshell, DICE agents tag themselves and any involved object with qualities that indicate the move they want to play in a coordination game, while their meta-level, cognitive models would try to achieve or stop pursuing aptly tagged goals and plans according to the agent's own moves in the game as well as of those entities perceived in the environment. The specification of policies is expected to substantially reduce the coding required by models and to allow the reuse of the same coordination patterns in many different situations, e.g. a single policy for queuing to pass through a gate (which will be part of the navigation models) as well as for queuing at the entrance of an office or at the cashier in a supermarket (which are decision-making behaviours not related to navigation goals).

A simplistic (but already available and of great practical use) coordinated behaviour exploiting qualities is goal delegation from an agent to another agent.

By means of the PRESTO API, any entity in a game can submit a goal to be pursued by any other entity; when the goal is enriched with a few predefined parameters, the destination DICE agent publishes the fact that it has accepted a goal or that has achieved it (or failed to achieve or refused), allowing the submitter (or any other observer, including PRESTO's session script engine) to monitor and coordinate behaviours without the use of any additional agent protocol.

In the PRESTO ontology, qualities are represented as endurant or perdurant, depending on their lifetime – static characteristics are endurant while stative, behavioural and coordination qualities are perdurant.

As a final note, it is worth mentioning that PRESTO uses ontologies, in addition to classifications and qualities as discussed above, for other purposes such as:

- To represent individual, rather than objective, perspectives on the world. Currently, an ontology is used to capture the possible values used by DICE models to appraise entities that may have an influence on behaviours. These values range from positive to negative at different levels, from "friendly" to "dangerous, to stay distant from". For reasons similar to those that led to the management of qualities in PRESTO, the relationships between ontological classifications and appraisal values are captured by configuration files at various level of granularity (shared by all NPCs of a certain type rather than specific for an individual) rather than within the ontology;
- Software engineering practice, e.g. to allow the definition of certain APIs in a language-independent format, with the automatic generation of software in some cases, and similarly for independence from the game engine when accessing commonly available resource types (e.g. animations, as mentioned above) by means of an engine-neutral syntax.

6   Related Work and Conclusion

In this paper, we focused on the experience of using Semantic Web techniques, and in particular lightweight ontologies, for the description of the artificial entities and their behaviours in gaming with the aim of uncoupling the description of virtual reality scenarios from their physical implementation in charge to the developers.

With respect to the literature, where ontologies are often used for a detailed description of the geometrical properties of space and objects [7], we focused more on how the description of the entities of a VR scenario can be easily represented and managed from the practical point of view. Indeed, the literature addressed such problems only marginally by focusing mainly on the use of ontologies for managing the representation of virtual reality scenarios themselves [2,17], even if in some cases a clear target domain, like the management of information related to disasters [1], is taken into account. The description of character behaviours has been supported by using ontologies for different purposes like as support for UML-based descriptions [3] or as a "core" set of structural behavioural concepts for describing BDI-MAS architectures [10].

However, all these works do not take into account issues concerning the practical implementations of flexible systems for building virtual reality scenarios. The proposed solution demonstrated the viability of using Semantic Web technologies for abstracting the development of virtual reality scenarios either from the point of view of the 3D-design and from the modeling of character behaviours.

References

1. Babitski, G., Probst, F., Hoffmann, J., Oberle, D.: Ontology design for information integration in disaster management. In: Fischer, S., Maehle, E., Reischuk, R. (eds.) Informatik 2009: Im Focus das Leben, Beiträge der 39. Jahrestagung der Gesellschaft für Informatik e.V. (GI), 28.9.-2.10.2009, Lübeck, Proceedings. LNI, vol. 154, pp. 3120–3134. GI (2009). http://subs.emis.de/LNI/Proceedings/Proceedings154/article2822.html
2. Bille, W., Pellens, B., Kleinermann, F., Troyer, O.D.: Intelligent modelling of virtual worlds using domain ontologies. In: Delgado-Mata, C., Ibáñez, J. (eds.) Intelligent Virtual Environments and Virtual Agents, Proceedings of the IVEVA 2004 Workshop, ITESM Campus Ciudad de Mexico, Mexico City, D.F., Mexico, 27th April 2004. CEUR Workshop Proceedings, vol. 97. CEUR-WS.org (2004). http://sunsite.informatik.rwth-aachen.de/Publications/CEUR-WS/Vol-97/IVEVAFinal_S1_01.pdf
3. Bock, C., Odell, J.: Ontological behavior modeling. J. Object Technol. **10**(3), 1–36 (2011). http://dx.doi.org/10.5381/jot.2011.10.1.a3
4. Bratman, M.E.: Intention, Plans, and Practical Reason. Harvard University Press, Cambridge (1987)
5. Busetta, P., Ghidini, C., Pedrotti, M., Angeli, A.D., Menestrina, Z.: Briefing virtual actors: a first report on the presto project. In: Romano, D. (ed.) Proceedings of the AI and Games Symposium at AISB 2014, April 2014
6. Calanca, P., Busetta, P.: Cognitive navigation in presto. In: Proceedings of the AI and Games Symposium at AISB (2015)
7. Chu, Y.L., Li, T.Y.: Realizing semantic virtual environments with ontology and pluggable procedures. In: Applications of Virtual Reality. InTech (2012)
8. Dragoni, M., Ghidini, C., Busetta, P., Fruet, M., Pedrotti, M.: Using ontologies for modeling virtual reality scenarios. In: Proceedings of ESWC (2015)
9. Evertsz, R., Pedrotti, M., Busetta, P., Acar, H., Ritter, F.: Populating VBS2 with realistic virtual actors. In: Conference on Behavior Representation in Modeling & Simulation (BRIMS). Sundance Resort, Utah, March 30 –April 2 (2009)
10. Faulkner, S., Kolp, M.: Ontological basis for agent ADL. In: Eder, J., Welzer, T. (eds.) The 15th Conference on Advanced Information Systems Engineering (CAiSE 2003), Klagenfurt/Velden, Austria, 16–20 June, 2003, CAiSE Forum, Short Paper Proceedings, Information Systems for a Connected Society. CEUR Workshop Proceedings, vol. 74. CEUR-WS.org (2003). http://sunsite.informatik.rwth-aachen.de/Publications/CEUR-WS/Vol-74/files/FORUM_44.pdf
11. Fernández-López, M., Gómez-Pérez, A., Juristo, N.: Methontology: from ontological art towards ontological engineering. In: Proceedings of Symposium on Ontological Engineering of AAAI (1997)

12. Gangemi, A., Guarino, N., Masolo, C., Oltramari, A., Schneider, L.: Sweetening ontologies with DOLCE. In: Gómez-Pérez, A., Benjamins, V.R. (eds.) EKAW 2002. LNCS (LNAI), vol. 2473, pp. 166–181. Springer, Heidelberg (2002). http://dl.acm.org/citation.cfm?id=645362.650863
13. Gruber, T.R.: Toward principles for the design of ontologies used for knowledge sharing? Int. J. Hum. Comput. Stud. **43**(5–6), 907–928 (1995). http://www.science direct.com/science/article/pii/S1071581985710816
14. Guarino, N., Welty, C.: Identity and subsumption. In: Green, R., Bean, C.A., Myaeng, S.H. (eds.) The Semantics of Relationships: An Interdisciplinary Perspective. Information Science and Knowledge Management, vol. 3, pp. 111–126. Kluwer, The Netherlands (2001)
15. Rao, A.S., Georgeff, M.P.: Bdi agents: from theory to practice. In: Proceedings of the First International Conference On Multi-agent Systems, ICMAS 1995, pp. 312–319 (1995)
16. Ritter, F.E., Bittner, J.L., Kase, S.E., Evertsz, R., Pedrotti, M., Busetta, P.: CoJACK: a high-level cognitive architecture with demonstrations of moderators, variability, and implications for situation awareness. Biol. Inspir. Cogn. Architect. **1**, 2–13 (2012)
17. Xuesong, W., Mingquan, Z., Yachun, F.: Building vr learning environment: an ontology based approach. In: First International Workshop on Education Technology and Computer Science, ETCS 2009, vol. 3, pp. 160–165, March 2009

Modelling and Simulation in the Autonomous Systems' Domain – Current Status and Way Ahead

Jan Hodicky[✉]

NATO Modelling and Simulation Centre of Excellence, Rome, Italy
jan.hodicky@seznam.cz

Abstract. A first Modelling and Simulation for Autonomous System Workshop (MESAS 2014) was organized by NATO Modelling and Simulation Centre of Excellence in Rome 2014. The main findings were related to the missing ontologies for AS deployment, a legal and cultural gap in the AS deployment and the request to launch the cross panel project under NATO Science and Technology Organization aimed at the AS development supported by modelling and simulation. The article is focused on the main findings form the 2015 edition based on the analysis of presented papers and final panel discussion in the workshop. The experimental frameworks for the AS development and deployment is mentioned and its perspective as well. The next part is explaining the differences in the autonomous system and human behavior modelling. The last part is focused on the AS concept of operation and the potential consequences.

Keywords: High Level Architecture · Autonomous System · Operational field · Modelling and simulation · Experimental framework

1 Introduction

Modelling and Simulation to support development and deployment of systems with autonomous capabilities proved to be valid concept during the 2014 Modelling and simulation for Autonomous Systems workshop [1]. 50 papers were submitted and 32 were later included into the proceedings. The main aspects touched by proceedings and by the final round about discussion session were the technology progress of the unmanned systems, a need for the common vocabulary to be shared between Autonomous System and Modelling and Simulation domains and the cultural and legal gap in the Autonomous System operational deployment. Among others the need to create cross panel activity under the NATO Science and Technology Organization (STO) was identified. STO is currently composed of more than 3500 Scientists and Engineers from NATO and its partners working on approximately 140 research activities. Autonomous System (AS) concept, design and implementation are covered by System Analysis and Studies (SAS) panel. M&S as a scientific discipline is under governance of NATO M&S Group (MSG) panel.

Where we have moved in these specified areas after one year?

In spite of the identified gap, missing the AS ontology to be used in the Modelling and simulation domain, no effort has been identified. AS ontologies or taxonomies are

© Springer International Publishing Switzerland 2015
J. Hodicky (Ed.): MESAS 2015, LNCS 9055, pp. 17–23, 2015.
DOI: 10.1007/978-3-319-22383-4_2

being heavily developed without taking into an account the need to reflect it both in the operational and technical field and importance of shaping it based on the M&S aspects as well. As an example of such approach that defines the AS ontology technologically oriented without touching the operational portion and M&S domain is in [2]. The result is that in the Modelling and Simulation domain the main taxonomy is based on the distributed simulation standards like DIS, HLA [4, 5] and still doesn't reflect the need to incorporate the autonomous domain in. On the other hand, vice versa, the AS taxonomy and ontology doesn't contain natively modeling and simulation aspects and therefore the experimentation cannot effectively and unanimously employ the M&S. One of the proposed actions might be a new working group under the STO composed of the member from the SAS, MSG and Human Factors and Medicine (HFM) panel. The last one, HFM, is critical for success. The human behavior specialist must be part of the ontology/taxonomy design; otherwise the objective to reproduce the human behavior in the AS will not happen. HFM, should as well clarify the role of the public opinion in the AS operationalization.

The last year MESAS motto picture, Fig. 1, defined the cultural gap between Systems with limited Autonomous Capabilities and System with autonomous Capabilities or Fully Autonomous System. The gap was explained as a fear of systems without human in the loop and potential consequences.

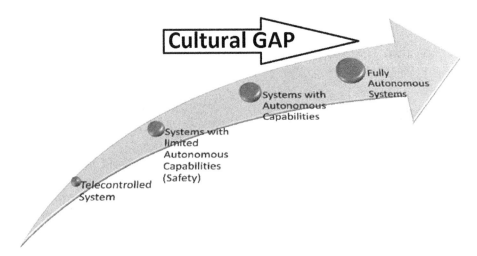

Fig. 1. AS technology progress dimension and cultural gap (NATO M&S COE source)

This year a gap was slightly modified based on the fact that in some areas the systems with full autonomous capabilities are already operational. As an example, the train control without conductor; human in the loop; might be taken. Therefore the issue of a cultural gap seems to be overcome; not it is moving into the psychological domain. We are refusing the employment of AS in the air domain without being able to accept in our minds that in some areas AS are regular part of our life.

Legal gap was identified last year and it remains on the list. After one year there is still missing a clear AS policy or legal documents, or even the same terminology that might be used by lawyers when justifying/banning the need for AS. An importance of public opinion involvement into the discussion about AS was identified to overcome the gap. It is not anymore sufficient to employ into discussion only classical triangle - Military, Industry and Academia (MIA), but a Public (P) should be integral part of it. We are speaking about MIAP square of community of interest around AS.

The technology progress dimension is not the only one that is comprised by the AS paradigm. The level of autonomy is another one and level of collaboration between AS is the third dimension. These findings are reflected in the Fig. 2.

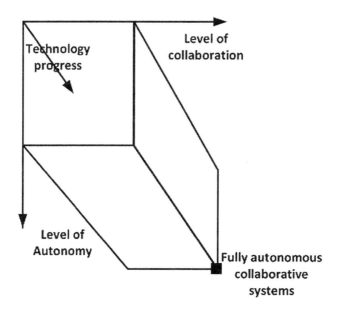

Fig. 2. Three dimensions of AS paradigm (author's source)

Technology progress is a main driver to reach the status of fully autonomous system with collaborative behavior being employed in the battlefield. The main obstacles to reach such state is legal/psychological gap identified earlier and the computational limits of current methods used to implement AS.

2   Experimental Frameworks for Autonomous Systems

To test, evaluate, analyze and optimize AS behavior and cooperation in the operational field, M&S experimental frameworks plays the most important role [1, 3]. The general experimentation AS framework uses as a backbone distributed simulation environment with support of distributed simulation standards like DIS, HLA and DDS [4–6]. The main actors of the M&S experimental frameworks are following:

- Combination of physical and virtual replications of entities
  - Human Operator/Being,

- C2 system,
- Communication node,
- AS.
- Combination of physical and virtual Environmental features
  - terrain,
  - atmosphere,
  - weather,
  - etc.

Lack of single standard for data exchange mechanism in the experimental frameworks corresponds to the current status in the distributed simulation domain. Experimental frameworks are usually design to natively support only one of the aforementioned standards which complicates the way of its reuse and double use [1].

Another challenge in the M&S experimental frameworks is different requirements for quality and granularity of environmental data from each replicated entity point of view. Demand on having micro and macro environmental data about operational area is computationally very demanding.

The M&S experimental frameworks from the future perspective require following interfaces:

- Human machine interface,
- C2 interface,
- Weapon systems interface,
- Unified interface to the knowledge management systems,
- Real time operational interface for scenario development, description or replication.

Operational interface is currently not developed topics. Without permanent connection to the C2 system and all sensors on the battlefield it is complicated to optimize the cooperation and collaboration of AS and human being to achieve particular mission objective. The operational scenario must be replicated in the synthetic environment comprising all physical and virtual entities. Based on real data a mission rehearsal and planning of AS and human being resources might be done effectively.

3   AS Behavior Modeling Versus Human Behavior Modelling

Do we need to model AS behavior? Current approach in the experimental frameworks is based on the idea of using the autonomy algorithms for simulation as well as the real world environment. Therefore if a universal native API is available, than there is no need to reinvent model of AS. The core AS behavior would be transferred from and to virtual/real AS by employing simple copy and paste technique. Moreover developing special AS behavior model cannot reveal any new findings from the system point of view. AS just reflects execution of an algorithm. It doesn't pose any human being creativity and only follows code instructions. Attempt to bring closer the creativity to the AS is clashing with the proven theory of Algorithmic Information Theory [7].

However to study and implement model of AS cooperation and collaboration is useful. If AS, represented by system of systems, cooperate and collaborate each other, the simulation study might reveal AS parameters, optimal algorithms and techniques to be implemented in the operational environment.

4   Algorithms for the AS

Algorithms for autonomous system correspond to the functionalities provided by it. One of the algorithms' classifications might be done based on the cooperative subsystem of AS and external factors:

- algorithm for AS sensors, like Light Detection and Ranging (LIDAR) [8], IMU Inertial Measurement Unit (IMU) [9];
- multi sensor data fusion algorithm [10];
- machine learning/motivated learning for building knowledge database of meta modeling data to assure the object recognition [11];
- mission [12], global [13] and local planning algorithm [14];
- cooperative algorithm [15].

The domain of the collaborative algorithms between ASs and AS and human being as well is the most important and not yet solved from the operational point of view. It goes behind the idea of cooperation; the common planning is not sufficient anymore. It contains algorithms that are able to share the real time battlefield picture and based on its understanding make a collaborative decision resolved in action plan.

Another critical and not developed algorithms' domain is focused on the reliability and robustness of the solutions that might be targeted in the near operational future. Diversity of field conditions causes AS performance failures. Therefore the next AS generation must primarily touch the issues of a failure detection and recovery. It is the only way to come closer to the fully autonomous system or at least to minimize human supervision on unmanned systems.

Another critical factor in the successful implementation of AS is to develop algorithms for reliable communications and redundant sub systems or systems. Without having in place such robust algorithms, the cooperative and collaborative algorithms would not be applicable.

Among other an issue related to the implementation of ethical features into the AS is appearing. A need to implement algorithm, ethical adaptor, being able to proactively modified behavior of AS similar to the human moral emotion, is crucial to enable fully operational deployment of AS [16]. Therefore there is a clear indication of moving towards the cognitive algorithms domain. Main focus is classification of dangerous local AS behavior and selection of a better one to fulfil the global objective.

Algorithms carrying out the building of knowledge database should use the big potential of gaming environment. Online gaming engine might be used to collect behavior of players trying to cooperate and collaborate and may define the behavioral patterns for AS collaboration in the operational environment. It is one of the ways to increase the quality of knowledge database system used for AS decision making.

5 Concepts of Operation

M&S is playing the most important role in pre-deployment phase of collaborative AS into the battlefield. We still do not cover perfectly the potential of isolated AS being deployed. The collaborative AS in the battlefield opens a new era of operational use. M&S via an experimental framework might clarify effectiveness of using collaborative fully autonomous systems versus highly automated systems or their mixture. Moreover massive using of the MS experimental framework for AS collaboration might overcome the psychological block to trust AS. Experimental frameworks employment might define limits of AS deployment and increase a trust in AS.

Important aspect is to use experimental frameworks to train trainers. Trainer is in charge of supervision of deployment of cooperating not fully ASs. Trainer must be able to recognize that ASs are still cooperating in the correct way, not modifying their behavior in the way not to reach the global objective. It opens a new market for training system.

Methods of Verification Validation and Accreditation for ASs and for their cooperation and collaboration must be developed to build up an operational trust. Experimental frameworks are not unified and validation data set is not yet defined. First approach might be to define the best practice for the M&S experimental frameworks for AS and to define standard set of scenarios. Effectiveness of AS cooperation and collaboration might be validated against it. Such a set of scenarios might define acceptable conditions of AS operational use from public opinion point of view.

For a concept of operation of AS, it is important to create such taxonomy of AS that connects level of autonomy and the functional capabilities of ASs seen as an individual system and/or as cooperative entities as well. There should be an explicit definition of AS capabilities in the perspective of a particular level of autonomy.

Big issue still to be solved in the domain of fully ASs collaboration is the liability. Who will be responsible for course of action, if there are casualties because of failure of fully collaborative ASs. If there is not man in the loop, no one is liable for the collaborative decision.

6 Conclusion

M&S is playing the crucial role in the integration phase of ASs into the operational field. Therefore, the differences between fully autonomous system and highly automated AS are revealed with the perspective of its operational use. AS vitally needs to be connected to the knowledge management system. From that perspective there is a requirement to define unified interface between AS and knowledge management system to allow AS to get data, analyze it adopt it and make decision. Taxonomies and ontologies of AS are still not well defined. Critical is to use the common vocabulary in interdisciplinary use of AS and M&S and to model and implement collaborative algorithms between ASs and AS and human being. Using the identical algorithms for AS development in the physical and synthetic domain would assure decreasing cost of AS deployment. Liability of decision done by collaborative fully ASs without human in the loop must be solved very soon to enable its operationalization.

References

1. Hodicky, J.: HLA as an experimental backbone for autonomous system integration into operational field. In: Hodicky, J. (ed.) MESAS 2014. LNCS, vol. 8906, pp. 121–126. Springer, Heidelberg (2014)
2. Alonso, J.B.: OASys.: Ontology for autonomous systems. Ph.D. thesis, Universidad Politecnica de Madrid (2010)
3. Perhinschi, M.G., Napolitano, M.R., Tamayo, S.: Integrated simulation environment for unmanned autonomous systems—towards a conceptual framework. Model. Simul. Eng. **2010**, 12 (2010). Article ID 736201
4. IEEE Standard for Distributed Interactive Simulation–Application Protocols. IEEE Std 1278.1-2012 (Revision of IEEE Std 1278.1-1995), pp. 1–747 (2012)
5. STANAG 4603. Modelling and simulation architecture standards for technical interoperability: High Level Architecture (HLA). Brussels: NATO Standardization Council (2009)
6. DDS Object Management Group (OMG). Data Distribution Service for Real-time Systems – version 1.2 (2007)
7. Chaitin, G.: What is creativity? (2010). http://www.philosophytogo.org/wordpress/?p=1872
8. Du, R., Lee, H.J.: A novel compression algorithm for LiDAR data. In: 2012 5th International Congress on Image and Signal Processing (CISP), pp. 987–991 (2012)
9. Chao, H., Coopmans, C., Di, L., Chen, Y.Q.: A comparative evaluation of low-cost IMUs for unmanned autonomous systems. In: Multisensor Fusion and Integration for Intelligent Systems (MFI), pp. 211–216 (2010)
10. Anitha, R., Renuka, S., Abudhahir, A.: Multi sensor data fusion algorithms for target tracking using multiple measurements. In: Computational Intelligence and Computing Research (ICCIC), pp. 1–4 (2013)
11. Raif, P., Starzyk, J.A.: Motivated learning in autonomous systems. In: Neural Networks (IJCNN), pp. 603–610 (2011)
12. Wang, J.J., Zhang, Y.F., Geng, L., Fuh, J.Y.H., Teo, S.H.: Mission planning for heterogeneous tasks with heterogeneous UAVs. In: Control Automation Robotics & Vision (ICARCV), pp. 1484–1489 (2014)
13. Liang, W., Xiao, A., Qian, H., Liu, G.: A global path planning algorithm based on rough sets theory. In: World Automation Congress (WAC), pp 1–4 (2012)
14. Sariff, N., Buniyamin, N.: An overview of autonomous mobile robot path planning algorithms. In: Research and Development, SCOReD 2006, pp. 183–188 (2006)
15. Gupta, S., Hare, J., Zhou, S.: Cooperative coverage using autonomous underwater vehicles in unknown environments. Oceans, 1–5 (2012)
16. Arkin, R.C., Ulam, P., Wagner, A.R.: Moral decision making in autonomous systems: enforcement, moral emotions, dignity, trust, and deception. Proc. IEEE **100**(3), 571–589 (2012)

Improving Robotic and Autonomous Systems Information Interoperability:
Standardizing Data Exchanges with XML

Steve Litwiller[1(✉)], Matt Weber[2], and Frank Klucznik[2]

[1] Joint Staff J6, Data and Services Division, Suffolk, VA, USA
steven.w.litwiller.civ@mail.mil
[2] Georgia Tech Research Institute, Atlanta, GA, USA
{matthew.weber,frank.klucznik}@gtri.gatech.edu

Abstract. A well-documented capability deficiency in Robotic and Autonomous Systems (RAS) is their lack of information interoperability within and between robotic systems, as well as between robotic systems and C2ISR networks. This inability stems from delivery of 'stove-piped' capabilities to meet urgent operational requirements, use of proprietary software, and bandwidth/payload constraints. This paper explains the use of a data-centric solution to improve information sharing through use of (1) a widely available translation language (eXtensible Markup Language (XML)) and, (2) a consistent implementation framework provided for within the National Information Exchange Model (NIEM). The paper also describes a recent collaborative simulation event called the Simulated Interactive Robotic Initiative (SIRI). This event used XML messaging between simulated ground vehicles, the ground vehicles and the Control Station, and also performed some preliminary use analysis of Efficient XML Interchange (EXI), as an alternative to hand-crafted binary messaging.

Keywords: XML · Information exchange · Data exchange · Messaging · Robotic and Autonomous Systems · SIRI · Efficient XML Interchange

1 Purpose

This paper explains the importance of implementing a standardized approach for performing data exchanges in Robotic and Autonomous Systems (RAS) capabilities. Specifically, it explains: (1) the use of eXtensible Markup Language (XML) as the common interface; and, (2) the use of a consistent design and implementation framework for building standardized data exchanges as provided within the National Information Exchange Model.

© Springer International Publishing Switzerland 2015
J. Hodicky (Ed.): MESAS 2015, LNCS 9055, pp. 24–39, 2015.
DOI: 10.1007/978-3-319-22383-4_3

2 Problem Statement

U.S. and multinational RAS lack the ability to effectively exchange information, resulting in 'stove-piped' operational command and control within platforms, systems or Services.[1] Platform or system-centric 'fixes' to this problem provide some improvement within specific mission areas, but are not applied across the full scope of RAS capabilities and are typically not scalable or reusable.

3 Background

Robotic and Autonomous Systems (RAS) capabilities include all unmanned airborne, ground, and maritime systems, system components, platforms, control stations, and information networks. RAS capabilities are integral to military operations, where they support mission accomplishment across the Joint Capability Areas, including Battlespace Awareness, Force Application, Force Protection, Command and Control, Force Support, Net-Centric, Building Partnerships, and Logistics. Their uses are embedded in all types of military and civilian missions, and are especially useful in performing "dull, dirty, or dangerous" missions [1].

Standardized data exchanges within and between systems/C2 networks are an important enabler for improving information sharing and understanding at the operational level. Additionally, standardized data exchanges enable automated, machine-to-machine interfaces between dissimilar information networks. Creating these data exchanges requires development of a common schema, which is tailored to the specific information sharing needs between the data sharing partners (Fig. 1).

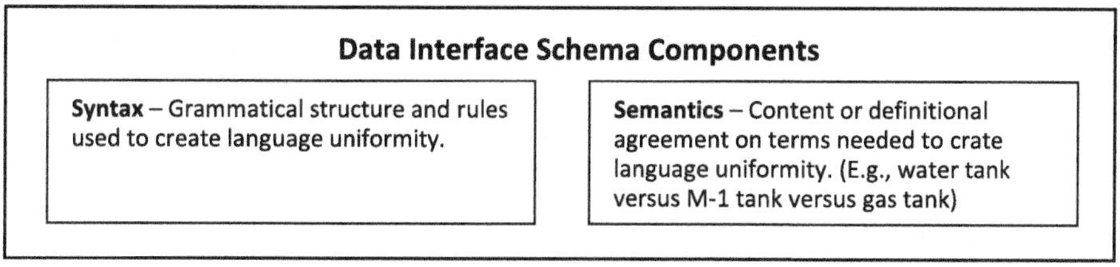

Data Interface Schema Components	
Syntax – Grammatical structure and rules used to create language uniformity.	**Semantics** – Content or definitional agreement on terms needed to crate language uniformity. (E.g., water tank versus M-1 tank versus gas tank)

Fig. 1. Data interface schema components

This approach of implementing standardized XML-based data exchanges supports the interoperability aspects of DOD's Net-Centric Data Strategy goals to make data visible, accessible, understandable, trusted, and interoperable [2].

4 Operational Need

The Unmanned Systems Integrated Roadmap (FY 2013-2038) [16] highlights command and control shortcomings in unmanned systems:

---

[1] Military Services are referred to as "Service(s)".

"Operational lessons learned, detailed analytical studies, after action reviews, JUONs, and combat mission need statements over the past 10 years of global combat operations have repeatedly shown C4 infrastructure shortfalls in our ability to support unmanned platforms."

Elsewhere, the Open Business Model for Unmanned Aircraft Ground Control Systems states:

"Many systems today face interoperability issues due to proprietary interfaces and data formats, differing data models (i.e. deferring data context and meaning) and a failure to adhere to open standards that limit DoD's ability to communicate and transmit data and imagery across UAS platforms and the Services." [12]

These interoperability shortcomings are manifest in ineffective data exchanges:

a. From the Control Station to the Robotic System;
b. From Robotic System to the Control Station (both as control messages and as data sensor feeds);
c. From the Control Station to other Control Station and/or C2 System(s);
d. From/to alike Robotic Systems;
e. From/to dissimilar Robotic Systems.

5 DOD Intent

As expressed in the Unmanned Systems Integrated Roadmap (2013 – 2038), the DOD long term intent is to improve RAS information interoperability:

"Interoperability is integral to the continued success of missions using unmanned systems and represents a long-term objective of the Services and their stakeholders. The urgent needs in theater and corresponding rapid acquisition approach during recent years have resulted in the current fleet of unmanned systems that generally do not interoperate with each other or with external systems (underline emphasis added). The combat development community is calling for interoperability as a critical element to the future unmanned systems fleet. The ability for manned and unmanned systems to share information will increase combat capability, enhance situational awareness, and improve flexibility of resources. Interoperability will improve the ability for unmanned systems to operate in synergy in the execution of assigned tasks. Properly stabilized, implemented and maintained, interoperability can serve as a force multiplier, improve warfighter capabilities, decrease integration timelines, simplify logistic, and reduce total ownership costs." [16]

The Roadmap also specifically addresses the requirement to introduce consistent and uniform standards to information exchanges:

"DOD is working to accomplish unmanned systems interoperability by standardizing critical interfaces within the overall UAS architecture by implementing standard IOPs. Since "standards are ever evolving," key enablers in this effort will be to clearly and consistently define the communication protocols, message formats, and implementation methods across these interfaces for new start efforts and system upgrades. In addition, development of middleware that can translate the multiple system inputs and outputs will be a key enabler. This effort will facilitate the mandated acquisition, technology, and logistics lifecycle management efficiencies across current and future unmanned programs." [16]

Further, the Roadmap lists several near term (2013-1017) 'desired capabilities' pertaining to data standards and command and control, to include increased interoperability, effective information fusion, and increasingly networked systems [16].

6 Discussion

Numerous initiatives are ongoing to improve RAS information sharing, to include leveraging the Defense Information Systems Networks (DISN) core as a baseline networking infrastructure to improve RAS access to existing networks, and also increasing reliance on Government-owned enterprise assets and use of common control and data dissemination systems. Some systems use well-known data standards for transmission of data, such as image data. However, most data exchanges in RAS do not rely on well-known standards, and there is no requirement mandating a common standard across the RAS communities.

The National Information Exchange Model (NIEM) is a community-driven, standards-based approach for exchanging information between different governmental organizations (e.g., Federal, State, Local, and International). It is an operationally relevant and proven approach for improving information interoperability and understanding between disparate users through the structured use of XML-based data exchanges. NIEM provides a coherent framework using consistent naming and design rules and repeatable developmental processes for creating data exchanges. It maintains repositories in the NIEM Core and Domains through which data interface tools are stored for re-use by the original information exchange partners or by new users.

Key attributes of NIEM include:

a. Broad range of U.S. government agency and non-government organization users.
b. Aligned with the Whole-of-Government approach.
c. Repository of schema specifications available for ongoing and future production of data interfaces. This reusability results in reduced mediation effort, faster implementation times, and lower development costs.
d. Ability to rapidly modify the data exchange composition/scale.
e. Usability independent of pre-existing system and platform data management design. The NIEM approach works on all computing architecture and operating system (OS) platforms.
f. Compatible with common programming languages and tools like Java, C #, C ++, Ruby, Simple API for XML (SAX), and Python. XML is a means of translation with other XML-based languages, such as KML or UML.
g. Federated design supports implementation of automated, machine-to-machine information exchange without need for a central controlling function between systems.

Figure 2 depicts the NIEM structure, and additional details on NIEM procedures and methodology are available at: https://www.niem.gov.

The NIEM Military Operations Domain provides a DOD-focused venue for military organizations and COIs to implement data exchanges. Under the auspices of the NIEM and Domain rules, users are able to specify the data elements within their prospective exchange that will enable the desired information sharing requirements. The Domain retains a repository of data schema components, able to be reused as needed for new users to and existing exchange or for a new exchange with different users. The data schema specifications currently in the Military Operations Domain

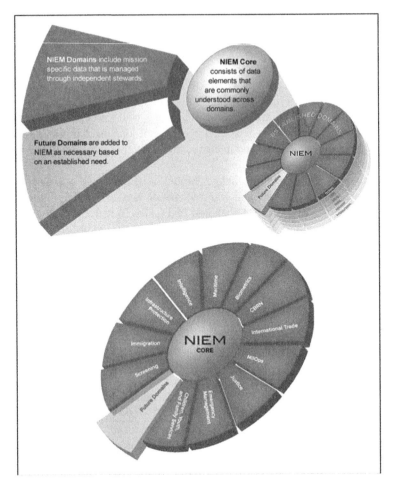

Fig. 2. NIEM domains

includes data concepts and definitions from within the Warfighter Mission Area (WMA) domain, to include doctrinal publications, military standards (MIL-STDs), industry specifications, and community vocabularies.

7   DOD Guidance on Adopting NIEM

The March 2013 DOD CIO memorandum [3] on the adoption of NIEM within the Department of Defense states:

> "... DoD will adopt the National Information Exchange Model (NIEM) as the best suited option for standards-based data exchanges. This adoption will involve a series of phased implementations by Components/Programs using NIEM content, guidance, and tools in an integrated effort to transition current DoD data exchange standards, specifications, and policies to a NIEM-based approach.", and,

"DoD organizations shall first consider NIEM for their information sharing solutions when deciding which data exchange standards or specifications meet their mission and operational needs."

Additional guidance on NIEM adoption and implementation is expected in a forthcoming DOD Instruction (8320.ff).

8 Implementation of XML-Based Data Exchanges in RAS

Transition to NIEM-conformant XML-based data exchanges is expected to occur on an incremental basis throughout DOD organizations and programs as systems, capabilities and networks undergo modernization/upgrade. Use of the NIEM approach and Military Operations Domain will generate developmental efficiencies as increased numbers of DOD users choose to employ NIEM Life-Cycle best practices, enterprise standards, policies, shared semantics and common representation.

Implementation issues and advantages specific to RAS include:

a. Flexible Adaptation – Data exchanges in RAS might involve operational control signals between the platform and Control Station, or sensor reporting from the platform, or transmission of data between operational command and control networks. The utility of XML for these data exchanges is determined by the system/program managers. It is anticipated that some forms of data exchange will be demonstrably more effective without an XML interface.

b. Operational Constraints – RAS is uniquely demanding in the operational environment due to payload and bandwidth limitations associated with the capabilities. XML typically uses a large amount of coding to perform its data exchange function, and this may make XML a sub-optimum option. A possible mitigation is applying Efficient XML Interchange (EXI), which is the W3C standard for XML data compression. EXI has been tested and validated in previous experiments and shown to produce near-optimum message size and often smaller than hand-crafted binary formats.

c. Partial Solution to a Big Problem – The use of XML-based data exchanges is a data-layer solution to the broader problem of 'stove-piped' RAS information. XML-based data exchanges, once implemented, can provide a ubiquitous option for exchanging data at different levels, but it does not address other information interoperability shortcomings, such as poor global connectivity; SATCOM availability; or insufficient enterprise-level gateways. Use of an XML-based data exchange must be determined by the practitioners/managers managing the specific robotic system.

d. Open Source/Widely Accessible/Mission Partner Friendly – NIEM is uniquely suited to support data exchange needs between US and mission partners, as it is freely accessible and not constrained by export or proprietary restrictions. XML is already widely used in industry and international militaries, and expected to be the basis for information interoperability in future mission networks and with Coalition partners. Additional synchronization between the NIEM Military Operations Domain exchange documentation and existing military data standards, such as

STANAG 4586 (relevant to unmanned airborne systems) and Joint Architecture for Unmanned Systems (JAUS) (relevant to unmanned ground systems) is ongoing.

e. Limited Modification Required – A key advantage of using XML-based data exchanges is that the information sharing partners are not required to change their existing data stores or standards. Implementation of an XML-based data exchange does necessitate a line of effort and resources to create/manage the exchange, but it is not a wholesale change of the existing system.

NIEM-conformant XML-based data exchanges may foster a migration from currently fielded data gateways and interfaces, particularly where initial real-time data exchange is not required, to a common framework with aligned requirements across multiple tactical standards (e.g., USMTF, Link 16, Link 11, and VMF). NIEM is also independent of transport, which means systems can use it with their existing network capabilities.

9 Implementation Actions

The Joint Staff J6 C5I Deputy Directorate is engaging in the following actions to promote increased standardization of XML data exchanges using the NIEM approach:

a. Plan and execute developmental series of Robotic Systems data exchange experiments/demonstrations. (2015, 2016 events). Specifically:

- A simulation event was conducted from April 2014 – April 2015 to determine the feasibility of using XML-based exchanges in RAS. The evaluation was a collaborative effort between the NATO Modeling and Simulation Center of Excellence (M&S COE) in Rome, Italy[2] and the Joint Staff J6, with support from the Georgia Tech Research Institute in Atlanta, GA.[3] The event involved exchanging XML-based messages between simulated unmanned ground vehicles (UGVs) and a mission monitoring station, as well as sending XML-based command messages from the mission monitoring station to the UGVs. Results showed that NIEM-conformant XML messaging is technically feasible within a robotic system, but may not be the optimal solution due to bandwidth and payload constraints. The use of XML between robotic systems and C2 mission systems is likely a more optimal use of XML to improve RAS information interoperability. The event also showed that using XML in combination with Efficient XML Interchange (EXI) may offer benefits of reduced message payloads over existing binary data exchange formats. See Appendix A for additional details.

b. Plan and execute RAS Information Interoperability Workshop. (2015 event).
c. Plan and execute inclusion of Robotic and Autonomous Systems with ongoing Tactical Infrastructure Enterprise Services (TIES) Joint Concept Technology Demonstration (JCTD) events. (2015, 2016 events).

---

[2] "NATO Modelling and Simulation Centre of Excellence." https://www.mscoe.org.
[3] "Georgia Tech Research Institute." http://www.gtri.gatech.edu.

d. Develop engagement strategy for the Services and in each RAS community (airborne, ground, and maritime). (2015, 2016-18 events).
e. Leverage and assist in harmonization of ongoing DOD efforts, including:
   - DOD CIO Joint Information Environment (JIE);
   - DOD CIO Unmanned Airborne Systems (UAS) Encryption (DODI 4660.04);
   - DOD Common Data Link (CDL) PSA/EA Standards;
   - OUSD AT&L UAS Control Segment (UCS) architecture model;
   - Joint Staff J6 Warfighter Mission Area (WMA) DODAF architecture federation;
   - Joint Staff J6/J8 Digitally Aided Close Air Support (DACAS) coordinated implementation;
   - Joint Staff Robotic/Autonomous Systems Team (JRAST);
   - Joint Staff JRAST Joint Concept for Robotic/Autonomous Systems (JCRAS) document;
   - NGA GEOINT Functional Manager's Seal of Approval (metadata compliance certification).
f. Develop, as early as possible within the JCIDS and development cycles, NIEM conformance criteria and implementation instructions to assist program offices in implementing XML-based data exchanges.
g. Coordinate with OSD AT&L and Services to develop generic POM justification language to support the resourcing requirements associated with NIEM adoption.

10 Use Cases

NIEM-conformant XML-based data exchanges are in operational use in numerous mission and functional areas. Some examples include:

a. Map Based Planning Service (MBPS): MBPS provides comprehensive collaborative planning tools for mission and contingency planning at strategic and operational headquarters. In 2014, the program used a NIEM-conformant XML-based data exchange to swap planning information.
b. Tactical Infrastructure Enterprise Services Coalition Warfare Program (TIES CWP): At the 2014 Coalition Warrior Interoperability, eXploration, eXperimentation, and eXamination eXercise (CWIX) event, NIEM-conformant XML-based data exchanges were used to improve interoperability and information sharing between the U.S. and coalition partners. Position Reports, Air Track information and Observed Position Reports were exchanged through a request-response web service environment.
c. Maritime Information Sharing Environment (MISE): MISE provides an ongoing internet-accessible, unclassified information sharing framework for interested parties on vessel tracking and information. Effective information exchange times have been reduced from weeks to days, and in some cases, to hours. MISE is leveraged by over 12 active partners within the federal and defense community, to include a US State partner.
d. Open Geospatial Consortium: NIEM support of the future Intelligence Command and Control environment was demonstrated in two Open Geospatial Consortium

(OGC) events in 2013. The GEO4NIEM [5] pilot showed that NIEM supports exchanging geospatial data represented in GML. Using NIEM in conjunction with the OGC technical framework, the MilOps Interoperability Experiment (MOGIE) [6] demonstrated data from a variety of message types can be fused without introducing error and displayed on a variety of devices including mobile handheld, web-browser, and computer workstations.

11   Appendix A – Simulated Interactive Robotics Initiative

The Simulated Interactive Robotics Initiative (SIRI) assessment was conducted to evaluate the feasibility of using XML-based messages in an RAS environment. SIRI involved comparing message sizes, serialize/marshal/encode times and deserialize/ unmarshal/decode times of various types and standards used in SIRI environment supporting UGVs. The purpose of this assessment was to provide a preliminary assessment of how XML and XML-EXI compare to the binary data standard used in the simulated unmanned system for the event.

SIRI is different from other studies done with EXI in that it compares performance with equivalent types in BEE-DDS. It is not meant to be a thorough study of performance for any of the used standards. It is also not the intention to compare fully optimized implementations of these standards as the focus was on the implementations used in SIRI. For a more complete study of EXI see [7–9].

11.1   SIRI Overview

To facilitate the SIRI experimentation of XML-based data exchanges and messaging, the M&S COE support team developed a Multi-Robot Simulator and also performed an interoperability test between Robotic Operating System (ROS)-based Multi-Robot Simulator BEE-DDS. The GTRI team developed an OGC conformant client using NIEM.

The Cooperative Multi-robot Information Exchange Demonstrator (COMIED) established and set-up a demonstrator to assess the key Information Exchange for Cooperative Multi-robot System (CMS) interoperability. The CMS is composed of a squad of networked Unmanned Ground Vehicle (UGV), and one or more Command and Control Stations (C2). A typical squad size is 5–10 UGVs.

The V-UGVs were developed based on the ROS/Stage simulation environment, which provides for different typologies of virtual ground robotic platforms which host the actual software component, providing the autonomous capabilities listed above.

The Data Exchange and the distributed robotic capabilities, such as the Dynamic Task Assignment, are based on the Open Management Group (OMG) Data Distribution Services (DDS) standard. The COMIED adopted the DDS protocol implementation used by the MSCOE support team which is called, "BEE-DDS." [15]

11.2   EXI Background

Efficient XML Interchange (EXI) is a binary XML format adopted by the W3C in 2011. The use of EXI enables messages implemented in XML to be represented in a compact binary format. This drastically reduces the time required to send messages across a data connection, enabling the use of XML in scenarios requiring high performance. EXI types can be completely defined in an XSD and can be converted to and from XML instances. This means EXI is ready to be used with existing NIEM type definitions with little to no modification.

EXI is not compression. While EXI messages are much smaller than their XML equivalents, the messages are not merely compressed text. EXI is an actual binary format that allows data to be encoded and decoded to and from EXI in a single step. With compressed XML, the text data is first marshalled into text and then compressed before it is transmitted. When received, the data must be uncompressed and then unmarshalled before it can be used by a machine. When using EXI, data is encoded in EXI, sent across the wire and then decoded back into machine memory. No compression is required and XML does not even have to be used in the process. Figure 3 illustrates this point. For a more exhaustive explanation of EXI see [4].

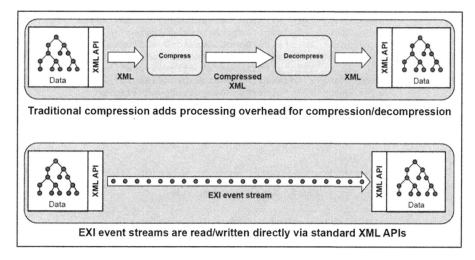

Fig. 3. EXI vs compression ("AgileDelta Efficient EXI FAQ." http://www.agiledelta.com/index. html.)

RobotStateType. When SIRI began, the RobotState type was defined to represent the status of the unmanned vehicles. Location, time and other information was sent from the UGVs to the MMS via RobotState message instances. RobotState was originally defined with the name StatoRobotDataType. This data type was exchanged between UGVs and between UGVs and their control station using Java serialization and is defined in Fig. 4.

```
struct StatoRobotDataType {
  long robotId; // RobotID
  string statoRobot; // RobotStateText
  string descrizioneEstesa; // RobotStateDescriptionText
  boolean esegueTask; // RobotPerformingTaskIndicator
  boolean robotAttivo; // RobotActiveIndicator
  double px; // RobotLocationCoordinate (x axis)
  double py; // RobotLocationCoordinate (y axis)
  double pa; // RobotOrientationMeasure
  double vx; // RobotVelocityMeasure
  double vy; // RobotSideSpeedMeasure
  double va; // RobotAngularSpeedMeasure
};
```

Fig. 4. StatoRobotDataType

```
<xs:complexType name="RobotStateType">
  <xs:complexContent>
    <xs:extension base="structures:ObjectType">
      <xs:sequence>
        <xs:element ref="siri:RobotID"/>
        <xs:element ref="siri:RobotStateText"/>
        <xs:element ref="siri:RobotStateDescriptionText"/>
        <xs:element ref="siri:RobotPerformingTaskIndicator"/>
        <xs:element ref="siri:RobotActiveIndicator"/>
        <xs:element ref="siri:RobotLocationCoordinate"/>
        <xs:element ref="siri:RobotOrientationMeasure"/>
        <xs:element ref="siri:RobotVelocityMeasure"/>
        <xs:element ref="siri:RobotSideSpeedMeasure"/>
        <xs:element ref="siri:RobotAngularSpeedMeasure"/>
        <xs:element ref="siri:RobotStateDateTime"/>
      </xs:sequence>
    </xs:extension>
  </xs:complexContent>
</xs:complexType>
```

Fig. 5. NIEM RobotStateType

Using the StatoRobotDataType above, GTRI defined a NIEM conformant complex type (i.e., RobotStateType) to match the fields as closely as possible, except that the type and element names are in English. The XSD and a sample instance are shown below. This data type was used in the simulation experiment as well as this assessment.

11.3   Experiment

The data used for this assessment was recorded as NIEM RobotState XML instances from the robot simulator used in COMIED. There are 2,126 RobotState instances which represent the path that five simulated UGVs followed during the simulation. Each RobotState instance was stored in its own file using the UTF-8 character encoding with no unnecessary white space characters. Figure 6 shows an actual sample instance used in the assessment (formatted for readability).

```
<ns2:RobotState xmlns:ns5="http://release.niem.gov/niem/niem-core/3.0/" xmlns:ns2="http://m
  <ns2:RobotID>0</ns2:RobotID>
  <ns2:RobotStateText>idle</ns2:RobotStateText>
  <ns2:RobotStateDescriptionText>Homing</ns2:RobotStateDescriptionText>
  <ns2:RobotPerformingTaskIndicator>false</ns2:RobotPerformingTaskIndicator>
  <ns2:RobotActiveIndicator>true</ns2:RobotActiveIndicator>
  <ns2:RobotLocationCoordinate>
    <ns3:Point srsName="http://metadata.ces.mil/mdr/ns/GSIP/crs/WGS84E_2D" ns3:id="noId">
      <ns3:pos>40.524525699740714 17.283559843392446</ns3:pos>
    </ns3:Point>
  </ns2:RobotLocationCoordinate>
  <ns2:RobotOrientationMeasure>
    <ns5:MeasureDecimalValue>2.6533156082878064</ns5:MeasureDecimalValue>
  </ns2:RobotOrientationMeasure>
  <ns2:RobotVelocityMeasure>
    <ns5:MeasureDecimalValue>0.0</ns5:MeasureDecimalValue>
  </ns2:RobotVelocityMeasure>
  <ns2:RobotSideSpeedMeasure>
    <ns5:MeasureDecimalValue>0.0</ns5:MeasureDecimalValue>
  </ns2:RobotSideSpeedMeasure>
  <ns2:RobotAngularSpeedMeasure>
    <ns5:MeasureDecimalValue>0.0</ns5:MeasureDecimalValue>
  </ns2:RobotAngularSpeedMeasure>
  <ns2:RobotStateDateTime>2015-01-05T12:00:37.900-05:00</ns2:RobotStateDateTime>
</ns2:RobotState>
```

Fig. 6. Example RobotState XML instance

No assumptions about required precision are made resulting in many values with overly high precision. The effect of precision on message size is discussed in a later section on optimization. There are five recurring values for RobotStateDescriptionText: "Homing" occurs 542 times, "Path Inspection" 1320 times, "Threat Found" 72 times, "Threat Mitigation" 132 times and no value occurs 60 times. There are two recurring values for RobotStateText: "idle" occurs 2042 times and "busy" occurs 84 times.

The processes described below often refer to RobotState JAXB objects and StatoRobotData objects. It is important to note that while all tests were executed with the same data, the DDS measurements used the StatoRobotDataType defined in Fig. 4 and the XML and EXI measurements used JAXB classes generated from the Robot-StateType defined in Fig. 5.

EXI Analysis. The EXI alignment type was set to bit-packed[4] and the strict option[5] was enabled. All other EXI options are left as the default (Fig. 7).

The EXI message size, shown in Fig. 8, was determined by recording the byte array length of all of the encoded XML instances and taking their average. The encoding time, for a single RobotState, was measured as the time taken to encode an instantiated RobotState JAXB object into a byte array. The decoding time, for a single RobotState instance, was measured as the time taken to decode the same byte array back into a RobotState JAXB object. The average time, for both encoding and decoding, was determined by measuring the respective time for all 2,126 instances a total of 10 times and taking the average. To rule out time introduced by JVM warm up overhead, the same process was executed ten times prior to the timed test described above. The encode and decode times are shown in Fig. 9.

---

[4] http://www.w3.org/TR/exi/#key-unaligned.

[5] http://www.w3.org/TR/exi/#key-strictOption.

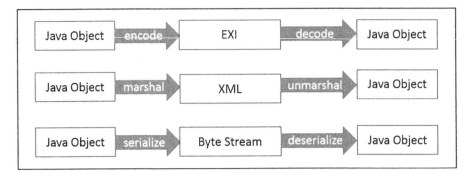

Fig. 7. Encode/decode, marshal/unmarshal, serialize/deserialize

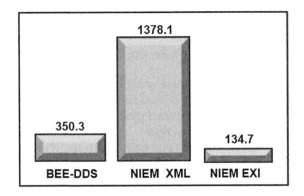

Fig. 8. Average message sizes in bytes

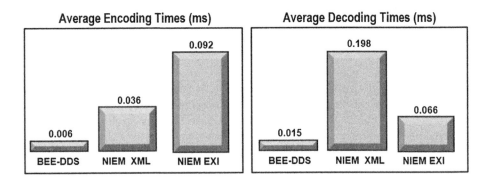

Fig. 9. Average message encoding and decoding times

XML Analysis. The XML message size was determined by recording the character length of all 2,126 XML instances and taking their average. The unmarshalling time, for a single RobotState, was measured as the time taken to unmarshal the instance, as a string in memory, into the JAXB object. The marshalling time was measured as the time taken to marshal the same JAXB object back into a string. The average time for both marshalling and unmarshalling was determined in the same manner described above, by measuring all instances ten times after JVM warmup and taking the average.

DDS Analysis. The DDS message size was determined by recording the byte array length of all of the 2,126 serialized StatoRobot objects and taking their average. The serialize time, for a single StatoRobotData instance, was measured as the time taken to serialize the StatoRobotDataType into a byte array. The deserialize time, for a single StatoRobotData instance, was measured as the time taken to deserialize the same byte array back into a StatoRobotDataType object.

11.4 Findings

Message Size. The chart below illustrates the average message sizes. EXI binary representation of SIRI state data defined in NIEM XML generated the smallest data package, which was 62 % smaller in size than the binary BEE-DDS, and 90 % smaller than the NIEM XML. The EXI message sizes range from 109 – 142 bytes. The XML message sizes range from 1339 – 1390 bytes. The DDS message sizes range from 338 – 355 bytes.

Encoding/Decoding Performance. The cursory performance analysis produced results that are not necessarily consistent with other evaluations. Particularly encoding EXI took over twice as long as marshalling XML. The charts below show the results.

These results reflect the performance of the implementation and software stack used in SIRI. Since the EXI performance has been shown to be much faster, these values are provided to illustrate their insignificance when compared to transfer times. The chart and table below show the end to end message processing times including transferring the message across a one Mbps data link. Transfer times shown are calculated using the average message size values without overhead so they represent the minimum amount of time the message would take to transfer (Fig. 10) (Table 1).

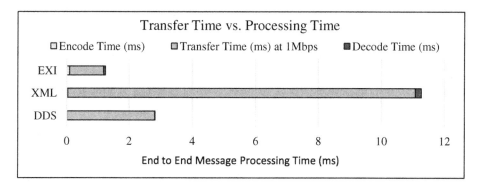

Fig. 10. Comparison of transfer and processing time

Table 1. Comparison of transfer and processing time

	Encode time (ms)	Transfer time (ms) at 1Mbps	Decode time (ms)
DDS	0.006	2.8024	0.015
XML	0.036	11.0248	0.198
EXI	0.092	1.0776	0.066

Optimization. Recommendations for future optimizations were identified to reduce the EXI message size. They were not included in the comparison above because they were not used during the SIRI simulation. The optimizations fall into two categories: Enumerations instead of strings and precision reduction.

Precision. Precision was initially not managed which resulted in many of the values having high precision. Post processing of the data to set maximum precision for the values reduced the message sizes by about 20 bytes. Specifically the latitude and longitude precision was reduced from 16 fractional digits to six and the other four values were reduced to one fractional digit (Table 2).

Table 2. EXI message size comparison based on precision

	High precision	Low precision
EXI	134.7 bytes	114.1 bytes
XML	1378.1 bytes	1333.8 bytes

This optimization only requires that the values are set to the optimal precision when the data is encoded. No modifications to the schema are necessary.

Enumerations. The XML instances had three string fields with recurring values. Modifying the schema to represent RobotStateDescriptionText, RobotStateText and srsName as enumerations reduced the average EXI message size to 67.4 bytes. This optimization requires the schema modifications which may not always be practical. It also limits the number of values that can be used to those defined in the enumeration.

12   Appendix B – Definitions

Data	A representation of facts, concepts, or instructions in a formalized manner suitable for communication, interpretation, or processing by human or machine means.
Information	Data placed in context and thereby given meaning.
Syntax	Grammatical rules applied to a computer language to create uniformity.
Semantics	The vocabulary used in a specific computer language.
Schema	The organizational pattern or structure (e.g., the schema for agreed Information Exchange Package Descriptions (IEPDs) used for the unmanned aircraft systems information exchanges includes rules for syntax and semantics).

References

1. Work, R.O., Brimley, S.: 20YY: Preparing for War in the Robotic Age. Cener for a New American Security (2014)
2. Stenbit, J.P.: Department of Defense Net-Centric Data Strategy. DTIC Document (2003)
3. DOD CIO Memorandum, Adoption of the National Information Exchange Model (NIEM) within the Department of Defense (DOD) (2013)
4. Schneider, J., Kamiya, T., Peintner, D., Kyusakov, R.: Efficient XML interchange (EXI) format 1.0, 2nd edn. W3C (2014)
5. Martell, R.: Summary and Recommendations of the Geospatial Enhancement for the National Information Exchange Model (Geo4NIEM) Interoperability Program Pilot. Open Geospatial Consortium (2013)
6. Klucznik, F., Weber, M., Houtmeyers, R., Brackin, R.: OGC® Military Operations Geospatial Interoperability Experiment (MOGIE). Open Geospatial Consortium (2013)
7. Binary Extensible Markup Language (XML) Technology Overview and Recommendation for Army Tactical Network Binary Data. CECOM Life Cycle Management Command Software Engineering Center Enterprise Solutions Directorate (2012)
8. Joint Staff J6 JFD Comparison of Compression Techniques for FFI-MTF XML. CECOM Life Cycle Management Command Software Engineering Center (SEC) Army Net-Centric Data Strategy Center of Excellence (ANCDS CoE) (2013)
9. Snyder, S.: Efficient XML Interchange (EXI) Compression and Performance Benefits: Development, Implementation and Evaluation. Naval Postgraduate School, Monterey (2010)
10. Unmanned Interoperability Initiative (UI2) Capabilities Based Assessment (CBA) (2012)
11. Christensen, H.I., Batzinger, T., Bekris, K., Bohringer, K., Bordogna, J., Bradski, G., Brock, O., Burnstein, J., Fuhlbrigge, T., Eastman, R.: A Roadmap for us Robotics: From Internet to Robotics. Comput. Community Consort. Comput. Res. Assoc., Washington, DC (2009)
12. An Open Business Model for Unmanned Aircraft Ground Control Stations. OSD AT&L, Unmanned Aircraft Systems Task Force, Interoperability IPT (2014)
13. Initial Capabilities Document (ICD) for Unmanned Systems. Joint Requirements Oversight Council (2010)
14. Joint Staff J6 Memorandum, DOD Adoption of the National Information Exchange Model (NIEM) and Establishment of the NIEM Military Operations Domain (2013)
15. Weber, M., Klucznik, F., Burkhart, L., Roth, S.: Simulated Interactive Robotics Initiative, Experiment with National Information Exchange Model eXtensible Markup Language, v1.2 (2015)
16. Unmanned systems integrated roadmap: FY2013-2038, US Department of Defense, Washington, DC US (2013)

Modeling and Simulation for UAS Integration into the United States National Airspace System and NextGen

Richard S. Stansbury[1]([✉]), John Robbins[1], Massood Towhidnejad[1],
Brent Terwilliger[2], Mohammad Moallemi[1], and Jayson Clifford[1]

[1] Embry-Riddle Aeronautical University, Daytona Beach Campus,
Daytona Beach, FL 32114, USA
{stansbur,robbinsj,towhid,moallemm,clifforj}@erau.edu
[2] Embry-Riddle Aeronautical University, Worldwide Campus,
Orlando, PA 32826, USA
terwillb@erau.edu

Abstract. Airspace integration is a major challenge that must be addressed for wider unmanned aircraft system (UAS) acceptance and one-day ubiquitous operations. Both research and training play a role in addressing these challenges, which are cross-disciplinary. Embry-Riddle Aeronautical University (ERAU) is heavily invested in promoting the safe integration of UAS into both the United States National Airspace System (NAS) as well its future under the FAA NextGen programs planned upgrades. This paper surveys ERAUs use of modeling and simulation (M&S) to address the relevant challenges including development of flight management systems (FMS) for UAS to operate amongst manned air traffic, the development of aircraft performance models for various UAS categories, the application of simulator technologies to UAS flight crew training, and the creation of virtual labs to provide realistic training experience for UAS system configuration and testing.

Keywords: M&S · UAS · Airspace integration · Training · NextGen

1 Introduction

Safe integration of unmanned aircraft into the National Airspace System (NAS) remains one of the greatest technical and regulatory hurdles for routine operations of unmanned aircraft systems (UAS) within the United States. The Federal Aviation Administration (FAA) NextGen program also creates a moving target as air traffic management (ATM) systems evolve with greater focus upon automation, interconnectivity, and higher density utilization of airspace and airport surfaces.

A greater number of opportunities exist for research focused UAS operations including the issues of a Certificates of Authorization (or Waiver) for operation of public operators or parties with Sect. 333 Exemptions, or alternatively a Special

© Springer International Publishing Switzerland 2015
J. Hodicky (Ed.): MESAS 2015, LNCS 9055, pp. 40–59, 2015.
DOI: 10.1007/978-3-319-22383-4_4

Airworthiness Certificate-Experimental. The FAA has also made available six UAS Test Sites. These options require a more mature system and often have significant constraints upon the operations performed under test. Because of these limitations, modeling and simulation (M&S) continues to play a major role in UAS research and training.

Embry-Riddle Aeronautical University (ERAU) is significantly active in education and research related to UAS as well as the FAA NextGen program. M&S is used in several relevant areas including aviation automation, airspace integration, performance analysis, and training. This paper provides an overview of ERAU, its aviation mission, and several key facilities supporting M&S. A brief literature review of M&S for UAS for the verification, validation, and demonstration of advanced flight management systems (FMS); airspace integration into the United States National Airspace System and its NextGen variant; UAS performance analysis; UAS pilot/crew training; and distance training for future UAS mission planners / managers. Next, a survey of research activities t ERAU iin each of these areas as performed s discussed. The paper concludes with a summary of ERAU's current M&S capabilities for UAS-NAS integraton.

2   Background

This section provides a brief background about ERAU and its role in unmanned aircraft systems academics and research.

2.1   Academics

ERAU is comprised of three main campuses: Daytona Beach, FL (ERAU-DB), Prescott, AZ (ERAU-PC), and Worldwide (ERAU-W). ERAU-W is comprised of more than 150 campuses around the world as well as distance delivery through online programs and courses. Across the three campuses, ERAU has developed a reputation for academics within the unmanned system community.

ERAU-DB launched a minor in UAS attached to its Bachelor of Science degree (BS) in Aeronautical Sciences in 2009. The minors success led to the offering of a BS in Unmanned Aircraft System Sciences (BS-UASS). This academic program prepares students for career as UAS operators or support crewmembers under a variety of roles and responsibilities. The use of flight simulators to provide students with UAS flight/operations experience is discussed further in Sect. 4.3. ERAU-DB also launched in Fall 2013 a Master of Science degree (MS) in Unmanned and Autonomous Systems Engineering (MS-UASE) in the College of Engineering. The MS-UASE degree program promotes systems thinking and engineering best practices for students of all undergraduate engineering backgrounds, and applies these concepts to the engineering of unmanned systems (including UAS) and related systems.

ERAU-W offers online a Bachelors of Aeronautics with a UAS minor. It also offers a MS in Unmanned Systems (MS-US) and an MS in Aeronautical Science with a UAS specialization. The MS-US degree provides students with a broader understanding of unmanned systems including UAS, their sub-components, and their integration. It also provides an understanding of the business and logistics aspects of UAS operations. Section 4.4 discusses the development of online tools to provide a laboratory experience for students through distance delivery. ERAU-W also provides UAS Workshops worldwide.

2.2   Research

UAS related research is prevalent across ERAUs three campuses. Fifty-five ERAU researchers (faculty and staff) have published papers related to unmanned and autonomous systems including UAS. ERAU was the lead university for the FAAs Center of Excellence for General Aviation Research (CGAR), which supported a portion of the FAAs UAS portfolio until 2012 when the program ended.

ERAU provides over a decade of UAS-related research. It is a founding member of the 19 university ASSURE Coalition [7]. ERAU has established partnerships with a number of key stakeholders including FAA, NASA, NOAA, and numerous industry partners. UAS M&S research is conducted on the Daytona Beach, FL campus in a number of state-of-the-art research facilities including the Next Generation Advanced Research (NEAR) Lab, a for-hire aviation research facility, and the UAS Training and Research Laboratory, with its high-fidelity UAS simulation capabilities for research and aircrew training. Section 4.1 discusses relevant UAS M&S research in the NEAR Lab while Sect. 4.3 discusses the development of high-fidelity simulators for training. ERAU with the support of NEAR also manages the Florida NextGen Testbed, an FAA facility to evaluate, test, and demonstrate FAA NextGen concepts and technologies.

ERAU-Ws faculty and collaborators are also actively involved in UAS related research. Section 4.2 discusses a major ERAU-W faculty collaboration to develop UAS performance data and metrics verified through M&S techniques. Through industry collaboration, they are also developing a laboratory experience for the MS-US degree for distance delivery as discussed in Sect. 4.4.

3   Literature Survey

This section provides a brief survey of literature relevant to M&S for aviaton automation, air traffic management, UAS performance modeling, pilot/crew training, and distance delivery for education.

3.1   M&S for UAS Flight Management Systems (FMS)

Due to the high costs of testing, verifying, and validating UAS automation hardware/software and strong safety assurances typical of aviation, M&S plays an important role in UAS design and development. Several commercial and open-source computer-based simulators have been developed in the past two decades [8]. Key discriminators between UAS simulators are categorized as functional fidelity, physical fidelity, ease of development, and costs. Functional fidelity explains the degree of accuracy in modeling the aircrafts flight dynamics and control surface functionalities, while physical fidelity deals with the accuracy of the aerodynamics and physical properties of the environment in which the aircraft flies [3].

The low cost and risk-free nature of M&S-based research and development (R&D) of UAS technologies has led to the development of simulation-based FMSs capable of steering the aircraft using a simulated autopilot. A survey of simulation-based autopilots for UAS can be found in Chao et al. [6]. An autopilot is a closed-loop system comprised of two parts: the state observer and the controller. Simulation-based autopilots rely on aerodynamic data calculated by the simulation engine as the simulation evolves, instead of receiving real-time data from the aircrafts sensors, inertial measurement unit, or GPS. The simulation engine also incorporates the control commands generated by the autopilot to compute the forces applied to the UAS, based on the vehicle specifications, engine thrust, and control surface measurements.

A fault-tolerant UAS autonomous control algorithm accompanied by a simulation environment developed under Matlab/Simulink is proposed in [16]. A recent comprehensive study of UAS autonomy challenges (sensing, control, cooperative control algorithms, software-in-the-loop and hardware-in-the-loop simulations) and certification issues are discussed in [30].

3.2   M&S for UAS/ATM Integration

As a result of a variety of challenges with UAS integration into the NAS, the FAA has failed to develop new regulation, policies, and procedures for UAS operation under current and near-future ATM systems [15]. A comprehensive study of the limitations, hurdles, and safety issues in integrating UASs into the NAS has been presented in Valavanis et al. [29]. The authors of that paper note that a major requirement for a UAS to be fully integrated into any NAS is noted broadly as the ability for a UAS to function as if a human pilot is onboard the aircraft [29]. UAS operation by remote control or applying current automation technologies has not fulfilled this vital requirement, which strengthens the need for M&S research to help address this gap.

M&S allows researchers and policy makers to verify technologies and procedures under pervasive ATM scenarios related to UAS/NAS integration in a risk-free setting including scenarios that would be physically impractical due to cost or risk. M&S has the tools and techniques that can support a number of key challenges for UAS ATM integration including, but not limited human factors associated with remote pilots interacting with air traffic control, methodologies for regulatory compliance and harmonization, and the modeling of hazards and risk.

3.3 M&S for Performance Modeling

The significant growth of UAS acquisitions and application, the dynamic regulatory requirements of UAS, and UAS technological and method advancements exhibit a need to better understand the ability of unique platform configurations to perform given tasks or functions [20]. Recent advances in UAS technology, coupled with methods for optimally exercising capabilities, have led to potential safety and efficiency gains [20]. Designs for command, control, and communication (C3), airframe, propulsion, and sensing elements have benefited from technological gains in the areas of microminiaturization, processing, sensing fidelity, and materials development [28]. Such enhancement of designs and their associated capabilities has fostered the availability of lower-cost, lightweight, more powerful, and stronger components available for integration into UAS [28]. UAS are now being considered and used to support a wide-range of applications, including mapping, inspection, emergency response, and precision agriculture [9,20]. Increased interest and use has focused efforts to better apply, regulate, and certify to further improve capacity to achieve desired results [9,20].

Despite the potential advantages and gains of improved UAS technology and techniques, there have been a number of cases where UAS have been acquired and underutilized or used in a manner the design was unsuited for, resulting in reduced effectiveness, cost inflation, and increased risk to persons and equipment [4,14,26,27]. Achieving advantageous UAS use is dependent on increasing awareness of the innate performance and operational constraints [20], which can be studied using M&S tools and techniques [17,21,31]. Through development and employment of a robust, high-fidelity set of performance models and analysis framework, the limitations and abilities of UAS (experimental treatments) can be isolated and manipulated in a manner supporting identification of studied effects on attributes (criterion) [20]. The knowledge gained from such investigation supports improved understanding of UAS configuration capabilities, identifying and addressing issues, developing improved conceptual operation (CONOP) plans, and creating new applications, strategies, or methods to ensure the safe, efficient, effective, and appropriate application of UAS [20].

3.4 M&S for Pilot/Crew Training

Flight simulators have been designed and constructed to meet user requirements in three areas: (a) entertainment; (b) personnel training, selection and testing; and (c) aircraft systems research and development [22]. Early uses of simulation technologies have led to breakthrough implications above traditional pilot training. World War II era motion platform applications of flight simulation technologies provided a reasonable method to train and hone the skills of military aviators. This technology afforded pilots the opportunity to fly missions in Instrument Flight Conditions (IMC) and led to studies into the transferability of training between varying platforms. Today, simulation technologies are commonplace in the aviation community. High-fidelity, full-motion platforms have become mainstream and an industry standard to both train new pilots and provide re-currency for existing aviation professionals. Empirical evidence suggests training accomplished in high-fidelity flight simulators promote a positive transfer of learning into the actual flight environment for manned aircraft [10]. ERAU has worked to dedicate significant resources and education in an effort to revolutionize the future of UAS as infrastructure continues to grow. High-fidelity simulation technologies have been used in flight training for decades, but with the further use of semi/fully autonomous systems in aviation, they have become a modern necessity to future aviators. McCarley and Wickens [13] state UAV flight presents many human factors challenges different from manned aircraft and the demands placed on the operators for civilian and commercial applications will vary with the characteristics of the specific flight mission. UAS pilot/sensor technologies will provide both cognitive and psychomotor skill enhancement at a significant value, guarding safety and efficiency as a priority. Simulation technologies allow users to fulfill a plethora of mission profiles that may be difficult or impossible to replicate safely in real-world? training environments. UAS application is threaded by a new generation of pilots who have seen the benefit of technology and automation from an early age. New entrants to the industry likely have a significant technological background, adding to a transfer of applicable skills relevant to industry need and standards.

3.5   M&S for Education Distance Delivery

The growth of asynchronous education, in terms of topical coverage and depth of experience, has led to the development of tools to better support learning achievement in an online environment. Historical research has exhibited positive performance when students engage in learning using interactive and active strategies, compared to conventional or passive methods, such as lecture [12,19]. Tools such as virtual laboratories, incorporating M&S techniques and capabilities, have been shown to support knowledge discovery and conceptual knowledge transfer [11]. The use of online virtual laboratories provides a means to support interactive, engaged learning among a geographically dispersed population of students, in turn providing new curriculum options to a wider population [5].

4   Survey of Modeling and Simulation for UAS-NAS Integration at ERAU

This section surveys specific M&S efforts at ERAU-DB and ERAU-W.

4.1   Development of Advanced Autonomy and Airspace Integration

Researchers at ERAU-DBs NEAR Lab haVE developed a simulation-based FMS with a number of embedded flight dynamic models (FDMs) of a variety of aircraft classes in the JSBSim M&S tool [1]. JSBSim is an open-source M&S software for flight dynamics modeling that implements physical equations of motion in fluid dynamics and aerodynamics, as well as ideal Proportional-Integrative-Derivative (PID) control theories. Models and controllers are written using C++ supported by XML model specification language.

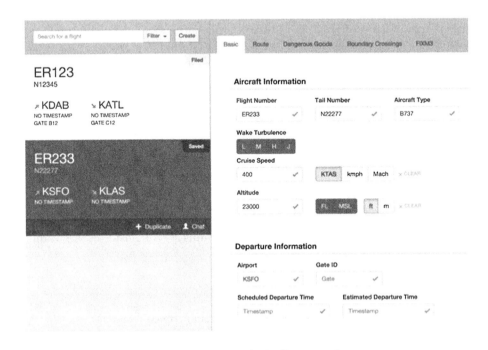

Fig. 1. NEAR-FMS flight filing interface

The NEAR-FMS is capable of storing flight plans using 3D waypoint trajectories (latitude, longitude, and altitude), as well as spawning multiple simulated real-time aircraft. Figure 1 shows the interface for adding a new simulated flight into the NEAR-FMS simulation environment. The arrival and departure airports and aircraft type as well as altitude, speed, and wake turbulence can be entered to the system. A flight plan trajectory can be provided for autonomous navigation of an aircraft. NEAR-FMS software allows UAS operators to create, modify and cancel flight plans. Flight plans can be defined using the Flight Information Exchange Model (FIXM) 3.0 flight plan format. FIXM 3.0 is an FAA developed data exchange model for transporting flight information across FAA NextGen systems. FIXM 3.0 defined flight plans. UAS telemetry will be converted to FIXM 3.0 and published to Flight Object Exchange Services (FOXS) via a Global Enterprise Messaging Service (GEMS). The utilization of NextGen technologies allows this simulator to be integrated into a variety of FAA NextGen research, verification and validation, and demonstration projects.

The NEAR-FMS operates and controls a high-resolution flight simulator / ground control station (GCS) mockup. The simulator provides high-resolution wide-angle virtual reality visualizations across three monitors displaying real-world terrain using Cesium 3D [2]. Additional simulation features include an auxiliary primary flight display (PFD), joystick control, and an autopilot switchboard as shown in Fig. 2.

Fig. 2. NEAR-FMS simulation console and display unit

The real-time NAS Aircraft Situational Display to Industry (ASDI) feed is incorporated into the system, facilitating the integration of the simulated UAS flights into the real-time state of the NAS. The control unit can switch between each simulated flight and take over the control for that particular aircrafts simulation. Once the control is released, the simulated aircraft goes back to autonomous control and follows the provided flight plan. Figure 3 depicts the NAS Flight Display Integration Console, where real-time flights are displayed along-side the simulated ones, created through the NEAR-FMS flight filing interface (Fig. 1). This capability allows the FMS to fly in a realistic ATM environment and test simulated scenarios that are correlated with real flight activities within the NAS.

Currently, three different aircraft categories were modeled based upon the Boeing 737, Bombardier Global 5000, and Cessna 172p. These aircraft models were selected to verify the conformity of the 4D trajectory of the simulated flight with assigned flight plans. In order to leverage the simulated FMS, autopilot scripts have been developed using fine-tuned PID controllers. The autopilot code is comprised of four main control loops that command the control surfaces and throttle. Detailed aircraft performance characteristics (available as public data)

Fig. 3. NEAR-FMS NAS flight display integration

are integrated into the autopilot script to mimic the realistic behavior of the aircraft. The autopilot control loops are as follows:

- Roll loop: commands the ailerons to control the roll angle,
- Pitch loop: commands the elevator to control the pitch angle (up and down),
- Yaw loop: commands the rudder to control the yaw angle (left and right), and
- Speed loop, commands the throttle to control the speed.

Figure 4 shows the altitude and velocity outputs for a two hour flight of a B737 as well as the corresponding elevator and throttle commands generated by autopilot. The elevator command value is bound to the the interval of (-1, 1). The value is then converted to the degree of deviation from normal position. The throttle value is limited to the interval of (0, 1), which is converted to the thrust of the engine by the simulation engine. For the test in Fig. 4, the altitude was set initially to 30,000 ft., then changed to 40,000 ft. after 976 s from the start of the simulation. Finally, it changed to 20,000 ft. after 2,079 s from the start of the simulation, as can be seen in the figure. The speed was set to 400 fps, which was changed to 350 fps, later at 2,079 s from the start of the simulation. The autopilot commands to elevator and throttle to hold the desired altitude and speed are depicted, respectively. Figure 5 depicts the flight path of the simulated B737 in this test. Note that the autopilot was able to maintain the altitude and speed despite of the sharp maneuvers on its route.

NEAR has further development plans for the simulation. First, the team plans to develop models for UAS platforms including 'Shadow 400" and "Gale" [18], which have been simulated in a previous version of the simulator, but have

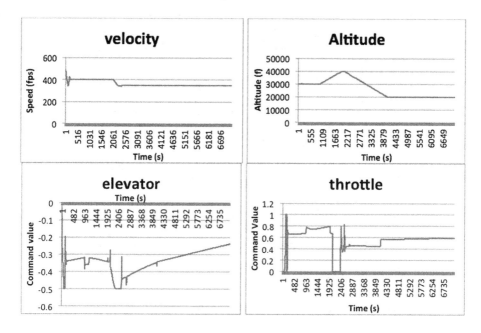

Fig. 4. NEAR-FMS autopilot commands and outputs for B737

not been reimplemented for the upgraded system. The simulation models of these aircraft in NEAR-FMS will provide cost-efficient rapid testing of various scenarios. Simulation results will help ratify design issues by providing detailed insight into the aerodynamics and strength of some of the parts of the UAS that are 3D printed in the lab.

The R&D team is also working on equipping NEAR-FMS simulated flights with full FIXM 3.0 published messages as well as Aeronautical Telecommunication Network (ATN) Baseline 2 messages. These capabilities will enable future projects en-route negotiations and Dynamic Required Navigation Performance (D-RNP) implementations on a simulated FMS prior to testing on actual avionics, paving the road for ATM integration of UAS.

4.2   Development of UAS Performance Models

This ERAU-W research project was initiated to improve collective understanding of the implications, limitations, constraints, and benefits of potential UAS application. Specifically, the research investigates the effects of using UAS configuration types to perform a given function. M&S concepts, techniques, and tools were applied in the development of a series of category representative performance models, termed attribute performance models (APMs), to establish a baseline for treatment, statistical analysis, and observation within an experimental framework.

Fig. 5. Flight path of the simulated B737 demonstration

The APMs represent various categorical segments of 282 commercial off-the-shelf (COTS) Group 1–3 UAS platform configurations ($N_{UAS} = 282$). Each APM consists of a series of attributes used to calculate performance or capability to execute a given function or application, including speed (cruise and maximum), altitude (operating and maximum), endurance, range (one-way and round-trip), weight (payload capacity, empty, and maximum takeoff), wind limit, and system cost. Each APM attribute is calculated by determining the mean score of individual UAS platform configuration attributes within the category. The attributes of the individual configurations were obtained from publically available sources, through communication with a manufacturer, or derived based on other related data.

In some instances, an attribute was unavailable and insufficient data existed to calculate (derive) the performance metric. To measure the potential strength of the models and identify weak attributes (low reporting rate), a series of metrics were calculated to indicate the percent of samples reported for each attribute and APM. The mean reporting rate of all attributes was 77.77 percent, with 2851 of 3666 total attributes identified or calculated. The attributes with the lowest reporting rate (out of 282 possible) were the maximum altitude (115; 40.78%), wind limit (67; 23.76%), and system cost (76; 26.95%). Those attributes that could be captured or derived were examined and used to produce the following APMs (developed to date):

- Group 1–3 UAS (100% of N_{UAS}; 77.77% of attributes reported)
- Group 1 Fixed-wing (19.86% of N_{UAS}; 77.47% of attributes reported)
- Group 1 Vertical Takeoff and Landing (VTOL; 15.96% of N_{UAS}; 77.95% of attributes reported)
- Group 2 Fixed-wing (15.96% of N_{UAS}; 75.90% of attributes reported)
- Group 2 VTOL (15.96% of N_{UAS}; 74.87% of attributes reported)
- Group 3 Fixed-wing (16.31% of N_{UAS}; 70.23% of attributes reported)
- Group 3 VTOL (15.96% of N_{UAS}; 68.55% of attributes reported)
- Small UAS (sUAS; sub-55lbs; 67.73% of N_{UAS}; 76.60% of attributes reported)
- Fixed-wing sUAS (35.82% of N_{UAS}; 76.77% of attributes reported)
- VTOL sUAS (31.91% of N_{UAS}; 76.41% of attributes reported)
- Electric sUAS (52.48% of N_{UAS}; 77.81% of attributes reported)
- Internal Combustion sUAS (15.25% of N_{UAS}; 79.96% of attributes reported)
- Tube-launched (4.26% of N_{UAS}; 60.90% of attributes reported)
- Optimal platforms to support a specific aircraft rescue fire fighting (ARFF) response application (4.96% of N_{UAS}; 94.51% of attributes reported)

Effective use and study of the APMs, within context of a given use, required the development of an application analysis framework, titled Capability Analysis and Effectiveness Response for Unmanned Systems (CAERUS). CAERUS was designed to support experimentation and detailed examination of UAS configuration performance and suitability to perform envisioned applications. The framework features the loading of applicable platform configuration details (APMs or individual UAS configurations), creation and execution of experimental scenarios (trials), implementation of unique theories of operation (CONOPs), and the ability to control extraneous conditions, while observing and measuring effects on criterion. CAERUS was designed to be tailored for a given application and tested using a conceptual theory of operation to deploy UAS in support of ARFF response operations (UAS-ARFF case study; see Fig. 6) [20].

The development and use of CAERUS provided significant benefits, including the ability to prototype and evaluate CONOPs without purchase or risk to cost-intensive UAS platforms, observe the effects of controllable parameters (environmental conditions and distances) on experimental treatments (APMs) as they were calculated (traceability), control extraneous factors, visualize UAS routes and maneuvers, and review automatically generated statistical analysis results, e.g., analysis of variance (ANOVA), [20]. It was also possible to achieve gains in efficiency (cost and time) as the framework automatically performed critical calculations and output data that could be used to assess individual APM performance for the development of application requirements and recommendations. In addition, the use of CAERUS provided the means for several members of the research team to work on individual aspects of the research concurrently, without requiring colocation at a common UAS operational site, as

Fig. 6. View from simulated UAS in orbit over stationary object of interest (target), generated using CAERUS framework featuring Google earth API

well as insight regarding the inherent appropriateness of individual and types of UAS to perform in a given environment.

While significant benefit was achieved through the use of the APMs and CAERUS, both are still developmental and would benefit from further revision, improvement, and evaluative validation (using actual UAS). As previously noted, the data associated with the individual UAS configurations is not complete with 22.23 percent of the attribute values unknown. Furthermore, the overall strength of the statistical models is based upon the overall sampling size (N_{UAS}), which could be improved through the addition of new platforms and configurations as they become available on the market. The CAERUS framework currently features limited trajectory and maneuver calculations, environmental effects, visualization capability, and user interface to load or manipulate data, due to constraints during initial development. Future revisions are planned to improve the user interface and add more complex M&S features, such as higher-fidelity calculations, visualization, and environmental (weather) condition effects.

4.3 UAS Pilot/Crew Training

ERAU-DB, in collaboration with URS, has built a state of the art high-fidelity UAS laboratory for research and aircrew training. ERAUs lab is outfitted with URSs Generic Unmanned Aerial System Trainer (X-Gen) [24], which is designed and built around the X-IG image generator [25]. XIG is capable of rendering 400,000 fully-textured, shaded and anti-aliased polygons to visualize an environment with six degrees of freedom at 60 Hz. This system supports geodetic exported terrain and rapid placement of database features using the Environmental Modeling Editor [23]. The XIG is used for real-time rendering of the UAS sensor view together with controls, displays, and a 2D moving map display for air vehicle operations.

The X-Gen simulator accurately reproduces GCS hardware and UAS flight characteristics. The lab has fourteen networked workstations that simulate a generic aerodynamic model profiling based upon a Medium Altitude Long Endurance (MALE) UAS. Each workstation can simulate either a UAS pilot station or sensor operator station, and can be linked to simulate a full crew station. Figure 7 shows two students using the simulator with one pilot, one payload operator, and one observer. The X-Gens operating system allows researchers to pull performance data to include aircraft attitude, location, altitude, and airspeed at 1 Hz. Multiple variables may be altered within the simulation including weather, latency, and system malfunctions. All crew stations are equipped with TeamSpeak software allowing for recordable voice and text based communications between crewmembers.

Fig. 7. BS-UASS studetns operate X-Gen simulators for classroom training experience

ERAU faculty have worked to develop scenarios to further the effectiveness of simulation-driven training environments. Simulations are dependent on a number of variables that support high levels of cognitive and psychomotor skill development, while also promoting human interaction through proper crew resource management (CRM). The synergy of these skillsets is paramount to the successful usage of simulation technologies to enhance student capability. ERAU has developed in-house training scenarios that are capable of replicating high-fidelity environments with multiple "real-world" scenarios. Students can directly benefit

Fig. 8. Student UAS flight crew plan mission prior to operating simulator

from insight derived from actual operational scenarios that strongly replicate actual UAS mission profiles. Figure 8 shows students conducting a pre-mission brief prior to executing the prepared mission scenario using the laboratory's simulators.

AS220 (Unmanned Aircraft Systems Operations), AS235 (UAS Operations & Cross-Country Data Entry), and AS473 (UAS Flight Simulation) are courses that ERAU offers that are heavily reliant on this simulation environment. Curriculum design was assessed to include high levels of simulation involvement to promote the required knowledge, skill, and ability profiles set forth by direct industry input. These courses provide different levels of exposure to include tactile and psychomotor skill development, cognitive assessment, and mission planning at the application level.

4.4   Distance Delivery of UAS System Integration Training

ERAU-W offers unmanned systems related curricula at both the undergraduate and graduate levels featuring synchronous, asynchronous, and mixed-modality delivery (e.g., classroom, online, and EagleVision networked video and audio). An integral aspect of such content delivery is the ability to achieve and support interactive learning. Work was recently completed on the University's first virtual learning environment, the Virtual Crash Lab, which was developed in partnership with Pinnacle Solutions and has been fielded across several ERAU-W safety (SFTY) courses. The experience and insight gained from development and release of this first virtual laboratory environment was instrumental for initiating the next in the series, the Virtual UAS Lab.

The Virtual UAS Lab has been designed to enhance the learning environment and build student experience through exploration, manipulation, and examination of individual component-level elements, integrated subsystems, and unique UAS configurations within virtual environments and modules. The first module, Bench Level Experimentation, is designed to introduce students to the capabilities and characteristics of individual UAS components, such as sensors, data-links, and propulsion sources, in a simulated environment supporting isolation, control, and observation of relevant parameters (e.g., acceleration, rotation, power, thrust, signal strength and propagation). This module will feature placement of the elemental components in a setting replicating a real-world laboratory environment to manipulate testable features of the device. For example, a three-axis accelerometer will be placed on a simultaneous multi-axis vibration table (i.e., shake table) to observe and record variable effects on individual accelerometer output. The intent of this module is to familiarize students with the baseline component, theory of operation, and resultant effects of manipulation.

The second module, Integration and Assembly, has been designed to provide experimentation opportunities at the subsystem level for communications, powerplant, and sensor payloads. This module will feature placement and manipulation of various student selected component combinations (integrated into a subsystem) to determine their potential effects or implications. For example, for the powerplant subsystem a motor (electric or internal combustion), power control (electronic speed control [ESC] or servo-driven throttle body), propeller type, fuel source (battery or liquid), and sizing for each will be selected for placement on a test rack where input control variables will be manipulated to determine thrust produced, revolutions per minute [RPM], and power remaining or consumed. The intent for this module is to support improved student comprehension regarding potential relationships and dependencies among components in a subsystem and to observe resultant effects of manipulation.

The final module, Flight Experimentation, has been designed to provide a common simulated environment supporting flight test, evaluation, and observation of a user configured UAS to evaluate ability to perform as intended (in relation to a student defined flight plan). This module will provide the student with a workspace to examine the various options (subsystems and elements) for integration into a unified UAS configuration. It will feature intuitive drag and drop assembly and saving of unique configurations for sharing among the community of users (faculty and students). The student will also create a flight path (series of waypoints with altitudes; see Fig. 9) within the simulated environment to observe and record the capabilities and performance of the UAS configuration, based on telemetry and payload output.

ERAU-W developed the conceptual overview of this tool by establishing connections to current unmanned system and engineering program/learning outcomes and activities (traceability), consulting with the Pinnacle Systems to determine feasibility and cost, and obtaining subject matter guidance from faculty members engaged in administration and instruction of applicable courses. The degrees anticipated to be supported by Virtual UAS lab include the Master

Fig. 9. Flight planning and addition of waypoint locations in the virtual UAS Lab - flight experimentation module

of Science in Unmanned Systems (MSUS; 36 credits), the Bachelor of Science in Unmanned Systems Application (BSUSA; 120 credits), undergraduate UAS minor (18 credits), graduate UAS specialization (12 credits), Bachelor of Science in Engineering Technology (123 credits), and Associate of Science in Engineering Fundamentals (65 credits). The Virtual UAS Lab has completed preliminary design review (PDR) with software development occurring over the next six-months, followed by subject matter expert (SME) review and testing with the anticipation of being available to students by January 2016.

5 Conclusion

As this paper has shown, there is a strong need for M&S to address the challenges and issues associated with UAS, and how ERAU is providing the capabilities of technologies and crews to meet address some of these challenges. The challenges of developing autonomy software and validating that software under realistic scenarios both with and without ATM integration are currently being addressed at the ERAU-DB's NEAR lab. ERAU-W is working to better understand how UAS perform under a variety of contexts and developing simulation tools to evaluate unmanned systems under anticipated scenarios to determine that they meet the requirements of key stakeholders. ERAU-DB's UAS Simulation Laboratory is leading the way in providing realistic UAS mission training through state-of-the-art flight simulation tools and technologies. Finally, ERAU-W is developing a new virtual laboratory environment to train future UAS systems integration and mission management personnel.

Acknowledgements. The authors would like to acknowledge the following parties for their support in the research and training projects discussed in this paper: Embry-Riddle Aeronautical University and its leadership across its three campuses; faculty, staff, and students of the ERAU-DB NEAR Lab; faculty and staff of the UAS Simulation Laboratory, and the BS-UASS faculty; UAS performance modeling and application analysis research team, including Dr. David Ison, Dr. Dennis Vincenzi, Dr. Todd Smith, Dr. Rene Herron, Dr. Ken Witcher, and David Thirtyacre; and ERAU Virtual Labs (crash and UAS labs) development teams, including Dr. Brian Sanders (ERAU-W), Dr. Ken Witcher (ERAU-W), Dr. Katherine Moran (ERAU-W), Scott Burgess (ERAU-W), Mark Leary (ERAU-W), Jamie Sipe (ERAU-W), Becky Vazquez (ERAU), James Ohlman (Pinnacle Solutions), Tina Tucker (Pinnacle Solutions), and Michael Durant (Pinnacle Solutions). Additionally to the ERAU-W faculty who contributed to requirements analysis and development, including David Thirtyacre, Dr. Robert Deters, Stefan Kleinke, Dr. Patti Clark, Dr. Bruce Conway, and Ted Thompson.

References

1. Jsbsim flight dynamic modeling and simulation software, April 2015. http://jsbsim.sourceforge.net/
2. AIG: Cesium - WebGL virtual globe and map engine, April 2015. http://cesiumjs.org/
3. Alexander, A.L., Brunyé, T., Sidman, J., Weil, S.A.: From gaming to training: a review of studies on fidelity, immersion, presence, and buy-in and their effects on transfer in pc-based simulations and games. DARWARS Train. Impact Group **5**, 1–14 (2005)
4. Betson, A.P.: The case against a cargo unmanned aircraft system. Army Sustain. **44**(5), 28 (2012)
5. Cancilla, D.A., Albon, S.P., et al.: Reflections from the moving the laboratory online workshops: emerging themes. J. Asynchronous Learn. Netw. **12**(3–4), 53–59 (2014)
6. Chao, H., Cao, Y., Chen, Y.: Autopilots for small unmanned aerial vehicles: a survey. Int. J. Control Autom. Syst. **8**(1), 36–44 (2010)
7. Coalition, A.: Assure: Alliance for system safety of uas through research excellence, April 2015. http://www.assureuas.org
8. Craighead, J., Murphy, R., Burke, J., Goldiez, B.: A survey of commercial & open source unmanned vehicle simulators. In: IEEE International Conference on Robotics and Automation, pp. 852–857. IEEE (2007)
9. FAA: Notice of proposed rulemaking (nprm), operation and certification of small unmanned aircraft systems (docket no.: Faa-2015-0150; notice no. 15–01) (2015). https://www.faa.gov/regulations_policies/rulemaking/recently_published/media/2120-AJ60_NPRM_2-15-2015_joint_signature.pdf
10. Haritos, T., Robbins, J.M.: The use of high fidelity simulators to train UAS pilot and sensor operator skills. In: Society of Applied Learning Technologies: New Technologies (2011)
11. Harms, U.: Virtual and remote labs in physics education. In: Second European Conference on Physics Teaching in Engineering Education (2000)
12. Lukman, R., Krajnc, M.: Exploring non-traditional learning methods in virtual and real-world environments. Edu. Technol. Soc. **15**(1), 237–247 (2012)

13. McCarley, J.S., Wickens, C.D.: Human factors implications of UAVs in the national airspace. University of Illinois at Urbana-Champaign, Aviation Human Factors Division (2005)

14. Minder, B., Coleman, T.: Unmanned aerial vehicles: underutilized and untapped (opinion). Emergency Management, May 2012. http://www.emergencymgmt.com/disaster/Unmanned-Aerial-Vehicles-Underutilized-and-Untapped.html

15. Parsons, D.: Usa eases grip on UAV controls: faa issues several exemptions for civil and commercial applications ahead of expected launch of unmanned aircraft rules. Flight International (2015)

16. Perhinschi, M.G., Wilburn, B., Wilburn, J., Moncayo, H., Karas, O.: Simulation environment for UAV fault tolerant autonomous control laws development. J. Model. Simul. Ident. Control **1**(4), 164–195 (2013)

17. Perry, S.R., Taylor, J.H.: A prototype gui for unmanned air vehicle mission planning and execution. In: 19th World Congress, The International Federation of Automatic Extraneous. Cape Town, SA (2014)

18. Stansbury, R.S., Towhidnejad, M., Demirkiran, I., Clifford, J., Dop, M., Koung, T., Cione, J., Ash, N., DuPuis, M.: A p-3 deployable unmanned aircraft for scientific measurement of tropical cyclones. In: Infotech@ Aerospace 2011. AIAA (2011)

19. Stuckey-Mickell, T.A., Stuckey-Danner, B.D.: Virtual labs in the online biology course: student perceptions of effectiveness and usability. MERLOT J. Learn. Teach. **3**(2), 105–111 (2007)

20. Terwilliger, B., Vincenzi, D., Ison, D., Herron, R., Smith, T.: UAS capabilities and performance modeling for application analysis. In: Proceedings of the Association for Unmanned Vehicle Systems International 42nd Annual Symposium. Atlanta, GA, May 2015

21. Terwilliger, B., Vincenzi, D., Ison, D., Witcher, K., Thirtyacre, D., Khalid, A.: Influencing factors for use of unmanned aerial systems in support of aviation accident and emergency response. J. Autom. Control Eng. **3**(3), 246 (2015)

22. Tsang, P.S., Vidulich, M.A.: Principles and Practice of Aviation Psychology. Lawrence Erlbaum Associates Publishers, New York (2003)

23. URS: Environmental modeling editor (EME) for rapid database enhancements, April 2015. http://www.urs-simulation.com/pdf/EME_spec.pdf

24. URS: X-GEN – generic unmanned system trainer, April 2015. http://www.urs-simulation.com/products/xgen_uas.aspx

25. URS: X-IG – visual image generator, April 2015. http://www.urs-simulation.com/products/xig_image_generator.aspx

26. U.S. Customs and Border Protection: use of unmanned aircraft systems in the nations border security (report no. oig-12-85) (2012). http://www.oig.dhs.gov/assets/Mgmt/2012/OIG_12-85_May12.pdf

27. U.S. Department of Justice: audit of the department of justices use and support of unmanned aircraft systems (2015). http://www.justice.gov/oig/reports/2015/a1511.pdf#page=2

28. U.S. Department of Transportation: unmanned aircraft systems (UAS) service demand 2015–2035: Literature review and projections of future usage (report no. dot-vntsc-dod-13-01).   http://ntl.bts.gov/lib/48000/48200/48226/UAS_Service_Demand.pdf

29. Valavanis, K.P., Vachtsevanos, G.J.: UAV integration into the national airspace: introduction. In: Valavanis, K.P., Vachtsevanos, G.J. (eds.) Handbook of Unmanned Aerial Vehicles, pp. 2113–2116. Springer, The Netherlands (2015)

30. Valavanis, K.P., Vachtsevanos, G.J.: UAV modeling, simulation, estimation, and identification: introduction. In: Valavanis, K.P., Vachtsevanos, G.J. (eds.) Handbook of Unmanned Aerial Vehicles, pp. 1215–1216. Springer, Netherlands (2015)
31. Wu, P.P., Clothier, R.A.: The development of ground impact models for the analysis of the risks associated with unmanned aircraft operations over inhabited areas. In: Proceedings of the 11th Probabilistic Safety Assessment and Management Conference (PSAM11) and the Annual European Safety and Reliability Conference, ESREL 2012 (2012)

Modeling and Simulation Interoperability Concepts for Multidisciplinarity, Interdisciplinarity, and Transdisciplinarity – Implications for Computational Intelligence Enabling Autonomous Systems

Andreas Tolk[(✉)]

Chief Scientist SimIS Inc., 200 High Str. #305,
Portsmouth, VA 23604, USA
andreas.tolk@simisinc.com

Abstract. Modeling and Simulation is highly important to robotics. Modeling is creating a conceptualization that is implemented by the simulation. As such the insights are directly applicable to planning and decision logic of autonomous systems for complex situations. When autonomous systems collaborate, they not only need to be interoperable, i.e. able to exchange data and utilize service calls, but also composable, i.e. provide a consistent interpretation of truth. The collaboration of autonomous systems can happen in a multi-, inter-, or trans-disciplinary context, depending on the maturity level of interoperability that is defined in this chapter using the Levels of Conceptual Interoperability Model (LCIM). The results are coherent with the NATO Net-enabled Capability Command and Control Maturity Model (N2C2M2) that can show the degree of interoperation with and among autonomous systems. Finally, several computational constraints are discussed that limit the ability of autonomous systems: incompleteness, decidability, computational complexity, and their implications for the applicability of self-organizing command and control for autonomous systems.

Keywords: Autonomous systems · Command & control · Composability · Computational intelligence · Interdisciplinarity · Interoperability · Modeling & simulation · Multidisciplinarity · Transdisciplinarity

1 Introduction

Why does a book on Autonomous Systems feature a chapter on modeling and simulation (M&S) interoperability concepts for multi-, inter-, and transdisciplinarity? This chapter will hopefully answer this question by showing the pivotal importance of M&S for autonomous systems, not only for testing, but in particular when it comes to proving computational intelligence for the autonomous system: M&S will the brain of autonomous systems!

An autonomous system will observe its situated environment, create a perception, communicate eventually with its user or other systems to add or confirm information, decide on what actions to take, and then execute the action, potentially in

© Springer International Publishing Switzerland 2015
J. Hodicky (Ed.): MESAS 2015, LNCS 9055, pp. 60–74, 2015.
DOI: 10.1007/978-3-319-22383-4_5

orchestration with other systems. Military personnel immediately recognize the "observe – orient – decide – act (OODA)" loop as documented by Boyd [1]. But what is easy for the soldier needs to be supported in computable form for autonomous systems, and this is done by M&S.

In order to be able to do this, the models used to build simulations need to be appropriate conceptualizations of all important things, relations, and actions. Furthermore, the often independently from each other developed models utilized in the various autonomous systems that participate in an operation need to be able to work with each other. It is not sufficient that the computational simulations are interoperable, i.e., they can exchange data and call services from each other. It is also necessary that the conceptualizations used are not contradicting each other. The models need to be composable, i.e., resulting in a consistent representation of truth, such as defined in [2]. This observation leads to the need of understanding the different disciplinarity categories of multi-, inter-, and transdisciplinarity and how they are supported by different levels of interoperability as defined for model-based systems in the *Levels of Conceptual Interoperability Model* (LCIM) [3].

As simulations, when used as the brain for an autonomous system, are computer programs, there are several epistemological implications with far reaching theoretic and philosophical consequences. Computability, decidability, computational complexity, and other insights that limit computer programs in general are applicable to simulations used for decision making as well.

Finally, autonomous systems need to be integrated into the command and control processes of operations. The last section of this chapter will look at principles of self-organizations for current operations. The NATO Net-Centric Command and Control Maturity Model (N2C2M2) [4] can become a useful frame to look at command and control capabilities for military autonomous systems as well.

In summary, this chapter may be quite different from typical robotics contributions and specification. It has been contributed with the objective to make the developer and user of autonomous systems aware of some bigger guiding principles than those usually in the focus of finding very practical solutions to very real challenges. Hopefully, the reader will not only enjoy this new perspective, but will clearly see the importance of these ideas for the future of autonomous systems.

2   What is Modeling and Simulation

In this section, the important ideas regarding M&S for autonomous systems will be described. The focus will be on the use of M&S in autonomous systems, as an integral part for decision making. Additional aspects, such as the use of agent-based simulation systems for better testing, have already been discussed in [5].

M&S comprises two main activities: modeling and simulation. As shown in [2], the modeling part is of essential importance not only for the resulting implementation – the simulation – but also for the general applicability of the simulation in changing contexts and the ability to successfully collaborate with other model-based applications.

2.1 Modeling

Modeling is the task-driven, purposeful simplification and abstraction of a perception of reality that is shaped by physical/ethical and cognitive constraints. It results in a formal specification of a conceptualization and can be conducted in several phases. In detail:

- *Task-driven:* A model is created with a certain purpose in mind. Often, a research question or hypothesis needs to be answered. In the defense domain, the use for training or testing is also a frequent task. In any case, the task is implying a certain worldview that will drive decisions during the modeling processes.
- *Simplification:* The model will focus only on the important aspects to fulfill the given tasks. Everything that is not important can be deleted, resulting in a much simpler subset of relevant entities, relations, and events.
- *Abstraction:* The subset is normally further simplified by only modeling the core entities, relations, and events in full detail. Elements that influence the core, but that do not belong to the core, are often abstracted to reduce the overall complexity.
- *Purposeful:* Simplification and abstractions are purposeful decisions of the modeler (or the modeling team). As a result, decision parameters and motivation for certain solutions can be documented.
- *Perception:* The modeler or team does not have direct access to reality. Even when using the latest scientific insights, only a perception of reality can be used as the reference point. Our scientific models and insights are themselves perpetually evolving [6]. While physical models have been stable, social models are far from having the same degree of maturity.
- *Physical/ethical constraints:* The access to empirical data is often limited by physical and by ethical constraints. Frequently, not all attributes of interest are accessible or observable. Sometimes, new instruments help to make better observations. Similarly, ethical limits may obstruct optimal data collections, in particular when the welfare of human beings in endangered.
- *Cognitive constraints:* While simplification and abstraction is done purposefully, cognitive constraints of the modeler or the team or not necessarily immediately obvious. However, an expert in the domain will collect far more relevant information than a novice. A model can only be as good as the domain expertise that is utilized to create it.

Another important aspect is the multitude of approaches that can be used and that often shape the facet under which a problem is evaluated and analyzed. Fishwick [7] presents examples of the many modeling paradigms regarding modeling methodologies – such as discrete event systems, system dynamics, or agent based approaches – and model types – such as ordinary differential equations, process algebra, temporal logic, etc. A hidden danger is that modelers become very comfortable with their favorite paradigms and types and, as a result, are perceiving the task through these favorite approaches. The manner of speaking *"if you only have a hammer, everything looks like a nail"* is applicable in this context as well.

The result of the modeling phase is a formal specification of the conceptualization that can be implemented as a computer program. This conceptualization captures all entities and their properties, the relations between entities, and events as detailed as deemed necessary based on what could be found out about the task. For the simulation, this conceptualization becomes its reality: whatever is not in the model cannot be understood or taken into consideration.

Even when we assume a coherent positivistic worldview, i.e., that only one reality exists that is equally exposed to several modelers, based on the constraints discussed in this subsection they will likely come up with very different conceptualizations.

2.2 Simulation

Simulations implement models and execute them over time. They allow to gain numerical insight into complex system behaviors. But like the modeling process, many additional decisions are necessary during the implementation processes that may influence the reliability of the simulation.

Oberkampf et al. [8] document some typical errors and uncertainties in M&S. They identify mathematical modeling, discretization and algorithm selection, computer programming, and numerical solutions as pivotal activities that all contribute to potential errors and uncertainties. In particular when solving stochastic differential equations numerically, the approach taken has a significant influence on the quality of the implementation, as shown in [9]. Oberkampf et al. [8] show how the choice of partial differential equations, auxiliary physical equations, boundary and initial conditions, and non-deterministic representations contribute to uncertainties and errors during mathematical modeling activity. It is worth pointing out that these errors and uncertainties are not caused by human error or faulty hardware, but that they are systemic to the use of digital computers to implement models.

Similarly to the observations before it can be assumed that even when starting from the exact same conceptualization, which has been shown to be unlikely from the discussions in the last subsection on modeling, the resulting applications can differ significantly.

2.3 M&S and Autonomous Systems

The use of simulation to provide a safe and controlled environment for developing and testing autonomous systems is well established. An example of the state of the art is documented by Rentschler [10] who provided a realistic synthetic environment for autonomous underwater vehicles. Additional examples are given in [5]. The use of M&S for autonomous systems in this section, however, is focusing on providing intelligence for decision making to the system. The following Fig. 1 shows a taxonomy of an autonomous systems is suggested by Tolk [5].

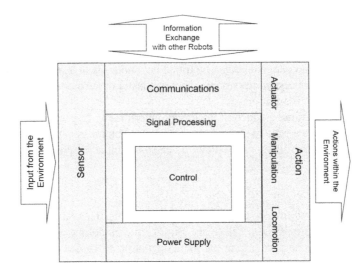

Fig. 1. Taxonomy of an autonomous system

Autonomous systems use sensors to observe the environment. In addition, they may communicate with the user and other systems to plan together or to orchestrate the execution of a common plan. This is done by the control unit that gets sensor data and communicated information via signal processing components. Once the decisions on how to act are computed, the necessary commands are generated and transmitted via signal processors to actuators, manipulators, or the locomotion system.

Many challenges have been solved recently, but the control unit is in many cases not smart enough to support real autonomy, not even as a backup when, e.g., remote control is interrupted. In order to support these ideas of autonomy, the systems have to understand the situation they are in and plan accordingly. The ideas represented in the

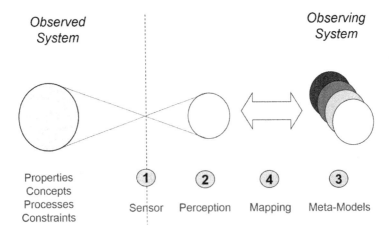

Fig. 2. Models and machine understanding

following Fig. 2 were first introduced by Zeigler in 1986 to demonstrate how models support the general concepts of machine understanding [11].

First, the autonomous system needs a set of sensors and signal processors (1) in order to support a perception (2). This is a nontrivial process and many good contributions from the domain of sensors and robotics introduce necessary solutions to hard physical and mathematical problems, such as the correlation and fusion of multi-sensors, or feature extraction in complex environment. In the context of this chapter it is of interest to know that an attribute can only make it into the perception of the autonomous system if three conditions are fulfilled:

- The attribute of interest is exposed in a form observable by the sensors of the autonomous systems.
- The target-background noise ratio for the attribute of interest is sufficiently small not to disturb the observation.
- The perception itself allows for capturing the observation of the attribute of interest.

Of particular interest is the third bullet, which is often overlooked in technically focused publications: the perception itself is a model, a conceptualization of everything that the developer thinks is of interest and observable. Like the researcher who conducts a data survey decides before he conducts the interviews on the data model he wants to use to capture the information, the designer of an autonomous systems must decide on the conceptualization of the perception, and whatever he simplifies, abstracts, or based on the cognitive and physical constraints excludes from the perception can never be perceived or taken into consideration by the autonomous system in following operations.

In order to make sense of the perception, a set of explanations needs to be provided in computable form. This happens in form of meta-models (3) that provide interpretations of the observation. A perceived object is recognized by the autonomous if a mapping (4) between the perception and an applicable meta-model can be established. This is normally done if the correlation between observed and assumed characteristic attributes passes a certain threshold: if something has a tracked locomotion systems, is armored, has a turret, and has a gun it is likely some form of military tank.

Again, these are models: conceptualizations of possible observations foreseen by the developers of the autonomous system. If an object shows up in the operational environment that has not been foreseen, it cannot be recognized. If, e.g., an android is observed, but the developers of the autonomous systems did not foresee that such a system would show up in the possible scenarios, the autonomous system may either assume the android to be a human – when the correlation of observed attributes, such as height or patterns of movements, is sufficient – or it is classified as unknown.

The meta-models are not only used to map observations to recognizable objects, they also attach assumed capabilities and behaviors to these objects. If a military tank is observed, certain behaviors expected from a tank is used to support planning and reaction. The recognized meta-models with a synthetic representation of the environment are used to support the sense-making (orient) as well as planning and decision making (decide).

In summary, models play a pivotal role for intelligent behavior of autonomous systems. Perceiving, sense-making, and decision-making are driven by implemented conceptualizations. As such, all the discussions on modeling and simulation, as individual phases as well as the M&S discipline, are directly applicable and necessary for gaining a better understanding of capabilities and constraints of autonomous systems.

3   Multidisciplinarity, Interdisciplinarity, and Transdisciplinarity

While the observations so far focused on individual systems, the following section will expand this discussion towards societies of autonomous systems. Of particular interest for this chapter are heterogeneous societies comprising a variety of autonomous systems with different tasks and capabilities. It is highly unlikely that their control units will use identical models and implementations, and still they have to work together. Orchestrating these tasks is comparable to the collaboration of several disciplines that also are characterized by different conceptualizations and methods. The LCIM helps to understand how heterogeneous M&S solutions can be utilized in support of these ideas. Following the same logic used in the last section the case will be made that these ideas and concepts are directly applicable to the control logic used in autonomous systems as well.

3.1   Understanding the Different Disciplinarity Categories

Science and engineering are conducted within several disciplines, although the proper criteria for organizing knowledge into disciplines is still open to debate. However, different disciplines can be distinguished by their topics of interests, the way they understand knowledge (ontology), the way they gain knowledge (epistemology), the methods and tools they are using, and other often very practical criteria. In order to cope with complexity, for several years science applied the principle of analyzing and describing a complex phenomenon by breaking them apart into smaller and simpler subsystems on a more fundamental level. This principle of reductionism supported the idea of several independent disciplines well, but in recent years the need to address problems systemically and holistically brought experts from several disciplines together to collaborate on solving problems.

The degree of collaboration of these experts and the disciplines can differ significantly. Stock and Burton [12] introduced definitions for multidisciplinarity, interdisciplinarity, and transdisciplinarity.

- In multidisciplinary approaches, experts from various disciplines are working together on a common question or topic of interest. Each discipline remains unchanged but simply contributes its knowledge, methods, and expertise.
- When common tools are developed and the participating discipline start to link to each other instead of juxtaposing, the effort becomes interdisciplinary. Permanent bridges between the disciplines are established.
- Finally, when the participating disciplines are systematically integrated to create new knowledge components in transcending and transgressing form, a new transdisciplinary effort emerges.

Figure 3 shows a comparison of these categories of disciplinarity. In multidisciplinary projects, the collaboration is deconflicted by clearly defined domains of responsibility and synchronized by the exchange of terms of a common controlled vocabulary. In interdisciplinary projects, common domains of mutual interest are identified in which the work is orchestrated by sharing methods and tools. In transdisciplinary projects, the borders between the disciplines vanish and a new discipline is born, in which all elements of the old disciplines are collaborating in well-orchestrated manner, each part being applied to the biggest advantage of the new body of knowledge.

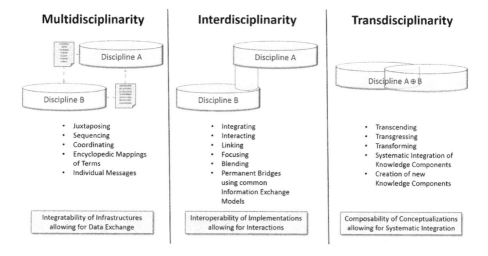

Fig. 3. Multi-, inter-, and transdisciplinarity

Disciplines are working with formal conceptualizations of their domains. The various levels of collaboration also imply a decreasing degree of alignment of the underlying theories, ontological means, and epistemological rules. In a broader sense, as postulated by Goldman in [6], these again are models and their implementations.

3.2 The Levels of Conceptual Interoperability Model

The LCIM [3] was developed to explain the various degrees of interoperability when building federations. It has been applied in various domains, from defense simulation to the evaluation of interoperability challenges for the next generation of the power grid, and has been recommended to be extended into an interoperability maturity model [13]. It underwent several changes since its original conception and now distinguishes between seven interoperability levels, forming three categories that are easily mappable to the multi-, inter-, and transdisciplinary principles just discussed.

- On the lowest level, systems are stand alone. There is no connectivity or exchange between the systems. Every system works for its own.
- Once signals can be exchanged, technical interoperability is achieved. However, the interpretation of these signals may differ within the various systems.

- On the level of syntactical interoperability, the interpretation of signals to communicate common symbols is agreed upon.
- Finally, the interpretation of these symbols provides a common semantic. Controlled vocabularies or information exchange data models help to reach this level that allows the exchange of data between the systems.
- However, only because data can be exchanged between the systems, this does not imply that the receiving system is reacting as expected. If the way the system is going to apply the received information is agreed upon, pragmatic interoperability is reached.
- In order to reach full transparency, the internal state changes need to be understood as well, which results in dynamic interoperability.
- Finally, all constraints and assumptions need to be shared in order to reach conceptual interoperability.

Figure 4 shows the LCIM.

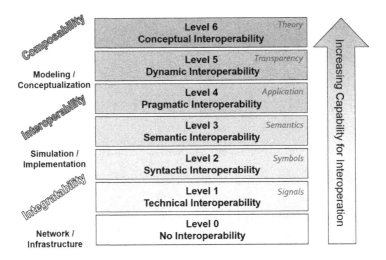

Fig. 4. The levels of conceptual interoperability model

King and Turnitsa [14] provide examples on assumptions and constraints that are necessary to ensure real collaboration, but that are often only captured insufficient or implicit. The initial work on the LCIM was generalized by Page et al. [15]. They introduced the three interoperability categories:

- *Integratability* contends with the physical/technical realms of connections between systems, which include hardware and firmware, protocols, networks, etc.
- *Interoperability* contends with the software and implementation details of interoperations; this includes exchange of data elements via interfaces, the use of middleware, mapping to common information exchange models, etc.

- *Composability* contends with the alignment of issues on the modeling level. The underlying models are purposeful abstractions of reality used for the conceptualization being implemented by the resulting systems.

Successful interoperation of solutions requires integratability of infrastructures, interoperability of systems, and composability of models. Successful standards for interoperable solutions must address all three categories.

   While interoperability is necessary for model-based solutions, it is not sufficient. As shown in [2], two interoperable systems can easily produce to different interpretations of truth, if their internal concepts are not well aligned. Interoperability is well understood as the ability to exchange information and to use the data exchanged in the receiving system. Interoperability can be engineered into a system or a service after definition and implementation. Composability is a different challenge. Composability ensures the consistent representation of truth in all praticipating systems. This requires that the underlying models need to be consistent. To engineer composability into a system may require a complete redesign of the models used.

4   Implications for Autonomous Systems

The two previous sections made the argument that intelligence needed to develop autonomous systems need to be model-based. If two autonomous systems have to collaborate, their possible degree of collaborations will be determined by the level of conceptual interoperability they can reach. Integratability allows for multidisciplinary collaboration of systems, interoperability supports interdisciplinary approaches, but for full cooperation, such as required for truly transdisciplinary efforts with full integration into a synergistic society of heterogeneous autonomous systems, composability is required. In order for autonomous systems to work like this, standards guiding their collaboration must address all three categories.

   These insights are well supported by the NATO Net-enabled Capability (NEC) Command and Control (C2) Maturity Model (N2M2C2) [4]. If autonomous systems reach the required level of computational intelligence, they can be integrated into the command cycle which is governed by similar constraints as the collaboration between model-based systems just presented in the previous section.

   Finally, some noteworthy computational limits of simulations that are applicable to model implementations for sense-making and decision-making in autonomous systems are given.

4.1   Command and Control for Autonomous Systems

With the N2C2M2, Alberts, Huber, and Moffat [4] introduced a concept for measuring the maturity of independent systems regarding their ability to support a common goal. They define five categories of interoperation visualized in Fig. 5.

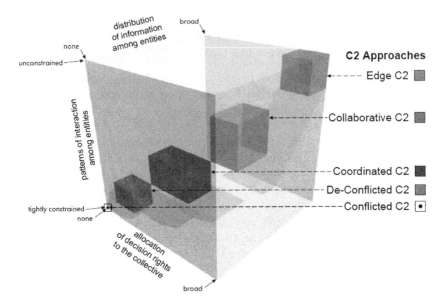

Fig. 5. The NATO NEC C2 maturity model

The dimensions used to place the five categories are the allocation of decision rights to the collective of entities (from none to broad), the pattern of interactions among these entities (from tightly constrained to unconstrained), and the distribution of information among the entities (from none to broad).

While currently the various systems are managed and governed independently, the resulting plans are conflicting. Each system exclusively focuses on its own resources and capabilities to reach their own objectives as if no other participant were present. Therefore, conflicts between participants are the rule. Their objectives are potentially mutually exclusive. Plans and execution will compete with each other.

Limiting the responsibility to each sector of the system results in de-conflicted operations. It ensures that organizations avoid interfering with one another. However, this partition is artificial and suboptimal, as it excludes synergism. The orchestration of activities in each sector will be supported by special nodes in intersecting domains specifically designed for this task. Nonetheless, orchestration will be limited to synchronizing the execution of operations.

Coordinated operations require joint planning driven by a shared intent. The synchronized plan allows decision-making on lower levels. However, each component is still acting on the participant's behalf, leaving the governance intact. The execution of the plan remains the responsibility of the local system. Coordinated operations require a common intent and a common awareness, supported by broader access to shared sensors for the sake of gathering and fusing information into a common picture. This is where sociability starts to make a real difference.

Collaboration requires one not only to share the planning process, but also the execution process. Shared situational awareness supported by joint common operational pictures requires a unifying system of systems that integrates the heterogeneous contributions of all systems. Information shall be shared seamlessly. While the execution process is still limited to the better component or better service in the coordinated approach, the collaborative approach synchronizes planning and execution vertically and horizontally.

Coherent operations are characterized by rapid and agile decision-making processes based on seamless and transparent information-sharing. Smart and social components of each system will have access to all information they need to make the decision, regardless of where they are, which components they use to gain access to the information, or where the information came from.

As before, the ideas of multi-, inter-, and transdisciplinarity can be recognized. While in deconflicted command and control the autonomy of the participating entities remains and only controlled information is exchanged, in the coherent operations command authority is transcending, transgressing, and transforming, which equals interdisciplinarity. Similarly, if autonomous systems are to be integrated, they have to fully expose their assumptions and constraints ruling their sense-making and decision-making. This requires conceptual interoperability as defined in the LCIM. As shown in [13], the level of interoperability directly influences to highest possible level of interoperation.

As such, proprietary solutions for autonomous systems are potentially endangering the operational freedom of the military decision maker, as limited interoperability equals limited collaboration ability.

4.2 Computational Limits of Computational Intelligence

The idea of intelligent autonomous systems that take over the decision authority is topic of many novels. However, there are computational limits that developers of this applications need to be aware of. They have been enumerated for simulations in [16]. As has be argued so far, they are also applicable to autonomous systems.

- *Gödel's Incompleteness Theorems* have significant implications for computational intelligence [17]. In very simple form they state that in a non-trivial system a true statement can exist that is not part of the axioms and that cannot be derived by applying the rules. If such rules are introduced, the system will become inconsistent. This means for autonomous systems that they cannot derive all true statements by applying logic, or if they can, they will end up with inconsistencies in their knowledge base. Their knowledge is therefore limited.
- *Turing's Halting Problem* showed that certain problems cannot be solved by any algorithm [18]. He used the example to decide if a program with a certain data input will halt or run into a loop. By only assuming that such an algorithm exists, Turing creates a contradiction, which shows that the assumption must be false and the algorithm cannot exist. Many problems have been found since then to be not decidable by an algorithm, such as if a requirement set is complete, if two algorithms are equivalent, etc. If a problem is known to be undecidable, an autonomous system cannot decide it either.
- *Computational Complexity* deals with time and resources needed by a computer to find a solution [19]. Just because an algorithm can find a solution to a problem, this does not mean that it can do it within reasonable time and resource constraints.

Computers continue to get faster and more powerful, but if a solution requires exponential time or resources, it is not generally applicable.

- *Algorithmic Information Theory* proves that computers cannot be creative in the sense that they can find solutions in an unbounded solution space. It shows that all computers can do is transform input data into output date using the program code [20]. Everything the computer produces must therefore either be in the input data or in the transforming code.
- *Mathematical Model Theory* copes with equivalencies of models, in particular when expressed in different mathematical languages [21]. It provides the proof that composability cannot be engineered after the fact into a model-based system. If two conceptualizations are not consistent, no algorithm can exist to avoid inconsistency of truth representations.
- *Chaos Theory* has shown that if non-linear systems are bounded and folded back onto themselves, the resulting function is highly dependent on the initial conditions: even if two starting points lie arbitrarily close, after several iterations they will be on very different spots on the trajectories [22]. As computers use digitized numbers, there will always be a slight precision error, which limits the usefulness of computer-based extrapolations for chaotic functions.

This short list can neither claim exclusiveness nor completeness. It should also not be a discouragement for developer of control systems for autonomous systems. New developments in the domains of *Big Data* and *Deep Learning* is opening new opportunities that so far have not been heard of. In a recent article in the Business Insider Journal [23], Friedman predicted that IBM's Watson Supercomputer may soon be the best doctor in the world, as it is continuously updates his medical knowledge base with new text books, journals, etc. Each diagnosis will therefore take all the most recent knowledge into consideration.

5   Summary and Conclusions

Within this chapter, the applicability of many insights and research results in the domain of M&S were shown. In order to enable autonomous systems, sense-making and decision-making will be based on implemented formal specifications of conceptualizations. Models play important roles for the perception as well. The ideas of multi-, inter-, and transdisciplinary efforts can guide the degree of interoperations in scenarios that comprise autonomous systems. They are also constrained by the degree of interoperability as specified in the LCIM. Finally, the N2C2M2 can be integrated in this view consistently as well.

The implications for autonomous systems are far reaching technically and operationally, as their control functions have to incorporate model-based approaches as means of computational intelligence needed for real autonomy. They can use the full potential of computer implementations, but they are also constrained by their limitations. Developers need to be aware of these foundations and the curriculum for experts in robotics may be improved with some insights into the epistemological foundations of modeling, challenges of implementations, and the mathematical foundations of interoperability and composability as described in this chapter.

The earlier the autonomous systems community starts to work on and agree to standards to support all levels of interoperability as defined in the LCIM, the earlier it will enable the full and integrated use of autonomous systems in the orchestrated set of forces applicable for the military leader. If not all levels are supported, these limits will constrain the degrees of freedom of operations that include autonomous forces, as has been shown from the perspective of different categories of disciplinarity and the command and control ideas captured in the N2C2M2.

References

1. Boyd, J.: A Discourse on Winning and Losing. Air University Library Document No. M-U 43947, Maxwell Air Force Base (1987)
2. Tolk, A.: Interoperability, composability, and their implications for distributed simulation - towards mathematical foundations of simulation interoperability. In: Proceedings of the 2013 IEEE/ACM 17th International Symposium on Distributed Simulation and Real Time Applications, pp. 3–9. IEEE Computer Society, Washington, DC (2013)
3. Tolk, A.: Interoperability and composability. In: Modeling and Simulation Fundamentals: Theoretical Underpinnings and Practical Domains, pp. 403–433. Wiley, Hoboken (2010)
4. Alberts, D.S., Huber, R.K., Moffat, J.: NATO NEC C2 Maturity Model. Office of the Secretary of Defense. Command and Control Research Program, Washington, DC (2010)
5. Tolk, A.: Merging two worlds: agent-based simulation methods for autonomous systems. In: Autonomous Systems: Issues for Defence Policymakers, pp. 289–315. NATO Headquarters Supreme Allied Commander Transformation, Norfolk (2015)
6. Goldman, S.L.: Science Wars: What Scientists Know and How They Know it. Lehight University, The Teaching Company, Chantilly (2006)
7. Fishwick, P.A.: Handbook of Dynamic System Modeling. Chapman & Hall/CRC Press, Taylor and Francis Group, Boca Raton (2007)
8. Oberkampf, W.L., DeLand, S.M., Rutherford, B.M., Diegert, K.V., Alvin, K.F.: Error and uncertainty in modeling and simulation. Reliab. Eng. Syst. Saf. **75**(3), 333–357 (2002)
9. Talay, D., Tubaro, L.: Expansion of the global error for numerical schemes solving stochastic differential equations. Stoch. Anal. Appl. **8**(4), 483–509 (1990)
10. Rentschler, M.E.: Dynamic simulation modeling and control of the Odyssey III autonomous underwater vehicle. Doctoral dissertation, Massachusetts Institute of Technology, Cambridge, MA (2003)
11. Zeigler, B.P.: Toward a simulation methodology for variable structure modeling. In: Modeling and Simulation Methodology in the Artificial Intelligence Era, pp. 195–210. North Holland, Amsterdam (1986)
12. Stock, P., Burton, R.J.F.: Defining terms for integrated (multi-inter-trans-disciplinary) sustainability research. Sustainability **3**, 1090–1113 (2011)
13. Tolk, A., Bair, L.J., Diallo, S.Y.: Supporting network enabled capability by extending the levels of conceptual interoperability model to an interoperability maturity model. J. Defense Model. Simul. Appl. Methodol. Technol. **10**(2), 145–160 (2013)
14. King, R.D., Turnitsa, C.D.: The landscape of assumptions. In: Proceedings of the 2008 Spring Simulation Multiconference, Society for Modeling and Simulation (SCS), San Diego, CA, pp. 81–88 (2008)

15. Page, E.H., Briggs, R., Tufarolo, J.A.: Toward a family of maturity models for the simulation interconnection problem. In: Proceedings of the Spring Simulation Interoperability Workshop (2004). Paper No. 04S-SIW-145

16. Tolk, A.: Learning something right from models that are wrong - epistemology of simulation. In: Yilmaz, L. (ed.) Concepts and Methodologies for Modeling and Simulation - A Tribute to Tuncer Ören, pp. 87–106. Springer, London (2015)

17. Murawski, R.: Gödel's incompleteness theorems and computer science. Found. Sci. **2**, 123–135 (1997)

18. Weber, R.: Computability Theory. American Mathematical Society (AMS), Providence (2012)

19. Papadimitriou, C.H.: Computational Complexity. Wiley, Hoboken (2003)

20. Chaitin, G.J.: Algorithmic Information Theory. Wiley, Hoboken (1982)

21. Prestel, A., Delzell, C.N.: Mathematical Logic and Model Theory: A Brief Introduction. Springer, London (2011)

22. Smith, L., Smith, L.: Chaos: A Very Short Introduction. Oxford University Press, Oxford (2007)

23. Friedman, L.F.: IBM's watson supercomputer may soon be the best doctor in the world. In: Business Insider, Science (2014). http://www.businessinsider.com/ibms-watson-may-soon-be-the-best-doctor-in-the-world-2014-4. Accessed May 2015

MS Experimental Frameworks for AS

Interoperability Issues Reduction in Command and Control for Multi-robot Systems

Francesco Fedi[1](✉) and Francesco Nasca[2]

[1] Selex ES, Rome, Italy
francesco.fedi@selex-es.com
[2] NATO Modelling and Simulation Centre of Excellence, Rome, Italy
mscoe.cd04@smd.difesa.it

Abstract. Multirobot systems are a promising step forward in supporting human operators, since they can provide a wider set of capabilities and an improved system performance in terms of adaptability, resilience and scalability, without increasing the complexity of the single system element. Team heterogeneity is a multirobot system strength, but it raises interoperability problems which need to be solved to avoid the overall system performance and costs to be impacted by issues such as vendor dependency, high integration costs, high system maintenance costs. Moreover, interoperability is mandatory for a sound integration of multirobot systems as components of System of System architecture where both legacy and innovative segments need to coordinate each others. This paper describes the outcome of the Simulated Interactive Robotics Initiative (SIRI), a project aimed at providing a first assessment of the interoperability between Multirobot and legacy Command & Control Systems. The project developed an interoperability solution which is based upon the following key standards: the Data Distribution Services for Real Time Systems (DDS), which addresses the data exchange service interoperability, and the National Information Exchange Model (NIEM), which addresses the data models interoperability. SIRI provides a preliminary demonstration of the interoperability advantages stemming from the synergic adoption of the mentioned standards in multirobot system and paves the way for a more consolidated and robust framework which follows the system architecture drivers of Interoperable Open Architecture (IOA) a set of guidelines which has been already resulted in cost saving in the procurement of many large defence systems.

1 Introduction (by LTC Francesco Nasca)

The actual technological progress is moving towards an increasing availability of systems with wider capabilities of autonomy. Today Robotic & Autonomous Systems (RAS) are entering our everyday life with capabilities which tend to reach the paradigm of fully autonomy. This idea fascinated millions of science fiction readers, but now is being taken in serious consideration whenever a RAS is "inter-operating" with our daily activities. This is the case also for military activities, where RAS are starting to be considered as part of an operation, especially in areas where humans are not supposed to enter, such as contaminated areas, dangerous activities, etc.

© Springer International Publishing Switzerland 2015
J. Hodicky (Ed.): MESAS 2015, LNCS 9055, pp. 77–89, 2015.
DOI: 10.1007/978-3-319-22383-4_6

An example is the mitigation of an explosive threat, in which robots are actually used to approach, manage and deactivate unknown explosive devices.

The use of RAS with new capabilities of autonomy implies higher risks of failure, due to the uncertainty of the results related with the lack of an extensive experimentation of these new systems. So the need to approach a risk reduction for the use of highly autonomous RAS made two different communities, the Robotics one and the Modelling & Simulation (M&S) community, to start discussing at MESAS 2014 about the use of M&S for Autonomous Systems. The discussion provided an input for NATO M&S Centre of Excellence (Rome, ITA) to start a new project in collaboration with the USA Defence Joint Chiefs of Staff and Selex ES Italian Industry. The project, named Simulated Interactive Robotics Initiative (SIRI), is aimed at studying the interoperability issues between Multirobot Systems and legacy Command & Control (C2) Systems through the use of M&S. This paper describes the outcomes of SIRI project, which resulted in the development of a simulator of swarms of robots interoperable with C2 Systems.

2   Interoperability Issues in Multirobot Systems

2.1   System Integrator Interoperability Issues (by Francesco Fedi Ph.D.)

Robotic and Autonomous Systems integration. Design systems and system-of-systems while satisfying the combined attributes of performance, scalability and reliability is hard. Adding non-functional requirements of interoperability, flexibility, modularity, and portability makes the problem even more difficult. This goal is not just for systems of a similar type but also for different mission specific systems, such as systems of systems, which need, want and use similar data. The more and more frequent adoption of Robotic & Autonomous Systems (RAS) in operations improves the operational efficiency and the soldiers safety. Multirobot systems are a promising step forward in supporting human operators, since they can provide a wider set of capabilities and an improved system performance in terms of adaptability, resilience and scalability, without increasing the complexity of the single system element. Team heterogeneity is a multirobot system strength, but it raises interoperability problems which need to be solved to avoid the overall system performance and costs to be impacted by issues such as vendor dependency, high integration costs, high system maintenance costs. Moreover, interoperability is mandatory for a sound integration of multirobot systems as components of System of System architecture where both legacy and innovative segments need to coordinate each others.

2.2   Operations Interoperability Issues (by LTC Francesco Nasca)

Modern military operations require the use of systems with autonomous capabilities, not just remotely con-trolled by a human operator, but also able to accomplish the mission with a specific autonomy. Therefore, the questions now are: "how such an autonomous system will behave in a specific operational scenario?", "how RAS will impact the military operational procedures?", "how RAS will interact with the human operators?".

The use of M&S is key to provide answers to these questions. In fact, the simulation of any kind of RAS in a virtual scenario, not only enables experimenters to predict, test and study RAS behavior in operational scenarios, but also provides a safe tool for risk assessment, risk reduction and experimentation. For this purpose, SIRI project resulted in the development of a Multi-Robot Systems (MRS) simulator. The MRS simulator is able to simulate the behavior of swarms of virtual robots, autonomous and collaborative also with possible real robots.

In order to perform such simulations, there are some interoperability issues to face. First of all, Multirobot Systems need to exchange information with C2 Systems. In a military operation, RAS must be commanded and controlled by human operators through a C2 System, which normally allows military staffs to manage the whole operation. So the first interoperability issue is raised by the information exchange between Multirobot systems' services and C2 Systems' services. In this paper, we are considering the interoperability issues faced by SIRI Project between Multirobot Systems' Data Distribution Services (DDS) standard and National Information Exchange Model (NIEM) standard compliant C2 Systems.

The second interoperability issue is raised by the use of M&S. The performance of a simulation in a virtual scenario implies the exchange of information between real RAS and simulation systems as well. Therefore, there is not only the need for interoperability between the most common simulation services (based on DIS, HLA, HLA Evolved protocols) with NIEM compliant C2 Systems, but also with Multirobot Systems' DDS standard.

The interoperability issues described above depict a need for a "tri-lateral interoperability" between RAS, C2 Systems and simulation systems. The SIRI project discussed in this paper faced only one side of the "tri-lateral interoperability", the RAS-C2 Systems interoperability, and there is still need for further developments in order to face also the other sides of the "triangle".

2.3   The Interoperability Open Architecture (by Francesco Fedi Ph.D.)

Open Infrastructure.   An Open Architecture (OA) is meant to deliver specific benefits – interoperability is perhaps the most important. For over 10 years government procurement agencies have been asking for Open Architecture solutions from their supply chains, and all they have got is a tick box exercise for the adoption of open standards, open systems and COTS technologies. All of these are components of an OA, but unless they are brought together within an open infrastructure, as we will describe herein, the full benefits of Open Architecture cannot accrue to the system customers, more importantly, to the system users.

Interoperability Definition and Goal.   Interoperability has become a loaded term in the de-fence industry. So before we proceed we should be clear what the term means.

Interoperability is the ability of systems, units, or forces to provide services to and accept services from other systems, units, or forces, and to use the services to enable them to operate effectively together.

Interoperability is a fundamental prerequisite for an open competitive supply chain. Defines an in-service system capability as much as an initial development capability. It enables integrators to connect multiple components developed by different parties **without changing them**.

Interoperable Open Architecture Definition. Interoperable Open Architecture (IOA) is a System of System Architecture (SoSA) based upon open standards that delivers interoperability among sub-systems and applications built and integrated at different times. To be meaningfully interoperable, different systems built at different times, with different hardware, different software architectures, different technologies, and different uses of the data and system information must be readily and meaningfully integrable.

System-Level Interoperability. IOA defines a SoSA through its data via the adoption of a data-centric middleware open standard. Typical Open Standard for SoS integration specifies both a wire protocol (for integratability) and programming interface (for portability). However, while this provides the basis for an interoperable OA, it is still insufficient. Advanced programs have recognized that application portability is a goal, but that system-level interoperability is the higher order functionality that is needed. Communication and connectivity may have been openly standardized, but the meaning of the information flow has not. To address this issue it shall be defined a System Data Model (SDM) that defines content and context of the data that is communicated around the System of System (SoS) – it is not a wire protocol but rather a full specification of the data and its meaning which can then be instantiated appropriately on different technologies to exchange information. Included in this SDM is a set of meta-data that defines the semantic information associated with every piece of data, this semantic data contextualizes it or allows it to be re-contextualized to the application using it.

System Interoperability Levels. IOA aims to achieve a fully interoperable system, via the provision of the following levels of interoperability:

- Technical Interoperability: Bits and bytes are ex-changed in an unambiguous manner via a set of standardized communication protocols
- Syntactic Interoperability: A common data format is defined for the unambiguous sharing of information
- Semantic Interoperability: The meaning of data is exchanged through a common information model and the meaning of information is unambiguously defined and shared

The UK MoDGeneric Vehicle Architecture as Example of IOA. The UK Ministry of Defence (MoD) adopted the In-teroperable Open Architecture (IOA) for its new Generic Vehicle Architecture (GVA) [MoD (2010)]. With the adoption of the IOA the MoD has raised the bar for systems-of-systems integration management by initiating a fundamental shift in perspective regarding collaboration between its procurement agency and System Integrators (SIs).

Communication between two subsystems of any type requires at least two common properties: the production and consumption of data. The MOD has assumed full responsibility for defining and maintaining a System Data Dictionary (SDD) of the complete vehicle defined on a subsystem-type basis (sensors, C4I, HUMSs etc.), a dictionary and vocabulary for communication between subsystems. This SDD—called the Land Data Model—forms the core of the MOD's strategically different engineering approach to systems architecture design.

The MOD mandated the use of the Object Management Group (OMG) Data Distribution Service (DDS) standard for the open-standard middleware for all data communication within the vehicle.

3 SIRI Interoperability Open Architecture (by Francesco Fedi Ph.D.)

3.1 Interoperability Principles in SIRI

SIRI Design Guidelines for Interoperability. The means of implementing system level interoperability via data and information flows is to use a data-centric design approach. SIRI adopts a Data-centric Interoperability that is based on the following architectural guiding principles:

- All data (that is to be exchanged in the system) are rigorously defined (with semantics), described, documented and available via a distributed repository which act as SDM. As described in the following paragraphs in SIRI the SDM provides for semantics and syntactic information of the Robotic segment, and its Command & Control subsystem. The SIRI Robot Data Model (RDM) has been based on the NIEM Standard (www.niem.gov).
- Data exists in the system fully independently of any application or function. Data is managed by a System Software Bus (SSB) infrastructure.
- The SSB infrastructure also acts as run-time data repository, and the single authoritative source of state information in the system. As described in the following paragraphs, the SIRI SSB is based on the Data Distribution Services standard. Specifically the BEE-DDS (www.beedds.com) product has been selected.

SIRI System-Level Interoperability. According to the SIRI principles, the SSB provides a system level interoperability by maintaining the system state in the architecture infrastructure and not within applications or in a specific sub-system. In fact the entire system state has to be made explicit within the SSB by every connected functional sub-system or application. This decouples not only the communication between subsystems, but also the state information. This allows any subsystem or application to obtain state information from the software infrastructure rather than from another subsystem or application, thereby reducing coupling and removing stovepipes.

SIRI Syntactic and Semantic Interoperability Delegation. Moreover, SSB provides one more key step. That is to delegate the syntactic and semantic interoperability to the RDM, a web-based repository which can be managed by either the prime SI or directly by the Government Agency (GA), as the case of GVA, and it is common to manufacturers at each system integration levels. Thus semantic and syntactic interoperability can now be maintained, like the run-time state, at the system level and not between 2 or more interoperating applications or sub-systems.

3.2 SIRI System Software Bus

The Data Distribution Service. "Data Distribution Services for real-time systems" (DDS) is an open-architecture for real-time middleware specified by the Object Management Group (OMG) [1, 2]. It is a sophisticated technology that implements a real-time publish-subscribe communication model and allows distributed processes to share data transparently among peer entities. It includes a complete set of Quality of Service (QoS) parameters for a complete control of the service performances and resource allocation.

DDS publish-subscribe model allows for sending and receiving data, events, and commands among the nodes. Nodes that are producing information (publishers) create "topics" (temperature and pressure in Fig. 3) and publish "samples". The DDS delivers the sample to all of those subscribers which declare an interest in that topic and that are compliant with the requested QoS. Any node can be publisher, subscriber, or both simultaneously.

Applications that use RT-DDS for their communications are entirely decoupled, therefore the designer shall spent very little effort on interface definition and testing, even in case of complex systems, e.g. System of Systems, Federation of Systems. DDS autonomously handles all aspects of message delivery without requiring any intervention from the application.

This is made possible by DDS allowing the user to specify QoS parameters as a way to configure automatic-discovery mechanisms and specify the behavior adopted in sending and receiving messages.

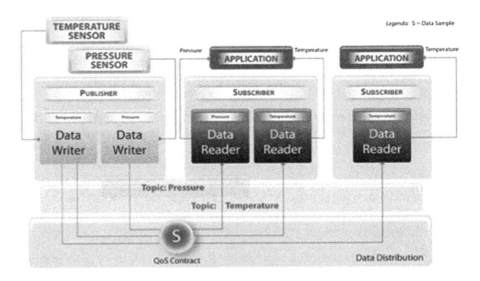

Fig. 1. A typical DDS usage

The BEE-DDS Product. Selex ES developed BEE DDS, a real-time middleware which is an implementation of the OMG's Real-Time Data Distribution Service (RT-DDS). BEE DDS provides all of the RT-DDS functions specified by the standard, and it is specifically optimized for mobile, mission critical applications where predictability, dependability, and security are key system requirements. BEE DDS includes proprietary solutions to improve the OMG's suite of QoS parameters for RAS systems addressing:

- Timing Requirements: data lifetime, data delivery deadline, maximum/minimum transmission rate at both sender and recipient endpoints;
- Availability requirements: resilient data delivery, data persistence in the system despite of either the temporary or permanent unavailability of the source, data distribution service availability via the hot swap of backed-up data sources;
- Partitioning which allows to split the system into different logical domains.

3.3   The SIRI System Data Model

The National Information Exchange Module.   In support of the overarching aim to improve system interoperability that is critical in achieving seamless C2 for the warfighter, the need for a common set of interface and messaging standards required for interoperability with respect to exchanging information is clear. Without a common semantic understanding of what data represents, however, there is a significant opportunity for lack of interoperability, even if the messages are correctly parsed and interfaces are followed. Therefore, a key aspect is the recognition that data modeling is a separate, core aspect for defining interoperable systems. This aspect includes specifying definitions, taxonomies, and other semantic information to ensure there is a common understanding about what information a specific data item imparts.

The National Information Exchange Model (NIEM) (www.niem.gov) is an inter-agency initiative that pro-vides the foundation and building blocks for national-level interoperable information sharing and data ex-change. NIEM uses the XML standard to define the content of messages being exchanged. It's about the data and how it's structured.

The extensible markup language (XML) based MilOps (Military Operations) data exchange is part of the web enabled, shared data modernization effort ongoing in DoD. The evolution to MilOps builds on that of fielded C2 military standards: message formats, symbology, and data links.

The intent for SIRI project with regards to the NIEM MilOps data standard is to determine the re-usability of current MilOps message formats to exchange various information between the virtual unmanned ground vehicles and the C2 mission stations, and to identify any new data elements to be incorporated into the MilOps domain as necessary.

The System Data Model Repository.   Communication between two subsystems of any type requires at least two common properties: the consumption and production of data. A given GA may assume responsibility for specifying and maintaining a Robotic System Data Model (RDM) that acts as a system data dictionary which is defined at subsystem-level (sensors, C2, HRI, etc.), and includes both a dictionary and a vocabulary for information exchange among subsystems. The RDM forms the core of the SIRI's engineering approach to architecture design for robotic systems. It is a fundamental change from the traditional Interface Control Document (ICD)-based approach, which defines the low-level protocol and messages characteristic of the stovepipe system architectures that have inhibited field responsiveness to changes in operational needs.

3.4   The SIRI Demonstrator

The System.   The SIRI objective is to realize an Interoperability Study for the integration of a Multi Robot Systems (MRS) in Multinational Coalition Scenario.

The Reference Scenario to develop is COMIED (Cooperative Multi-robot System (CMS) Information Exchange Demonstrator). The CMS is composed by:

- A squad of networked Unmanned Ground Vehicle (UGV), typical squad size is 5-10 UGVs
- One or more Command and Control Stations (C2)

Typical C2 Stations are:

- Planning Station, which provides for mission plan.
- Mission Management Station, which provides for monitoring of both the mission (e.g. task progress) and the related UGV parameters.

The Data Exchange and the robotic cooperation capabilities, i.e. the Dynamic Task Assignment, are based onto the BEE-DDS.

The COMIED operative nodes are:

- V-UGVs: Virtual UGVs whose robotic platform and operational environment are provided by the ROS-Stage (Robotic Operating System/Stage) simulation environment.
- BEE Planning Station (BPS), which provides for local UGV mission control
- Mission Management Station (MMS), which pro-vides for remote system mission control and is based on the FalconView Framework.

These nodes will be connected by means of a VPN that includes the following nodes: (Fig. 2)

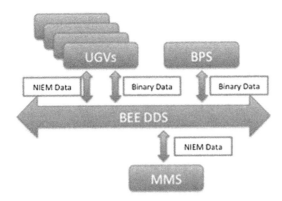

Fig. 2.   SIRI datacentric architecture

- A Mission Management node in U.S.
- A Multirobot node at NATO CoE in Rome, Italy
- A Simulation Control node including the BPS at Selex ES premises in Taranto, Italy

The Mission. The mission goal is to explore a given area to detect and neutralized possibly threats. The UGVs team coordinates to perform the mission tasks such as:

- To explore the area of mission in an accurate and complete way
- To detect, and locate threats
- To mitigate the discovery threat

Moreover each robot is able to execute specific operator commands such as:

- To stop execute any task
- To suspend the task execution and come back to its home position.

During the mission execution the UGVs dynamically allocate each task to be executed to coordinate each other and autonomously schedule/reschedule tasks execution.

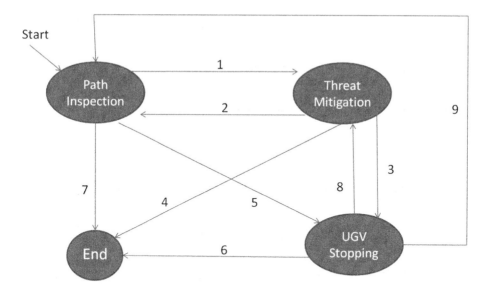

Fig. 3. SIRI mission tasks

The System Data Model. In Table 1 the main information flows that will be ex-change between the macro SIRI components have been identified:

Table 1. SIRI information flows

Information	Description	Publisher entity	Subscriber Entity
RobotStatus	It represents the data related to the UGV actual state according to its position, speed and executing task	UGV	UGV
			MMS
			BPS
Candidancy	Contains information about the UGV candidacy for the task to be executed	UGV	UGV
Coordination	Contains coordination service message among UGVs	UGV	UGV
TaskData	Contains all the information that identify a task to be executed by a UGV	V-UGV	UGV
		BPS	
		MMS	
UGV_Position	Contains the UGV position	UGV	BPS

4   Expected Benefits

4.1   System Integrator Benefits (by Francesco Fedi Ph.D.)

Innovative Approach to RAS Integration. SIRI aims to provide an innovative approach to robotic system integration. It will: increase robotic system effectiveness; enhance adaptability upgradeability and re-configurability in the face of ever-changing operational demands; and reduce whole life costs. The SIRI approach also aims to enable the retrofit of a wide range of products with the minimum of robotic system impact and logistic support in operations.

The System Integration Benefits

The system integration infrastructure remains un-changed

The SIRI philosophical change in approach does not fundamentally change the system integration infrastructure. There is still a need for a prime SI to bring together the various tier-2 and tier-3 SIs and manage the systems integration of future systems. However, now the SIs will work within the well known architectural guidelines as specified by the RDM. A publicly available RDM: enables ready sharing with the tier-N SI's, and opens the door to collaboration between nation states for multi-national operations.

...but the integration risks are mitigated

If it appears that a subcontractor will jeopardize the delivery schedule or contract deliverables, the prime SI now has the option and opportunity to seek alternative suppliers.

Because the RDM ensures interoperability, the SI knows integration will not be a significant issue and can therefore focus on functionality, usability, price, durability and so on. The business benefits to industry of mitigating the risk of subcontractor failure cannot be underestimated any more, also for large programs.

...and rapid R&D&I enabled

The SIRI enables rapid R&D&I outside the context of a **specific** robotic system programme, because now the SIs can have confidence that subsystems innovated taking into account the RDM specification can and will be viable in future robotic systems and their upgrades.

Legacy Subsystem can be integrated

Even legacy subsystems can be brought forward into the SIRI architecture. Figure 1 shows that legacy subsystems can be "wrapped" with a SIRI-compliant data gateway to become an integral part of robotic system that use more recent IOA system-integration technology. This provides a low-cost legacy transition mechanism for both the GA and SIs.

...to improve through-life maintenance procurement

As SIRI based systems are deployed, there will be a significant change in through-life maintenance procurement. Instead of 'big bang' upgrades, smaller maintenance and upgrade contracts can be initiated at much more regular intervals, the following paragraphs details the related benefits.

Through-Life Benefits

Integrated Logistics Support (ILS) simplification

Perhaps the biggest savings will come in through-life maintenance and upgrade cost reductions and Integrated Logistics Support (ILS) simplification. SIRI will create a market that is increasingly open for robotic components and subsystems, which in turn will drive a more competitive market and lead to cost reductions. Simultaneously, innovation will increase as suppliers work to differentiate their solutions.

Easy Integration of Simulation and Training Systems

Additionally, the existence of a standard logical data bus makes the development and integration of simulation and training systems orders of magnitude easier because a range of robotic simulation & training systems can leverage the actual robotic software components through the same SIRI interface and adopting the same data model via the common RDM.

Improvement in Robotic System Upgrading

Robotic systems will also become easier to enhance because integrating new functionality is as simple as defining an extension of the RDM. The logical data bus of SIRI ensures that new data providers and consumers can be discovered dynamically by the system. A new robotic function can select the data it needs from the SIRI data bus while adding itself as a provider of new sets of data to the robotic system environment. For full realization of the benefits of a new function existing subsystems may need to be enhanced.

4.2   Operational Benefits (by LTC Francesco Nasca)

SIRI proved to be a M&S tool that can effectively simulate not only the behavior of swarms of robots but also the procedures to command and control them in an operational scenario. This results in the development of a tool which enables human operators to:

- Perform operational training with risks limited to the possible use of real robots
- Develop concepts of operations and doctrines which include the use of swarm of robots
- Perform experiments and tests the behavior of new RAS or RAS with higher autonomous capabilities
- Study the employment of RAS in future military operations and their integration in military scenarios

5   Conclusions (by LTC Francesco Nasca)

SIRI Project provided a first assessment of the interoperability between MRS and legacy C2 Systems. The adopted technical solutions resulted into multiple benefits in terms of logistic integration, cost savings and interoperability. Therefore, SIRI provided a preliminary demonstration of the interoperability advantages stemming from the synergic adoption of the mentioned standards in MRS and paves the way for a more consolidated and robust framework which follows the system architecture drivers of Interoperable Open Architecture (IOA) a set of guidelines which has been already resulted in cost saving in the procurement of many large defence systems.

There is still a lot of work to do in order to mitigate the tri-lateral interoperability issues among RAS, C2 Systems and Simulation Systems. For instance, the interoperability between RAS services and the most common simulation protocols needs to be investigated. Moreover, the interaction with the human component is also another issue which needs to be taken in consideration and studied with the support of M&S tools in the development of autonomous systems.

In summary, there is room enough for more than one follow-up project, in order to implement the interoperability between RAS and other simulators and C2 systems, in order to develop a demonstrator which simulates the interaction between RAS and humans. This can be the outline for SIRI 2.0, a future Project which might support the implementation of a tri-lateral interoperability and possibly lead towards the study of how to train humans in the use of RAS and - why not - how to train Robots in the interaction with humans.

References

1. Object Management Group (OMG, 2007). Data Distribution Service for Real-time Systems – version 1.2
2. Object Management Group (OMG, 2008). The Real-time Publish-Subscribe Wire Protocol DDS Interoperability Wire Protocol Specification – version 2.0

3. Fedi, F.: The Real Time Swarm Intelligence Platform, in Polaris, pp. 12–16. SelexSistemiIntegrati, October 2012
4. UCS Executive Summary 2011: The Data Distribution Service (Reducing Cost through Agile Integration)
5. Ministry of Defence (2010), Generic Vehicle Architecture, Defence Standard 23-09, Issue 1, August 2010

Practical Applications and Experiments with the SyRoTek Platform

Miroslav Kulich[✉], Jan Chudoba, and Libor Přeučil

Department of Cybernetics, Faculty of Electrical Engineering,
Czech Technical University in Prague, Technicka 2, 166 27 Prague 6, Czech Republic
{kulich,chudoba,preucil}@ciirc.cvut.cz
http://www.imr.felk.cvut.cz

Abstract. SyRoTek is a platform for distant teaching and experimentation in robotics and related fields, which provides remote access to a group of thirteen fully autonomous mobile robots equipped with standard robotic sensors operating in the Arena – a restricted area with a set of fixed and retractable obstacles. Users of the system are able to control the robots real-time by their own developed algorithms and process and analyse data gathered with robots' sensors. The SyRoTek is after several years of development and operation a technically mature system providing all functionalities enabling and sweeten a whole development process: interfaces to robotic frameworks (namely ROS: Robot Operating System and Player/Stage), simulation environment based on Stage, on-line and off-line visualization of the current state of the Arena and the robots, web interface, tutorials and documentation, etc. Thanks to operation in 24/7 mode and easy interchangeability of the robots, the system is an ideal tool for performing a huge number of long-term and repeating multi-robot experiments.

This paper aims to introduce research activities made thanks to the system and to describe experiments performed with it by users from various institutions and application areas. Many of these experiments will not be possible or their realization will need order of magnitude more effort and/or time without the SyRoTek system. These applications are discussed as well as experiments performed.

Keywords: Distant experimentation · e-learning · Mobile robots · Robot programming

1 Introduction

Making experiments in the area of mobile robotics with a real robot is an expensive process not only due to high costs of specialized robotic hardware but also due to the need of continuous service and maintenance that requires human effort. This leads to higher demands on human resources and time needed to perform and evaluate experiments. Expenses are even much higher in case of multi-robot scenario, when long-term experiments are performed or experiments are repeated many times.

© Springer International Publishing Switzerland 2015
J. Hodicky (Ed.): MESAS 2015, LNCS 9055, pp. 90–101, 2015.
DOI: 10.1007/978-3-319-22383-4_7

These problems can be overcame by sharing of robotic hardware among several institutions, which can have (for applications where large environments are not required) a form of remote laboratories. Moreover, these laboratories bring another benefits – experiments can be performed remotely, scheduled for an arbitrary time (even during night) and they can be easily reproduced.

Early remote laboratories developed in the nineties enable a user to interact with a single hardware device (either a robotic arm or a mobile robot) [1,15,19,26]. University of Reading, U.K. introduced one of the first integrated, remotely controlled robotic systems called the ARL Netrolab project [14] in 1993. It allows control of a robotic arm and provides access to selected sensor equipment (sonars, infrared range finders, and a set of cameras). The e-laboratory project [27] combines a remote robotic platform with a virtual laboratory.

While there are many remote labs with robotic arms, remotely controlled mobile robots are not so common. One of most popular systems was developed in the RobOnWeb project at the Swiss Federal Institute of Technology in Lausanne (EPFL) [24]. In the REAL project [10], remote access to an autonomous mobile robot is provided allowing the user to control the robot by writing its own navigation module in C.

A Web-based remote laboratory that gives an opportunity to remotely experiment with various navigation algorithms on a mobile robot is described in [6]. The system consists of a Web interface for uploading the user's program to the robot, accessing the on-board video camera, and monitoring various state variables. The software framework provided is built on the Microsoft Robotics Studio.

A combination of a simulated environment with a physical set-up was applied in the LearnNet project [13]. The VRML technology was used to model the real environment at the user side, while only coordinates of objects are transmitted over the Internet. A set of robots is accessible for users in the Virtual lab project [17]. Several cameras monitored a playing field and a user can use a combination of several views to get better overview of the robots' movements. The robots can be controlled remotely via the ActiveX technology or by a program in C++, Delphi or Java. An open source solution based on the Player/Stage framework [9] was planned in another virtual robotic laboratory project [28], which unfortunately seems to be no longer active. Teleworkbench [25] is a complex system that allows multi-robot experiments with Khepera and Bee-Bot robots in an environment automatically built and controlled by a gripper. It provides precise robot localization based on image processing, on-line video stream and video recording, GUI with augmented reality (AR) for robot control, and a tool for experiment analysis.

Overwatch – a testbed for multi-robot experimentation primarily for educational purposes uses AR markers to localize robots and provides navigation capabilities to the robots [8]. Nevertheless, this system does not provides functionalities for remote control. Finally, robots built with the LEGO Mindstorms technology and controlled by user-defined code in Matlab are used in [2] allowing remote multi-robot experiments.

SyRoTek – a system for robotic e-learning and remote experimentation has been developed and carried on at Czech Technical University in Prague since 2006 [11]. It provides remote access to a group of thirteen fully autonomous mobile robots equipped with standard sensors (e.g. laser range-finders, sonar, infra-red sensors, cameras, floor sensors) operating in the Arena – a restricted area with a set of fixed and retractable obstacles. Users of the system are able to control the robots real-time by their own developed algorithms and process and analyse data gathered with robots' sensors. The SyRoTek is after several years of development and operation a technically mature system providing all functionalities enabling and sweeten a whole development process: interfaces to robotic frameworks (namely ROS: Robot Operating System [18] and Player/Stage [9]), simulation environment based on Stage, on-line and off-line visualization of the current state of the Arena and the robots, web interface, tutorials and documentation, etc. Due to operation in 24/7 mode and easy interchangeability of the robots, the system is an ideal tool for performing huge number of long-term and repeating multi-robot experiments.

In this paper, we aim to present research activities made with the system and to describe experiments performed with it by users from various institutions and application areas. Many of these experiments will not be possible or their realization will need order of magnitude more effort and/or time without the SyRoTek system.

The rest of the paper is organized as follows. Section 2 gives a short overview about the SyRoTek system itself. Several success stories are presented in Sect. 3. Finally, we conclude with remarks in Sect. 4.

2   System Overview

The SyRoTek platform consists of many components (both hardware and software) that cooperate and communicate with each other (see [11] for a detailed description). The main part of the system is the Arena – an enclosed space of size $3.5\,\mathrm{m} \times 3.8\,\mathrm{m}$, where robots operate. About fifty fixed obstacles that can be removed manually together with 37 retractable obstacles allow reconfiguration of the environment. Moreover, the Arena contains several supporting subsystems:

- **Charging:** When a robot finishes user's task (i.e., user's reservation has expired) it autonomously navigates into a docking station where its batteries are recharged.
- **Localization Cameras:** The system provides information about positions and headings of particular robots. This is done by an image processing algorithm that identifies patterns placed on the top of each robot in images from a camera located above the Arena.
- **Visualization Cameras:** Three visualization cameras located also above the Arena enable (1) on-line monitoring by providing visual information about the actual situation in the Arena and (2) creation of off-line records from the experiments.

– **Lighting:** Lights are installed to ensure (almost) constant illumination during a day required by the localization subsystem and to enable performing
experiments even in a night.

Fig. 1. Left: S1R robots "dancing" in the Arena. Right: S1R robot.

The SyRoTek robots [5] have a differential drive with a maximal velocity
$0.35\,\mathrm{ms}^{-1}$. The size of the robots is (length × width × height) $174 \times 163 \times$
$180\,\mathrm{mm}$. The on-board computer is the Gumstix Overo Fire module with the
ARM Cortex-A8 OMAP3530 processor unit. The robots communicate through
WiFi with the *Control computer* that mediates a user's access to the robots.
Moreover, *Control computer* provides key functionalities of the system – manages
the actual state of the robots and the Arena, prepares the robots according to
reservations, manages information about users and the tasks they solve, stores
teaching material and users' files, and so on (Fig. 1).

Four interfaces are provided to mediate the user access to the system:

– **Web page** (http://www.syrotek.felk.cvut.cz) is a main gate to the system. It
provides links to all material and documentation and to the robots by choosing
a task to be solved and creating reservation of robots and the Arena.
– **Command line interface** enables to control the robots by provided commands.
– **Player/Stage API** allows to write user's modules for the Player/Stage system. The developed code can be thus tested in a simulator first and then used
for a real robot without any modification.
– **ROS (Robot Operating System) API** enables the user to utilize a huge
set of functionality provided by ROS and to control robots withing the ROS
environment in a standard way.

3   Success Stories

The SyRoTek system has been in operation since 2011 when it started as a platform for practical labs of *Introduction to Mobile Robotics* course given within School of Informatics at University of Buenos Aires. The course was attended by 70 students who solved simple robotic tasks (e.g., collision-less wandering in an unknown environment). Since that, SyRoTek became a technically mature system which has been utilized not only for teaching but also as a platform for experimentation used by users from various universities. Some examples of successful usage are given in the next paragraphs.

3.1   Real-Time Action Model Learning

M. Certicky from Comenius University, Bratislava presents a novel on-line algorithm called 3SG(Simultaneouns Specification, Simplification and Generalization) for real-time action model learning [3]. Action model is a logic-based representation of action's effects and preconditions and its automatic action learning requires a lot of observations. Besides simulated experiments in the action game Unreal Tournament 2004, SyRoTek was used to learn behaviour of a real mobile robot.

The experiments were conducted with a single S1R robot equipped with a laser range-finder. Moreover, the SyRoTek localization system was employed to provide a global robot position. The robot randomly choose and performed one of the three actions: *move forward, turn left, turn right* and recorded laser readings for further use in the teaching process. 1250 trials were made each taking about 8 sec.. All the experiments thus took approximately 166 min.

The author of [3] was given about 30 min personal interview during which main functionalities needed to execute the experiments were explained to him. After that, he was able to experiment independently. Command line interface, especially `syr_control` command was used to control the robot. This command does exactly what is needed for the task: by calling `syr_control forward <id> <l>` moves the robot id by l meters forward, while `syr_control rotate <id> <r>` turns the robot id by r radians. Furthermore, `syr_control goto <id> <x> <y> <phi>` moves the robot to the desired position. Combination of these three commands in a single script enabled to perform all necessary trials without user's intervention.

3.2   Obstacle Avoidance Algorithms

A. Alspach and S. Mason from Drexel University, Pennsylvania implemented Smooth Nearness Diagram (SND) [7] during their 4-weeks stay at Czech Technical University (CTU). SND is a popular local navigation approach for reactive collision avoidance based on data from ranging sensors, e.g., laser range-finder. The algorithm determines new direction and velocity of the robot based on a distance from obstacles and the current goal whenever fresh ranging data are sensed. The process terminates when the goal is reached with a given tolerance.

Fig. 2. The robot avoiding obstacles employing Smooth Nearness Diagram in the Webots simulation environment. [Image courtesy of A. Alspach]

As the authors were familiar with the Webots framework (http://www. cyberbotics.com/webots), they decided to implement the algorithm in this framework using its interface to the MATLAB numerical computing environment first and then transfer it to the SyRoTek system. The transfer was straightforward as both SyRoTek and Webots have interfaces to ROS. Moreover, MATLAB can be integrated into ROS using `ipc-bridge` (https://www.github.com/ nmichael/ipc-bridge). This package employs IPC (interprocess communication) for inter-process communication and bridges communication between ROS and MATLAB. After the algorithm was developed, several test runs in SyRoTek were done to prove functionality of the code (Fig. 2).

V. Kozák continued to the topic [12]. He found best parameter settings and made an extensive comparison of three reactive obstacle avoidance algorithms (Smooth Nearness Diagram, Enhanced Vector Field Histogram – VFH+, and Dynamic Window Approach – DWA) in both simulation in Player/Stage and in the real environment of the SyRoTek Arena. A client to the Playr/Stage environment was written using SND and VFH+ drivers available in Player/Stage. The DWA driver for Player/Stage was written by the author.

More than 20.000 trials we performed in a simulator involving experiments in five environments (differing in density of obstacles) with a model of the S1R robot. After that, experiments in the SyRoTek Arena were done in two different environments. These experiments took approximately 120 h. Again, bash scripts were written to automatize running of particular trials in a batch. An interesting thing is that about 52 % of experiments were done between midnight and 02:30 AM and other 23 % from 20:00 to midnight. This will be impossible with standard (not remotely controlled) robots as university buildings are closed during nights.

3.3 Formation Control

A lot of work (and experiments) has been done in the area of formation control. M. Saska et al. designed formation driving approach designed for dynamic environments that enables to incorporate a prediction of positions of moving objects into the formation control and trajectory planning [21]. Besides numerous experiments in simulations they verified the developed algorithm in the SyRoTek system. A formation of three robots was moving in the Arena while avoiding a moving obstacle that was simulated by another SyRoTek robot – the obstacle motion was detected by the robots and the plan of the formation was changed.

The formation driving approach was improved recently [22] using a novel spline-based path planning method. The generated path in the form of a spline is used as an input for model predictive control that provides trajectories for the virtual leader of the formation and consecutively for the followers. This enables to solve a large set of formation driving tasks, e.g., obstacle avoidance in static and dynamic environments, temporary shrinking of the formation in a narrow corridor, or avoidance manoeuvre as a response to failure of one of the followers. Solution of all these tasks were verified with SyRoTek, for example, Fig. 3 demonstrates how members of a formation avoid a dynamic obstacle. Again, on-board ranging sensors were used to detect obstacles. Moreover, a dynamic environment was built using retractable obstacles that can be automatically and quickly rice up.

A practical application of formation control is autonomous airport snow sweeping by a formation of ploughs [23]. Again, a leader-follower approach was employed together with model predictive control to keep the formation in a compact shape. Formation coupling/decoupling was also possible to enable cleaning

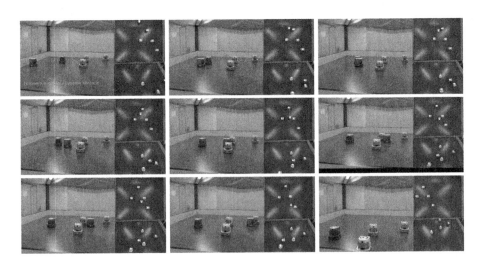

Fig. 3. Formation avoiding a dynamic obstacle (the blue robot going from left to right) with a course colliding with movement of three followers. [Image courtesy of M. Saska] (Color figure online)

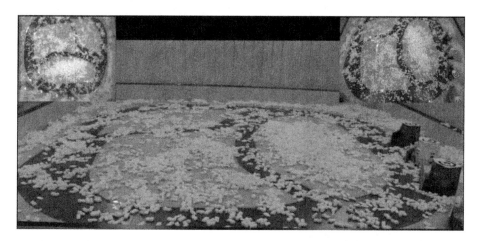

Fig. 4. Autonomous snow shoveling by a formation of robots.

Fig. 5. Particle swarm optimization for function optima finding.

of runways of arbitrary widths. The SyRoTek Arena was adapted to simulate an airport (see Fig. 4) – the Arena except of runways was covered by a paper to visualize runways and artificial snow was scattered over it. Furthermore, hand-made ploughs were created and attached to the robots. Of course, these experiments

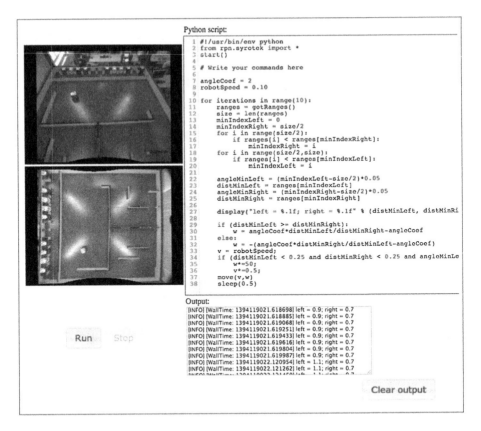

Fig. 6. Web user interface for running and editing pythons scripts. [Image courtesy of E. Cervera]

were not possible to make remotely as the artificial snow had to be scattered again after each trial, nevertheless the time needed to make experiments was significantly reduced comparing to experiments made in [20].

Principles of swarm control based on the particle swarm optimization were verified by V. Pavlik [16]. The task aims to find the whitest placed in the Arena, which was adapted by covering it with a paper with stains of various sizes and (gray-scale) intensities, see Fig. 5.

The key feature for making multi-robot experiments is an automatic preparation of robots, i.e. functionality that autonomously navigates the robots to their initial positions after each trial. This ensures repeatability of experiments as the robots start from the same positions every time and moreover enables to perform experiments in batches without user's intervention. This is greatly appreciated by SyRoTek users.

3.4   Robot Programming Network

Recently, an IEEE RAS supported initiative created a network of robotic education laboratories with remote programming capabilities – The Robot Programming Network (RPN, www.robotprogramming.net). The network thus enables an integrated environment for on-line robotic courses, several simulation environments and provides access to real robotic hardware developed by different institutions [4]. SyRoTek is one of the laboratories, which are being included into the network and are promoted within it.

As RPN uses ROS, SyRoTek integration based on `rosbridge_suite` package was straightforward. The RPN authors also adapted the existing SyRoTek widgets for visualization of an image from the Arena and developed a simple API for management of ROS topics that control the robots. Moreover, web interface was created that allows to edit python scripts and run them on the SyRoTek robots, see Fig. 6.

4   Conclusion

SyRoTek is a platform for making robotic experiments with real hardware developed at the Czech Technical University in Prague. Thanks to rich sensory equipment and advanced features it is an ideal tool for verification and testing of a huge number of problems, especially for experimentation with multi-robot systems or when long-term or a huge number of experiments are required to be performed. The system is open and free of charge to all institutions and individuals (only a simple registration taking few minutes is requested).

The aim of the paper is to promote the SyRoTek system to new users by introducing several projects done by SyRoTek users. We hope that the reader will be motivated and interested to try the system and use it for his/her purposes after reading the paper. Visit http://www.syrotek.felk.cvut.cz for more information, documentation, example codes, demo applications and videos created by the SyRoTek authors and users. Some videos can be also found at https://www.youtube.com/user/imrfel/videos.

While technical quality of the system is well advanced, documentation needs to be extended in order to attract a wide community of users. Fortunately, this is possible due to the CEMRA (Creation of Educational Material in Robotics and Automation) grant funded by IEEE RAS community that was received recently.

Acknowledgments. This work has been supported by the Technology Agency of the Czech Republic under the project no. TE01020197 "Centre for Applied Cybernetics".

References

1. Burgard, W.: RHINO-Project, 12 September 2012. http://www.iai.uni-bonn.de/rhino/tourguide
2. Casini, M., Garulli, A., Giannitrapani, A., Vicino, A.: A remote lab for experiments with a team of mobile robots. Sens. (Basel) **14**(9), 16486–16507 (2014)

3. Certický, M.: Real-time action model learning with online algorithm 3SG. Appl. Artif. Intell. **28**(7), 690–711 (2014)
4. Cervera, E., Martinet, P., Marin, R., Moughlbay, A.A., del Pobil, A.P., Alemany, J., Esteller, R., Casañ, G.: The robot programming network. J. Intell. Robot. Syst. **79**(248) (2015). http://www.link.springer.com/10.1007/s10846-015-0201-7
5. Chudoba, J., Faigl, J., Kulich, M., Košnar, K., Krajník, T., Přeučil, L.: A technical solution of a robotic e-learning system in the SyRoTek project. In: International Conference Computer Supported Education, pp. 412–417. INSTICC Press (2011)
6. Dinulescu, I., Popescu, D., Predescu, A.: Remote learning environment for visual based robot navigation. In: EAEEIE Annual Conference, pp. 26–30, July 2008
7. Durham, J., Bullo, F.: Smooth nearness-diagram navigation. In: IEEE/RSJ International Conference on Intelligent Robots and Systems, pp. 690–695, September 2008
8. Franklin, D.M., Parker, L.E.: Overwatch: an educational testbed for multi-robot experimentation (2013)
9. Gerkey, B.P., Vaughan, R.T., Howard, A.: The Player/Stage project: tools for multi-robot and distributed sensor systems. In: International Conference Advanced Robotics, pp. 317–323 (2003)
10. Guimarães, E., Maffeis, A., Pereira, J., et al.: REAL: a virtual laboratory for mobile robot experiments. IEEE Trans. Educ. **46**(1), 37–42 (2003)
11. Kulich, M., Chudoba, J., Kosnar, K., Krajnik, T., Faigl, J., Preucil, L.: SyRoTek - distance teaching of mobile robotics. IEEE Trans. Educ. **56**(1), 18–23 (2013)
12. Kulich, M., Kozák, V., Přeučil, L.: Comparison of local planning algorithms for mobile robots. In: Modelling and Simulation for Autonomous Systems (2015, to appear)
13. Mas'r, I., Bischoff, A., Gerke, M.: Remote experimentation in distance education for control engineers. In: Virtual University, Bratislava, December 2004
14. McKee, G., Barson, R.: NETROLAB: a networked laboratory for robotics education. IEE Colloq. Robot. Educ. pp. 8/1–8/3 (1995)
15. McLaughlin, M.L., Osborne, K.K., Ellison, N.B.: Virtual community in a telepresence environment. In: Jones, S.G. (ed.) Virtual Culture, pp. 146–168. Sage Publications, Inc. (1997)
16. Pavlík, V.: Swarm intelligence applied in multi-robot applications. Master's thesis, Czech Technical University in Prague, Faculty of Electrical Engineering (2012)
17. Petrovic, P., Balogh, R.: Deployment of remotely-accessible robotics laboratory. Int. J. Online Eng. **8**(S2), 31–35 (2012)
18. Quigley, M., Conley, K., Gerkey, B.P., Faust, J., Foote, T., Leibs, J., Wheeler, R., Ng, A.Y.: ROS: an open-source robot operating system. In: ICRA Workshop on Open Source Software (2009)
19. Robotoy, 7 March 2012. http://www.robotoy.elec.uow.edu.au
20. Saska, M., Hess, M., Schilling, K.: Efficient airport snow shoveling by applying autonomous multi-vehicle formations. In: Proceeding of IEEE International Conference on Robotics and Automation. Pasadena, May 2008
21. Saska, M., Spurný, V., Přeučil, L.: Trajectory planning and stabilization for formations acting in dynamic environments. In: Correia, L., Reis, L., Cascalho, J. (eds.) PAI 2013. LNCS, vol. 8154, pp. 319–330. Springer, Heidelberg (2013). http://www.dx.doi.org/10.1007/978-3-642-40669-0_28
22. Saska, M., Sputný, V., Vonásek, V.: Predictive control and stabilization ofnonholonomic formations with integrated spline-path planning. Robotics andAutonomous Systems (under review)

23. Saska, M., Vonásek, V., Přeučil, L.: Trajectory planning and control for airport snow sweeping by autonomous formations of ploughs. J. Intell. Robot. Syst. **72**(2), 239–261 (2013). http://www.dx.doi.org/10.1007/s10846-013-9829-3

24. Siegwart, R., Balmer, P., Portal, C., Wannaz, C., Blank, R., Caprari, G.: RobOn-Web: a setup with mobile mini-robots on the web. In: Beyond Webcams, pp. 117–135. MIT Press (2002)

25. Tanoto, A., Rückert, U., Witkowski, U.: Teleworkbench: a teleoperated platform for experiments in multi-robotics. In: Tzafestas, S., Tzafestas, S.G. (eds.) Web-Based Control and Robotics Education. Intelligent Systems, Control and Automation: Science and Engineering, vol. 38, pp. 267–296. Springer, Netherlands (2009)

26. Telescope, 27 July 2010. http://www.telescope.org

27. Tzafestas, C., Palaiologou, N., Alifragis, M.: Virtual and remote robotic laboratory: comparative experimental evaluation. IEEE Trans. Educ. **49**(3), 360–369 (2006)

28. Vlab, 26 September 2006. http://www.vlab.pjwstk.edu.pl

MedALE RTS Campaign: Data Analysis and Reporting

Marco Pasciuto[1(✉)], Giovanni Riccardi[1(✉)], Paolo Galati[2],
Fausto Pusceddu[2], Paolo Nurra[2], Maurizio Goiak[3], Emilio Banfi[4],
Francesco Grimaccia[5], Paolo Alviani[6], and Maurizio Romano[7]

[1] SICTA, Capodichino Airport, Naples, Italy
{marco.pasciuto,giovanni.riccardi}@sicta.it
[2] Alenia Aermacchi S.p.A., Turin, Italy
{paolo.galati,fausto.pusceddu,paolo.nurra}@alenia.it
[3] Selex ES, Ronchi dei Legionari, Gorizia, Italy
maurizio.goiak@selex-es.com
[4] Thales Alenia Space Italia S.p.A., Rome, Italy
banfi@thalesaleniaspace.com
[5] NIMBUS S.r.l., Lombardore, Italy
f.grimaccia@nimbus.aero
[6] ENAV, Rome, Italy
paolo.alviani@enav.it
[7] SICTA, Ciampino Airport, Rome, Italy
maurizio.romano@sicta.it

Abstract. The recently started Mediterranean ATM Live Exercise (MedALE) project among the SESAR Integrated RPAS Demonstration Activities, has the goal to provide to a wide spectrum of European Stakeholders indications and recommendations about the validity and limits of the existing RPAS assets, practices and operational procedure. In addition this project will provide an interesting contribution identifying the future necessary improvements or modifications to comply with the new ATM concepts that SESAR Programme is realizing. The MedALE demonstration programme adopted an incremental and complementary series of steps designed to demonstrate how RPAS may be integrated into non-segregated airspace. A combined approach has been adopted taking into account different levels of complexity and realism: Virtual and Constructive Real Time Simulation (RTS) and Live Trial (LT). RTS have been performed during November 2014 while LT activities are planned in May 2015.

This paper is focused on the Real Time simulation exercise that investigated the cooperation between ATC Controllers and RPAS Pilots in non-segregated airspace. In order to represent a real environment, a complex networked infra-structure composed by an integration of several remote simulation platforms was set up. In particular, ENAV ATC simulation system (hosted by NATO M&S CoE) and three RPAS simulator known as SKY-Y Full Mission Simulator (Male UAV), FALCO (Tactical UAV) and C-FLY (Light UAV), provided by Alenia Aermacchi, Selex and Nimbus respectively were linked ad hoc. The Operational Environment selected for the simulation exercise was the Decimomannu (LIED) airport located in Sardinia Island. During simulation campaign three type of scenarios have been considered. (1) Reference Scenario - reproducing the

J. Hodicky (Ed.): MESAS 2015, LNCS 9055, pp. 102–127, 2015.
DOI: 10.1007/978-3-319-22383-4_8

situation without the proposed solution. It means that the scenario didn't include the implementation of the RPAS. (2) Solution Scenario - represented by Reference Scenario with the introduction of three different types (with different performances) RPAS. This scenario was analyzed in both Line Of Sight (LOS) and Beyond Radio Line Of Sight (BRLOS) configurations. BRLOS scenario use RAPTOR simulation platform developed by Thales Alenia Space Italia, a SATCOM simulator in the loop emulating BRLOS C2 data link communications. (3) Non nominal Scenario - represented by Solution Scenario with the implementation of unusual events represented by RPAS loss of power, General Aviation Traffic (GAT) unusual situations and Loss of R/T Voice communication between RPAS Pilot and ATCO.

Making the comparison among these different scenarios interesting results have been obtained in terms of Safety and Human Performance Key Performance Area (KPA) with analysis of several indicators (Workload; Situational Awareness, Usability, Teamwork, Change of practices and procedure). The results collected from validation activities for both ATCOs and RPAS Pilots side, provided important feedback about technologies that support these Stakeholders and gave important elements on integration of RPAS traffic in a real ATM environment.

Keywords: RPAS · Real Time Simulation · Assessment and data analysis · SESAR ATM · ATC controller and RPAS pilot

1 Introduction

The development of Remotely Piloted Aircraft Systems (RPAS) has opened a promising new chapter in the history of aviation. These systems are based on innovative technologies developments, offering solutions which may open new and improved civil/commercial applications, as well as improvements to the safety and efficiency of civil aviation. In light of these significant benefits, the European Remotely Piloted Air Systems Steering Group (ERSG) has recognized a need to identify, plan, coordinate, and subsequently monitor the activities necessary to achieve the safe integration of RPAS into a non-segregated Air Traffic Management (ATM) environment.

Given that the full integration of RPAS into the European ATM System is vital and that the mission of SESAR is to create the new generation of ATM systems and operations, RPAS will need to be incorporated into the Single European Sky ATM Research Program (SESAR) solutions.

MedALE Project will be developed by a Consortium made by Alenia Aermacchi (Project Leader), Ente Nazionale per l'Assistenza al Volo (ENAV – Italian ANSP), Selex ES, Thales Alenia Space Italia, and Nimbus.

MedALE adopt an incremental and complementary series of runs and a real-world MALE flight trial in order to demonstrate how RPAS may be integrated into non-segregated airspace. The complementarities of the two approaches covered the path that starts from the analytical analysis, through the virtual simulation in a complex ground and flight environment with man-in-the-loop, and reaches the flight demo in a real and significant operational environment.

This paper provides the achieved results during the MedALE Real Time Networked Simulation Exercise. It describes the results of validations and how they have been conducted.

The simulations platforms interacted via standard DIS in a distributed virtual environment completely representative of the current ATM real one. In this virtual environment RPAS Pilots and ATCO controllers have been able to interact as in a real scenario, safely simulating different typologies of real contingencies evaluating operational procedures.

The networked simulation campaign addresses aspects of the RPAS-ATCO interaction, response to RPAS non-nominal conditions, and the impact on the RPAS Pilots, ATCOs workload and situational awareness due to the RPAS insertion.

2   Context of Validation

Nowadays, separation in controlled airspace is typically responsibility of the ATC, which issue clearances to the aircraft in order to maintain, at least, certain required separation values. Some systems, however, have already been proposed to increase the automation levels of these manual separation provision processes (i.e. specific tools that support the ATC to manage the desired separation levels).

The state of art indicates that several initiatives are in progress on the RPAS insertion at National and European Level but it is still missing a common approach that is agreed and recognized at European level, a necessary condition to make the insertion of the RPAS into ATM a reality. The majority of the emerging civil and commercial applications in Europe are undertaken with Light RPAS. Today the development of these applications depends on the capacity of national CAAs to develop the necessary regulation.

A true European Single Market for RPAS based on common rules is necessary to support the development of the European industry.

Currently from Italian ATCO point of view the RPAS are not managed. Furthermore taking into account current rules provided by ENAC (National Agency of civil aviation) the RPAS can fly only in segregated airspace. In case of the RPAS needs to fly in the not controlled airspace, ATZ and within 8 km of distance by the airport limit, it must provide request to ENAC (RPAS rules provided by ENAC). Such ENAC's Regulation is applicable to RPAS with weight $\leq$ 250 kg.

3   Conduct of Validation Exercise

3.1   Simulation Platform

MedALE Networked Simulation Exercise has the main scope to assess and evaluate the impact of introduction of three classes of RPAS (MALE, MAME and Light) in a simulated non-segregated airspace. This exercise has been carried out in a realistic environment with the RPAS Pilots and the integration of two human in the loop controllers working positions: Tower Controller (Military ATCO) and TMA controller (Civil ATCO).

The Networked Simulation is a complementary step to the Live Trial demonstration activity and, as far as possible, has taken advantages of existing network, called "SimLabs", managed by Finmeccanica companies (Selex ES and Alenia Aermacchi). SimLabs is a scalable and reconfigurable on-demand operating network among Finmeccanica simulation laboratories dislocated in Italy.

Effectiveness of SimLabs has been demonstrated via a "Constructive & Virtual" Distributed Simulation Experiment by federating the NATO Centre Of Excellence M&S of Cecchignola in Rome, acting as command center and interacting in a common scenario with the Finmeccanica Company's laboratories.

In order to reach the scope of the MedALE exercise, SimLabs network has been properly tailored in order to include the following actors:

ENAV ATC Simulation Platform provides the full set of capabilities allowing to operate in Real Time Simulations, including:

- Flight Data Processing (FDP), Arrival Manager (AMAN),
- Radar Data Processing (RDP),
- Safety Nets (STCA, MSAW and APW),
- Air Traffic Generator (ATG),
- Data Preparation and Data Log-ging.

It includes gateways that allow interoperability with external platforms via SVS or DIS standard.

The Unmanned Aircraft System (UAS) Full Mission Simulator is one of the main assets developed by Alenia Aermacchi S.p.A. for supporting the development of the UAS system and for the training of Operators. It is capable of simulating a complete mission of the Sky-Y Technological Demonstrator. An essential capability is the possibility of interconnection via standard HLA/DIS allowing to share a Synthetic Scenario and to be part of a distribute Simulation Environment. The Image Generator is able to show the entities in the scenario (e.g. other UAVs or manned civil traffic). The management of the simulation session (parameters and environment setup, failures injection, start, stop and freeze etc.) is feasible via a dedicated user interface operated by the specialists or by the instructor.

Nimbus UAS Simulator is realized by NIMBUS and it is capable of simulating a mission of the C-Fly Light RPAS Demonstrator. Six degrees of freedom flight dynamics model is complemented by integration of two visualization programs, data registration modules, control device interface, flight data display module, landing gear damage detector and indicator, crash condition detector and monitor, wind application module, automatic flight control module and soft real-time execution module.

Selex ES Falco Simulator is an advanced training system designed to train both RPAS Pilots and Mission Payload Operator for ISTAR missions in complex simulated scenarios. Falco Simulator provides a set of advanced tools to refine the Concept of Operations (CONOPS) and to fully explore the capabilities of the Falco RPAS in a completely simulated environment. Operators' Console Assembly is the same of the real Ground Control Station and it's the simulator main subsystem.

The Thales Alenia Space Italia SATCOM Simulator integrated with the Alenia Aermacchi UAS Full Mission simulator in order to allow the demonstration of the MALE RPAS operations and procedures in presence of BRLOS satellite data link performances. The Satellite Communication (SATCOM) simulator takes into account several factors of the SATCOM BRLOS datalink impacting its Quality of Signal.

The pictures below show the simulation concept and the simulation platforms location respectively (Fig. 1).

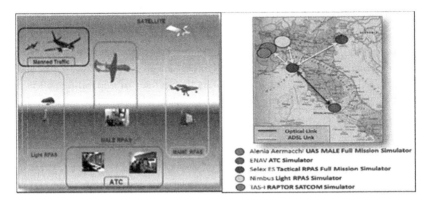

Fig. 1. MedALE simulation concept and platforms location

During the MedALE validation campaign the platforms interoperate via standard DIS in order to allow the sharing of a synthetic scenario and to exchange surveillance data (ATG traffic and RPAS aircrafts position). For the Voice communication VoIP software open source has been used.

3.2   RTS Preparatory Activities

Preparatory activities include:

- Exercise definition, including selection of the platform, airspace environment and scenarios definition, identification of the indicators and metrics to be measured and the identification of the success criteria for each objective identified and embedded in the exercise.
- Exercise preparation:
  - prototypes development/adaption and HMI modification based on defined specifications;
  - traffic scenarios definition and development in order to include the RPAS flights in the simulated manned traffic, also an high level performance model of the RPAS involved has been developed;
  - environmental data implementation (sectorisation, arrival and/or departures procedures, adaptations of the traffic, etc.) on the validation platform;
  - training preparation;

- Technical Acceptance Test/Operational Acceptance Test (TAT/OAT) of the validation platform.

3.2.1 Actors and Roles

Executive Controller "EW - Feeder". The EXE controller is part of the sector team responsible for the EW Area of Rome ACC sectors. He is responsible for the safe and expeditious flow of all flights operating within his area of responsibility. His principal tasks is to separate and sequence known flights operating within his area of responsibility and to issue instructions/information to pilots. Additionally, he monitors the trajectories of aircraft according to the clearances issued. He is assisted in these tasks by automated tools for conflict detection and trajectory monitoring.

According to these working methods the Executive:

- ensure that the required separation minima is maintained between all the aircrafts in the sector;
- is responsible for complying with all exit co-ordinations;
- is responsible for accepting/transferring all radar transfers;
- transfer the flight from feed Sector to the EW sector;
- ensure that aircraft resume own navigation to the first available point on its flight planned route following the issuance of radar vectors if the current instruction has diverted the aircraft from the previously assigned route;
- provide aircraft with instructions so as to keep clear of a TSA/R/D area when required;
- ensure that traffic exiting the sector on an ATC assigned routing is within the coordinated parameters, and ensure that all restrictions imposed by the receiving sector have been met prior to the sector boundary;

Executive Controller "APP". The APP EXE will receive traffic from EW via KOVAS, RAMEN from LIED a/d and the FIX LUKAD from LIEE airport. His/her task is to manage the final delivery of sequenced traffic. The APP EXE has the important role of assessing the quality of traffic delivery through the initial point of the SID and STAR. It is understood that the APP EXE will be very heavily loaded and therefore traffic may be deleted prior to landing for LIE and LIED.

Pseudo-Pilots. Pseudo-pilots are responsible for ensuring the realistic performance of the manned aircraft of the simulated environment by the timely input of controller instructions received over R/T or CPDLC. They manage aircraft interface when flying both EW and MEASURED airspace (Table 1).

RPAS Pilots

- RPAS flight path definition;
- Contribute to the definition of the performance expectations;
- Interaction with the ATCOs.

Table 1. Preparatory activities and actors

ACTOR	ACTIVITIES
Exercise Manager	• Manages the preparation process in order to ensure the execution of the exercise in line with objectives and timeline.
Exercise Technical Coordinator	• Sets the Technical platform according to project requirements. • Organises regular Technical and Operational Tests, according to the project schedule.
Exercise Operational Leader	• Supports the definition of the operational scenario applied. • Contributes to the definition of ATCOs' working methods and operational procedures. • Supports the definition and evaluation of the traffic samples. • Coordinates with the ACCs the ATCOs' availability during tests and exercise. • Manages the training preparation.
Scenario Preparator	• Prepares the operational scenarios for the exercise. • Prepares the traffic samples for tests, training and exercise. • Implements non nominal events in the traffic samples if needed.
Human Factors Analyst	• Contributes to define the organisations applied. • Contributes to select the data collection methods applied. • Prepares data collection materials (observation grids, scripts for debriefings, questionnaires). • Contributes to define the recording specifications. • Defines non nominal events to be introduced in the traffic samples, if needed. • Defines experimental design and agenda of the exercise. • Defines the ATCOs seating plan according to the experimental design
Safety Analyst	• Contributes to select the data collection methods applied. • Prepares data collection materials (observation grids, scripts for debriefings, questionnaires). • Contributes to define the recording specifications. • Contributes to define experimental design and agenda of the Exercise. • Defines non nominal events to be introduced in the traffic samples, if needed.
Other Analysts	• Contribute to define the recording specifications.
RPAS Pilots	• RPAS flight path definition. • Contribute to the definition of the performance expectations. • Interaction with the ATCOs.
Satellite Aerocom Expert	• Contribute to the definition of the SATCOM operational scenario (e.g. transition from LOS to BRLOS and vice versa) and not nominal events (e.g. external failure). • SATCOM simulator development/adaption and HMI modification based on experimentation needs. • Support to SATCOM integration with MALE RPAS simulator platform and to relevant acceptance tests.

Other Actors

3.2.2 ATC Constraints
Real ATC constraints are considered in the Operational Airspace. For all traffic departure from the following airports are considered:

LIEE departure:

All traffic departing LIEE destination Northbound and Southbound shall be coordinating at 3000ft

LIED departure:

All traffic departing LIED destination Northbound and Southbound shall be coordinating at 5000ft

3.2.3 Manned Traffic Preparation
Traffic samples used during simulation are based on a busy summer period typical morning and evening busy periods from weekday operations. The selected days are 13th and 20th of July during the 2013 year. The traffic for the validation exercises shall include a "Morning" 3 h busy period and an "Afternoon" 3 h busy period. Traffic samples have been devised to serve specific validation purposes as required. Two type of Traffic sample have been considered for the Validation purposes: TS1 and TS2. The TS3 will be used only for the non-nominal case.

The Traffic have been augmented in line with main Eurocontrol predictions of 3–4 % increase per year. More precise forecasts concerning Italy and the Milan Airports have been taken into account. This implies that simulated traffic levels have been at least 20 % higher than 2012 to represent 2015.

3.2.4 Radar Separations
Baseline procedures and working methods are the one used actually in Rome ACC. Separation standards are those in use today (Table 2):

Table 2. Horizontal and vertical separation

Horizontal separation	
Application	Separation
En route radar	5 NM
Vertical separation	
Application	Separation
En route radar	1000 ft (RVSM)
	2000 ft (No RVSM)

In particular, the minimum separation of:

- 5 NM radar separation at or above FL200;
- 5 NM spacing between subsequent landing aircraft on LIED and LIEE,

shall be provided unless increased longitudinal separation is required due to wake turbulence or due to specific requests.

3.3 Simulation Scenario

The Operational Environment is the Decimomannu LIED airport, in the south of Sardinia. All the RPAS aircraft land and departure from this Airport following the GAT/OAT procedures, then coordination between the civil and military units is granted. In detailed RPAS depart from a military airport and climb in no segregated airspace.

The simulation scenario is intended to be a "Round Robin" (take-off/landing from/to the same airport) during which three different RPAS (with different performances) fly in a mixed environment with other conventional manned aircraft in a controlled airspace. One of the main goal is to demonstrate how the Operational procedures of the RPASs are compatible within the selected non-segregated airspace.

The environment is Italy, in particular en-route and approach of the Sardinia Airspace sectors of Rome ACC. The Validation Scenario has been based on the simulation of two measured sectors of Rome ACC (namely EW) plus one approach sector defined as "Decimomannu APP". In addition, this Scenario will include 2 airports LIEE Cagliari Elmas and LIED Decimomannu.

These sectors have been slightly modified in order to customize the traffic in the appropriate sectors dimension. A portion of the Airspace is dedicated to the Feeder sector which will transfer the traffic into the measured sectors (EW) according the LoA and FLAS in Rome Area of Control.

The LIED Military Airport has been airport selected for the RPAS round robin route. Transition from segregated military airspace to the area of operations defined as a restricted area and transition again from the area of operations to segregated military airspace. Landing to LIED Airport.

For manned traffic purpose, also the LIEE Airport has been used (not for the RPAS). Airspace has been imported from the Eurocontrol SAAM v4.7 tool within the following coordinates:

- Top Left: 44°00' 00" N
- Bottom Right: 36° 00' 00" E

The vertical limits of the airspace are as follows (Table 3) (Fig. 2):

Table 3. Vertical limits of the airspace

Sector	Vertical limits
APP (TWR)	GND-FL245
EW	FL245-FL245

3.4 Exercises Execution

For each defined scenario, different runs has been planned with occurrences of specific non-nominal events. As there were two ATCOs involved in the validation activities and three validation scenarios, nine is the total number of runs.

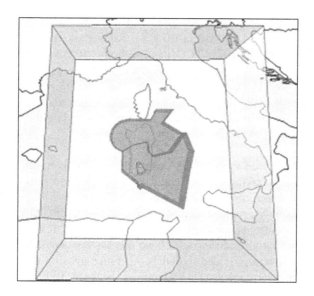

Fig. 2. Medale operational scenario

The scenarios included also non-nominal cases as loss of engine power, GAT unusual situations and loss of voice radio communications between RPAS Pilot and ATCO.

Other 2 or 3 runs have been considered for ATCO training. Furthermore 3 spare runs have been considered in order to replay eventual failure runs. In this way a total amount of runs is 14/15. Each simulation run has the duration from 1 h to 1 h and 30 min, having consequently four days of validation.

It is important to highlight that before to perform the Networked Real Time Simulation one week of Technical Acceptance Test (TAT) and Operational Acceptance Test (OAT) activities has been needed. The scope of TAT activities was to perform the technical tests on ground and airborne side as well as to verify the integration of the simulation platforms from the technically point of view.

The scope of the OAT activities is to involve the ATCO and validation expert in order to configure the validation platform and tune the operational scenario. It has to be performed around 15 days before the Networked exercise. After these steps the platform is ready to perform Networked simulation.

4   Results

ATCOs Networked Simulation Results. Networked Simulation is considered a V2 Real Time Simulation. RTS techniques are important in providing human-in-the-loop experience of a proposed concept in a relatively controlled and repeatable environment. Extensive training of participants was performed to reach levels of expertise and familiarity with the proposed concept and simulation tools. MedALE validation campaign was performed used a single platform composed by Air Traffic Controller part, known as ENAV ATC Simulation Platform, and Airborne part represented by three RPAS Simulators provided by Alenia (Sky-Y), Selex (Falco) and Nimbus (C-Fly). So RTS investigate both Ground (ATCOs) and Airborne (RPAS and RPAS pilot) point of view. This section of the paper is focused on ground segment. Ground analysis considered impact on ATCOs only for Falco and Sky-Y RPAS because their objective is to fly in the current traffic flow as well as in a Non Segregated Airspace. Otherwise C-fly objective is to made observation flights for various possibilities of use (e.g. control pipelines, coast, etc.).

Ground part was composed by APP/TMA controller as well as En-route controller. As highlighted by ATCOs, taking into account current RPAS performance, they impacted mainly APP/TMA sector, only in same cases RPAS have been managed by En-route controller. Consequently ground analysis was focused on APP/TMA controller, any-way also En-route controller feedback have been considered. It is important to high-light that 3 ATCOs took turns during tests. Two ATCOs was provided by ENAV (Civil ATCOs) and another was provided by Italian Air Force aviation (Military ATCOs).

The analysis had as object the comparison between Reference and Solution (BVLOS) scenarios. Were investigated both Safety and Human Performance KPA, taking into account the following indicators:

- Workload;
- Situational Awareness;
- Usability;
- Teamwork;
- Change of practices and procedure;
- Trajectory monitoring.

Regarding BRLOS conditions (simulation of the satellite link between RPAS pilot and Sky-Y) limited to Command and control aspects, we can say that they were transparent for the controller.

The analysis was performed taking only into account qualitative data. So data gathering was carried out through questionnaires (e.g. Nasa tlx, SASHA etc.). They were submitted to the ATCOs after each run. It is important to highlight that the analysis provided are related to the assumptions considered during RTS. So the results cannot be generalized and applied to other different situations.

Human Performance. The human performance KPA foresees the following vali-dation objectives:

- OBJ-RPAS04-001 - To evaluate the impact of introduction of RPAS flights in non-segregated airspace;
- OBJ-RPAS04-002 - To evaluate ATCOs workload related to the introduction of RPAS flights in non-segregated airspace;
- OBJ-RPAS04-003 - To evaluate ATCOs Situational Awareness related to the introduction of RPAS flights in non-segregated airspace;
- OBJ-RPAS04-004 - To evaluate ATCOs Teamwork related to the introduction of RPAS flights in non-segregated airspace.

HF literature underlines the relationship between Workload, Situational Awareness, Usability, Teamwork and the influences in between. Then, these objectives have been analysed taking into account Workload, Situational awareness and Teamwork indicators. Considering all the previous factors, these indicators have been evaluated taking into account qualitative data and compared with information collected during de-briefings as well as controllers' behaviour observed during the validation.

Workload.   Perceived Workload represents the effort spent by a human operator to achieve a particular level of performance. During simulation this indicator has been quantitative assessed through the standard questionnaire "NASA Task-load Index (TLX)" that includes the appraisal of mental, physical and temporal demand, performance, effort and frustration levels.

Next figure displays the workload of three ATCOs involved as APP/TMA controller during several runs. Particularly this figure ensure to made workload comparison between Reference (Blue line) and Solution - BVLOS (Red line) scenarios (Fig. 3).

Workload trend is gathered around the lower/middle part of the diagram, especially

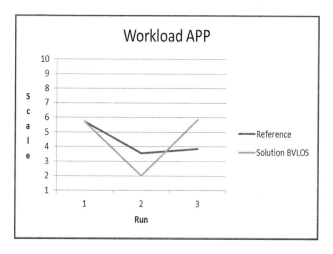

Fig. 3. ATCO's **workload**

from 6 to 2 values, for both Reference and Solution scenarios. It is important to highlight that negative values are never considered. Reference and Solution scenarios are included in the optimal range.

ATCOs workload average value for both Reference and Solution scenarios are about 3. It means that ATCOs achieved an excellent level of workload (very low/neutral) in both scenarios. Diagram show that workload value in the Reference and Solution scenarios are comparable and similarly distributed. This aspect allows to highlight that the inclusion of RPAS in the traffic flown doesn't impact on ATCO workload. The main elements that impact the RPAS inclusion in the traffic flow, are related to their performances.

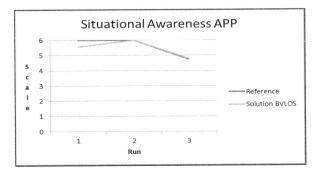

Fig. 4. ATCO's situational awareness

Table 4. RPAS performances

RPAS	Speed	Altitude	Endurance[a]	Range[b]
Sky-Y	110 Kts	FL120/140	≈ 40 min.	≈ 80/90 nm
Falco	110 Kts	FL120/140	≈ 40 min.	≈ 80/90 nm
C-Fly	27 Kts	1000/2000 ft	≈ 20 min.	≈ 10 nm

[a]Endurance is the maximum length of time that an aircraft can spend during flight.
[b]Range is a measure of distance flown

Below are reported currently MedALE RPAS performances (Table 4):

It is important to highlight that in order to include the RPAS in the traffic flow is required that their performances have to be improved.

Another important aspect is related to the lack of pilot on board, that seems doesn't create problems in not nominal case, but could be significant in case of unusual situations (e.g. RPAS loss of command and control).

Situational Awareness. Situational Awareness represents the perception of elements in the environment within a volume of time and space, the comprehension of their meaning and the projection of their status in the near future. During simulation this indicator has been quantitative assessed through the standard questionnaire "SASHA".

Figure 5 shows the situational awareness of three ATCOs involved as APP/TMA controller during several runs. Particularly this figure ensures to made workload comparison between Reference (Blue line) and Solution - BVLOS (Red line) scenarios (Fig. 4).

Situational Awareness trend is focused on higher part of the diagram, values are spread over between 5 (almost always) and 6 (always), for both Reference and Solution scenarios. Negative values are never noticeable. So it is possible to assert that Reference and Solution scenarios are included in the optimal range.

ATCOs workload average value for both Reference and Solution scenarios are about 5.5 which correspond to an high value of the scale. It means that ATCOs achieved an excellent level of Situational Awareness (very high) in both scenarios. Diagram shows that Situational Awareness value in the Reference and Solution

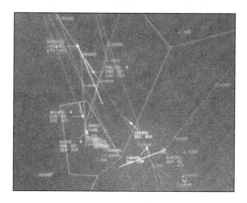

Fig. 5. RPAS flight in a simulated non-segregated airspace

scenarios are comparable and equally distributed. This aspect allows to highlight that the inclusion of RPAS in the traffic flown doesn't impact on ATCO Situational Awareness.

Anyway in order to avoid misunderstanding, ATCOs assert that RPAS have to be able to load flight plan in the Flight Management System (FMS), consequently RPAS have to be equipped with FMS. In this way RPAS are able to select both procedure indicated by ATCO as well as appropriate back up procedure in case of unusual situations. Of course back up procedure must be known to all actors involved.

Usability. Usability is defined as the extent to which a product can be used by specified users to achieve specified goals with effectiveness, efficiency and satisfaction in a specific context of use. In this case was investigated the RPAS information (e.g. track and waypoints) that should be shown to the ATCO on the CWP. Screenshot below shows ATCO point of view (CWP/HMI picture). This figure displayed RPAS flight in a non-segregated airspace that is GAT and RPAS (SKY452, FAL56 and NIM43) in the same airspace.

The information displayed by the label are represented in the figure below, they are: CALLSIGN, RPAS SYMBOL, ACTUAL FLIGHT LEVEL (ALV), EXIT FIX o SECTOR, CLEARED FLIGHT LEVEL (CFL) and EXIT FLIGHT LEVEL (XFL). ATCOs required that these information have to be shown also in case of RPAS aircraft (Fig. 6).

ATCOs assert that RPAS have to be able to perform Squawk ident (when RPAS pilot push a specific button the corresponding label on ATCO HMI blink). In order to perform Squawk ident, RPAS have to be equipped with transponder.

Furthermore ATCOs highlight that it is very important to discern between RPAS and GAT flights. Currently the label on the controller HMI report an hash as shown in the figure above (RPAS SYMBOL). Controllers assert that this symbol could be confused with asterisk that indicate "Sierra" mode. Consequently in order to discern between RPAS and GAT flights, ATCOs advise:

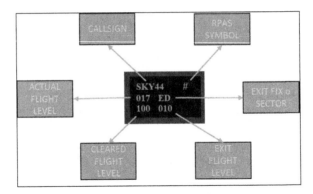

Fig. 6. RPAS label

- Underline the CALLSIGN;
- Use particular CALLSIGN that indicate the aircraft category as occurs for the postal flights. A proposal could be to have all RPAS CALSIGN that begin/end with the same letter (e.g. "U" of unmanned)

In order to facilitate the recognition of the RPAS flight, during first call RPAS pilot could use an official and standard phraseology. A proposal could be introduce the term RPAS/unmanned in the standard phraseology used during first call.

During the debriefing ATCOs confirmed that RPAS information on the CWP was very good.

Some questions of questionnaire related to the RPAS information have been selected:

- 4.1 → performed tasks of different level of complexity accurately;
- 4.5 → GAT/RPAS assured a flexible management;
- 4.7 → Current practices and Procedures are useful for RPAS;
- 4.8 → introduction of RPAS flights in non-segregated airspace is usable;
- 4.9 → How demanding is the management of mixed-mode aircrafts (GAT and RPAS) on your attention resources- Is it excessively demanding.

These questions have been selected because they provide evidences related to the RPAS information on the CWP.

Figure 12 shows the questions on the horizontal axis and the achieved scores on vertical axis. For each question the score is made up of different contributions (i.e. different answers) provided by ATCOs, stacked one over the other one to make the total value of 100 %. The scale of different colours and related meaning is reported on the right of the figure.

In the figure is showed also that the highest percentages of the answers provided by controllers are "always" or "almost Always". "Always" and "almost Always" answers are spread between 67 % and 100 % (It is important to highlight that the last column report always positive feedback). It means that RPAS information on the CWP are very good. Moreover, 100 % of ATCOs asserted that the RPAS information on the CWP were complete and useful (Fig. 7).

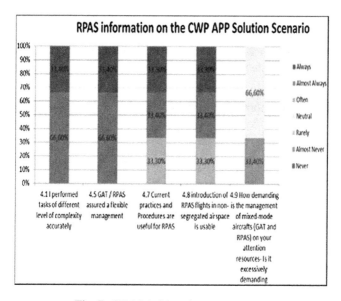

Fig. 7. RPAS information on the CWP

Teamwork. Teamwork represents the allocation of tasks between team members and the way information between team members is exchanged. A good design of tasks and activities on different actors is supported by positive level of teamwork. During simulation this indicator has been quantitative assessed through the standard questionnaire "STQ".

Figure 8 displays the teamwork of three ATCOs involved as APP/TMA controller during several runs. Particularly this figure ensure to made teamwork comparison between Reference (Blue line) and Solution - BVLOS (Red line) scenarios.

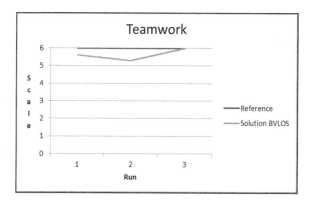

Fig. 8. ATCOs teamwork

Teamwork is focused on higher part of the diagram, values are spread over between 5 (almost always) and 6 (always), negative values are never noticeable. The average value is around 5.5 which correspond to an high value of the scale. It means that teamwork between En-Route an APP/TMA controller is not affected to the inclusion of RPAS flights.

Safety. The safety KPA foresees the following validation objectives:

- OBJ-RPAS04-001 - To evaluate the impact of introduction of RPAS flights in non-segregated airspace;
- OBJ-RPAS04-007 - To evaluate the safety level in case of the introduction of RPAS flights in non-segregated airspace;
- OBJ-RPAS04-008 - To Assess the safety impact associated to the communications between the RPAS flight crews and ATCOs

These objectives have been analysed taking into account change of practices and procedure as well as trajectory monitoring indicators. Furthermore in order to support this analysis, workload and Situational Awareness results, have to be considered. Considering all the previous factors, these indicators have been evaluated taking into account qualitative data and compared with information collected during de-briefings as well as controllers' behaviour observed during the validation.

Change of Practices and Procedures. Some questions of questionnaire related to the RPAS Change of Practices and Procedures have been selected:

- 5.5 → RPAS Concept, Rules, change of practices and Procedures are operationally feasible;
- 5.6 → The RPAS flyability is acceptable;
- 5.7 → Change of practices and Procedures are acceptable;

These questions have been selected because they provide evidences related to the RPAS Change of Practices and Procedures.

Figure 9 shows the questions on the horizontal axis and the achieved scores on vertical axis. For each question the score is made up of different contributions (i.e. different answers) provided by ATCOs, stacked one over the other one to make the total value of 100 %. The scale of different colours and related meaning is reported on the right of the figure.

Figure shows that 100 % of the answers provided by ATCOs are strongly agreed with the questions reported above. Furthermore during debriefing ATCOs confirmed that RPAS procedure have to refer to current procedures applied to GAT aircraft in order to minimize the change of practices from ATCO point of view. Furthermore ATCOs required to select and set standard/official procedures to apply to the RPAS flights.

Trajectory Monitoring. Some questions of questionnaire related to the RPAS Trajectory monitoring have been selected:

- 5.2 → I was ALWAYS able to follow the right track;

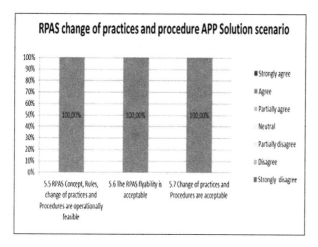

Fig. 9. Change of practices

- 5.3 → The GAT/RPAS allows to avoid Lateral and Vertical error respect to the predicted track;
- 5.9 → Integration of RPAS flights in departing/arrival airport traffic is safe;
- 5.10 → introduction of RPAS flights in non-segregated airspace is safe;

Figure 10 follows the same criteria explicated in the previous section, taking into account them the following diagram have been produced:

Figure 10 shows that the highest percentages of the answers provided by controllers are "Agree" or "Strongly Agree". "Agree" or "Strongly Agree" answers are spread between 66 % and 100 %. It means that ATCOs were able to provide or maintain safe service. ATCOs assert that RPAS follow the right track and have no sensible deviation

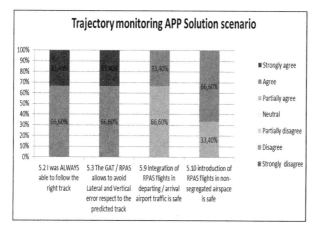

Fig. 10. Monitoring trajectory laterally/vertically preventing loss of separation with obstacles or terrain

from nominal path. Furthermore ATCOs highlight that RPAS pilot follow the clearances provided by ATCOs through R/T communication.

Unusual Situations. Unusual situations respect the following validation objectives:

- OBJ-RPAS04-010 - assess the procedure to use in case of "loss of engine power" of the RPAS;
- OBJ-RPAS04-011 - assess the procedure to use in case of loss of voice communication of RPAS between RPAS Pilot and ATCO;
- OBJ-RPAS04-012 - assess the flight procedure that the RPAS have to use in order to give way to an arriving conventional aircraft

The feedback provided by ATCOs about these scenarios are:

RPAS loss of engine power – when occurred RPAS loss of engine power, they had the right altitude, so RPAS arrived to the runway without problem. It should be emphasized that in this circumstance have been considered a low level of traffic in order to made a first test. Anyway ATCOs assert that in case of high traffic due to RPAS performance could occur some issues. Consequently ATCOs suggests to improve the RPAS performances;

Loss of R/T voice communication – we have simulated the loss of R/T voice communication between RPAS pilot and ATCO. In this case the official procedure to apply is that aircraft pilot squawk ident when receive the clearance. As the involved RPAS cannot provide squawk ident, ATCO requested to RPAS pilot to made a little turn on the right and on the left when receive the clearance. Taking into account this procedure, RPAS reached the runway without problem. Of course ATCOs request again that RPAS have to be equipped with transponder;

RPAS have to give way to an arriving GAT aircraft – RPAS performed the clearance in time, they have to give way to a GAT without problem. It is important to highlight that the current RPAS performance took some time to the controller in order to plan the unexpected event, so some better performance provide greater flexibility of decision and timing to ATCOs.

The aim of the activity was to verify concept feasibility from the Sky-Y operator point of view. Due to the availability of just one assessor, the collected results are mainly qualitative and no statistical considerations are provided.

System Usability. After simulation runs, RPAS pilots had to fill in questionnaires concerning aspects of system usability: 10 questions about usability aspects such as integration, ease-of-use, and complexity regarding the system under consideration. The questions alternated between positive and negative usability aspects and agreement could be indicated on a scale from 1 to 5. The application was judged to be easily usable, improving the RPAS pilot's situational awareness during flight operations, and proved to be very intuitive requiring reduced learning times and allowing managing aircraft operations also in the single operator configuration applied during the assessment.

It has been noted that the surveillance task related to the application is a secondary task in the en-route flight within controlled airspace primary mission, therefore the use of the system does not require a constant level of attention and conversely could cause a complacent attitude.

The Run 4 records a lower usability score was due the fact that the BRLOS time delay introduced in the scenario causes an increase of workload that forces the pilot to feel a bit of "Time Pressure": pilot was more focalized on primary tasks and consequently reduced the attention on the application, negatively affecting the final score.

Situational Awareness. After simulation runs, pilots had to fill in SASHA (Situation Awareness for SHAPE) questionnaire, which assessed the level of pilot situational awareness during the preceding simulation run.

The SASHA questionnaire consisted of 6 questions. The questions alternated between positive and negative aspects and agreement could be indicated on a scale from 0 to 6. The Situational Awareness level was always very high. The lower score collected during the Run 5 was due to the fact that an Engine failure was "requested" with a short notice, in this way happening as an unexpected event, even if not directly related to the surveillance application.

Workload Evaluation. Within the post-run assessment, the pilot workload was evaluated following the NASA-TLX method. NASA-TLX is a subjective, post hoc workload assessment tool. NASA-TLX allows users to perform subjective workload assessments on operator(s) working with various human-machine systems. NASA-TLX is a multi-dimensional rating procedure that derives an overall workload score based on a weighted average of ratings on six subscales. The subscales include Mental & Physical Demands, Temporal Demands, Own Performance, Effort and Frustration.

The task was judged as executable with a medium/low workload level, assuming a very short training/familiarization phase.

The global trend shows a stable workload mean value below 50 (on a 0 to 100 scale). Almost all the runs provided the same results: this was due to the fact that the surveillance task supported by the application was secondary with respect to the primary task to fly the RPAS within en-route controlled airspace and so only marginally affected the score.

For what concerns the trend of the single workload parameters (Fig. 19), we can note that:

- The perceived performance level was quite high and stable, meaning that the pilots were always able to adequately face the different test conditions.
- Mental demand and Effort are stable along all the runs
- Time Pressure was generally perceived as low in normal conditions.
- The perceived frustration level was negligible,
- Physical demand is perceived as less significant compared to other parameters.

Globally the task was perceived mainly as a mental low demanding one, requiring a reduced effort and within easily manageable time constraints (Fig. 11).

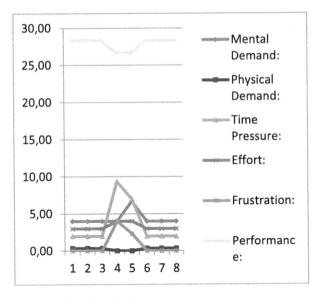

Fig. 11. Sky-Y pilot workload parameters results

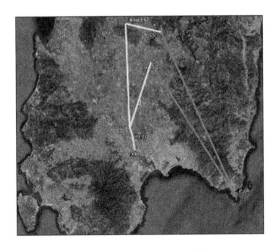

Fig. 12. LOS/BRLOS transition for SATCOM simulation

SATCOM Simulation Results. The SATCOM validation exercise involving the RAPTOR simulator (**R**pas s**A**tellite **P**laform for fu**T**ure c**O**mmunications infrast**R**ucture) is aiming at the verification of the BRLOS operation and BRLOS -ATM interactions depending on satellite communications relaying RPAS C2 (OBJ-RPAS04-001-013).

During the execution of the scenario the Sky-Y has been simulated extending its flight beyond radio LOS and switching C2 data communications to/from RPAS to satellite data link by means of SATCOM simulator.

The RAPTOR simulation platform is capable of assessing the SATCOM data link performances by evaluating key performance indicators (KPI) relevant to the link propagation conditions (e.g. clear sky or rain attenuation) and airborne SATCOM antenna illumination conditions from/to the satellite antenna. The different KPIs can be assessed when varying a number of link parameters and environmental conditions.

The MedALE BRLOS simulation exercise perfectly fits into the current RAPTOR capabilities.

The RPAS04-001-013 simulation objective is twofold:

- To verify that the communications during BRLOS operations are assured without any interruption (continuity);
- To verify that the quality of service is in line with the expected for the C2 applications (data link availability and performances).

Considering high level objectives of MedALE RTS exercise, it has been decided to evaluate the BRLOS performance by simulating the Satcom data link in qualitative terms only, without carrying out detailed performance analyses. This goal has been achieved by simulating representative RPAS communications based on Athena-Fidus space segment, a broadband communications satellite for civil and military users operating in Ka band, together with the companion Satcom terminal on the RPAS airborne side.

The simulated exercise started in LOS and then switched in BRLOS when approaching a predefined control station radio horizon. The environmental conditions scenario was initially set to 'nominal' (i.e. no rain, no interference) and then, at a certain point of the simulation, changed to 'degraded mode' (i.e. medium rain rate) to check that the Satcom data link performance were maintained.

Planned LOS/BRLOS Transition. The following picture shows the planned TS2 scenario with the Sky-Y route and relevant LOS and BRLOS flight segments.

The yellow segments represent the LOS path, the blue ones indicates the segments flown in BRLOS conditions. The switching from LOS to BRLOS has been done by the Sky-Y RPAS Pilot through the SATCOM simulator.

Considerations About BRLOS Datalink Availability. Along the BRLOS mission (Blue path), the SATCOM scenario conditions were intentionally changed (degraded) in order to check the system performance and robustness. This was achieved by sending commands to the RAPTOR simulator in real time, without impacts on the simulation from an operational point of view.

SATCOM BRLOS 'Nominal' scenario conditions:

- atmospheric condition: no rain;
- interference: no interference (both ground and onboard side);
- propagation delay: computed by RAPTOR simulator as function of actual geometry (about 350 ms);
- latency: none.

SATCOM BRLOS "Degraded" scenario conditions:

- atmospheric condition: medium rain rate = 5 mm/hr;
- interference: no interference;
- Propagation delay: same as above (about 350 ms);
- Latency: none.

In both "nominal" and "degraded" conditions the continuity and availability of command and control chain communications were maintained using the satellite data link and no apparent difference was observed by the RPAS Pilot during the two legs of the route.

Falco Simulation Results. RPAS Falco system is currently in use in many countries for surveillance and peace keeping operation where commercial traffic is absent.

The aim of the activity was to verify concept feasibility from the RPAS Falco Piloti point of view;

System Usability. After simulation runs, pilots had to fill in questionnaires concerning aspects of system usability.

The system usability questionnaire was the same for each RPAS Pilots Falco System was judged to be usable in simulated scenario and proved to be very intuitive requiring reduced learning times and allowing managing aircraft operations, even if it's suggested to improve the RPAS to increase the pilot's situational awareness during flight operations.

Falco system is not currently equipped with equipment that displays the nearby traffic; the only feedback for the pilots was given by the ATC through voice communication.

Situational Awareness. After simulation runs, each RPAS pilot filled in the same SASHA (Situation Awareness for SHAPE) questionnaire, which assessed the level of pilot situational awareness during the preceding simulation run.

The Situational Awareness level was always high. In Run 5 an Engine failure was "requested" with a short notice, in this way happening as an unexpected event; even if not directly related to the surveillance application this caused a lower score respect others runs.

Workload Evaluation. The task was judged as executable with a medium/low workload level, assuming a very short training/familiarization phase. the global trend shows a similar workload for both pilots with values around 50 (on a 0 to 100 scale).

For what concerns the trend of the single workload parameters, we can note that:

- The perceived performance level was quite high and stable, meaning that the pilots were always able to adequately face the different test conditions.
- Mental demand and Effort are similar for both.

- Time Pressure is double for second pilot due to the scenarios he was involved (Run 5 increased the pilot attention on time management).
- The perceived frustration level was negligible.
- Physical demand is perceived as less significant compared to other parameters (Fig. 13).

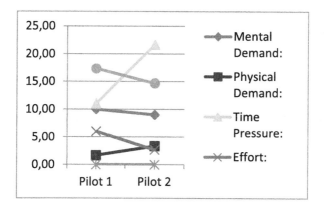

Fig. 13. Falco pilots workload parameters results

C-Fly Simulation Results. Two different pilots conducted the simulation runs (first pilot in runs from 1 to 4, and a second expert pilot qualified by Euro USC, in runs from 5 to 8).

The first pilot faced more difficulty because of his less experience and first involvement in a multiple-RPAs simulation environment, while the second one has taken the opportunity to monitor activities and procedures from the first set of trials (1–4).

Moreover, due to adaptation restrictions of the SW environment of the Nimbus C-Fly RPA simulator, the RPAS pilot was not able to see the surrounding air traffic scenario on the screen, but received updates and instructions only by ATCO communications via the designed radio channel.

For what concern the Situational Awareness the results are fairly comparable except for the first run of the first pilot who pointed out a less score because of the new activity, but he soon recovered on an average positive 4 like the other one.

Finally are shown the result about the workload following the method NASA-TLX evaluating the total workload based on the weighted vote of six categories named: Mental Demands, Physical Demands, Time Pressure, Performance, Effort and Frustration (Fig. 14).

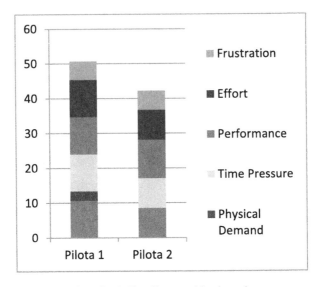

Fig. 14. C-Fly pilots workload results

5 Conclusion and Recommendation

Usually RPAS are operated mostly in controlled airspace and are handled as special exceptions. Policies and procedures must be set for how ATC can interact with RPAS without creating burdensome workloads.

Some high level conclusions can be summarised as follows:

- separation standards need to be reviewed and potentially altered;
- policies must be tuned for launch and recovery methods for departing/arriving airports and for different RPAS typologies;
- communications performance requirements necessary to meet safety requirements are needed;
- standardized methods must be established for how to pass RPAS performance characteristics and mission information to ATCO;
- procedures for emergency and/or non-nominal operations should be established.

Despite the positive end-user feedback and overall operational acceptability of the concept (even if need to be tested in other validation) some minor and general recommendations were provided:

(a) RPAS flight have to perform Squawk ident, so RPAS have to be equipped with transponder;
(b) In order to avoid misunderstanding, that impact on ATCO Safety and Situational Awareness, ATCOs assert that RPAS have to be able to load flight plan in the Flight Management System (FMS), consequently RPAS have to be equipped with FMS;

(c) ATCOs recommended that RPAS procedure have to refer to current procedures applied to GAT aircraft in order to minimize the change of practices from ATCO point of view. Furthermore ATCOs required to select and set standard/official procedures to apply to the RPAS flights.

References

1. Roadmap for the integration of civil Remotely-Piloted Aircraft Systems into the European Aviation System, June 2013
2. SESAR JU, Call Ref. SJU/LC/0087–CFP
3. Aeronautica and Difesa, pp. 60–61, July 2013
4. MedALE Project

Methods and Algorithms for AS

Collided Path Replanning in Dynamic Environments Using RRT and Cell Decomposition Algorithms

Ahmad Abbadi[✉] and Vaclav Prenosil

Department of Information Technologies, Faculty of Informatics, Masaryk University,
Botanicka 554/68a, 602 00 Brno, Czech Republic
Ahmad.Abbadi@mail.com, prenosil@fi.muni.cz

Abstract. The motion planning is an important part of robots' models. It is responsible for robot's movements. In this work, the cell decomposition algorithm is used to find a spatial path on preliminary static workspaces, and then, the rapidly exploring random tree algorithm (RRT) is used to validate this path on the actual workspace. Two methods have been proposed to enhance the omnidirectional robot's navigation on partially changed workspace. First, the planner creates a RRT tree and biases its growth toward the path's points in ordered form. The planner reduces the probability of choosing the next point when a collision is detected, which in turn increases the RRT's expansion on the free space. The second method uses a straight planner to connect path's points. If a collision is detected, the planner places RRTs on both sides of the collided segment. The proposed methods are compared with the others approaches, and the simulation shows better results in term of efficiency and completeness.

Keywords: Path re-planning · Motion planning · RRT · Cell decomposition · Multi RRT

1 Introduction

The motion-planning problem is an active subject in the robotics field. It attracts the researchers to develop and increase the motion independence of the systems. The high demand of autonomous system leads to develop many concepts of motion planning. They vary in the efficiency and the domain of applications. Examples of these algorithms are: local planners, e.g. Bug algorithm [1]; roadmap approaches, for example, visibility roadmap and Voronoi diagrams [2]; cell decomposition methods, which are divided the working space into manageable regions, and classified the workspace into free and obstacle areas. Other examples of motion planners are the randomized sample-based algorithms, these approaches try to approximate the workspace by taking samples from it randomly [3]. Recently, many researchers have studied the combination of these methods, in order to avoid the drawbacks and enhance the performance.

In this paper, our focus is to develop an efficient planner on slightly changed workspace. The proposed methods are designed for the robot's omnidirectional movement. The approximation cell decomposition (ACD) is used and combined with the RRT planner in order to enhance the robot's navigation. The ACD finds a spatial path on

© Springer International Publishing Switzerland 2015
J. Hodicky (Ed.): MESAS 2015, LNCS 9055, pp. 131–143, 2015.
DOI: 10.1007/978-3-319-22383-4_9

preliminary and stationary workspaces, and then the RRT is used to validate this path on the actual workspace.

Two methods have been proposed in this paper. The First one creates instances of RRTs and biases their growth toward the points of the ACD's path in ordered form. It updates the bias values based on the collision information. If changes are made to the workspace and a collision is found along the path's segments, the planner attempts to find a new sub-path locally by exploring the space around the collision place using RRT. The Second method uses a straight-line planner to connect the path's points. It creates local RRT trees on both sides of the collided segment of the path, if one is detected.

This paper organized as follows, The RRT algorithms and related developments are presented in Sect. 2. In Sect. 3, the principle of cell decomposition algorithms is reviewed. The proposed method and result is discussed in Sects. 4 and 5, respectively. Finally, we conclude the results.

2   Rapidly Exploring Random Tree (RRT)

The rapidly exploring random tree algorithm is a sample-based motion planner [4, 5]. It does not evaluate the workspace in an exact manner; rather, it deals with configurations that are taken randomly from the configuration space. The principle of RRT algorithms is to build a filling space tree and pulling the tree's growth toward unexplored regions. It takes a configuration randomly and then branching a new extension from the nearest node of the tree toward this configuration. The new branch's length is determined by the incremental step parameter. If this branch does not collide with obstacles or it does not break constrains, it is kept in the RRT tree. Thus, the tree is growing outward of the initial position. The principle of the basic RRT algorithm is shown in Fig. 1.

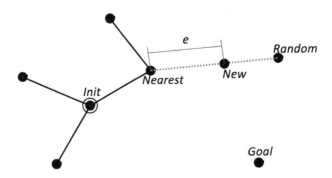

Fig. 1. RRT principle

In navigation problem, the RRT produces a feasible path between the initial position and the goal one, if these locations existed in the tree's nodes. The feasibility of the path comes due to the tree characteristic, where the tree is built up of valid connections between the tree's nodes. It starts from the initial location and explores the space until it finds the goal, then it produces the path. The tree's nodes from the root to the goal leaf represent the path's vertices.

The basic RRT algorithm is shown in Fig. 2. It takes as input parameters the initial location, the goal location, and the incremental step. In addition, it takes termination parameters such as a maximum number of attempts to grow branches, a time limitation, or other parameters based on the application. The output is a graph has a tree structure, where the nodes represent the tree's vertices, and the edges represent the connection between these vertices.

```
Algorithm: RRT
Input:    Initial, Goal, Max Iteration I,
          incremental distance ε.
Output:   The tree graph G.
1.  G:init(Initial)
2.  FOR (i = 1 TO I) BEGIN
3.      randomPnt = randConfiguration()
4.      nearestPnt = G.nearestVertex(randomPnt)
5.      newPnt = NewConfiguration(nearestPnt,randomPnt,ε)
6.      IF NOT isCollided(nearestPnt,newPnt) BEGIN
7.          G.addVertex(newPnt)
8.          G.addEdge(nearestPnt,newPnt)
9.          IF G.checkGoal(Goal)BEGIN
10.             RETURN G.success()
11.         END
12.     END
13. END
14. RETURN G.fail()
```

Fig. 2. RRT algorithm

The algorithm starts by placing the tree's root on the initial location, and then it takes a random sample from the configuration space. It finds the nearest tree's vertex to this sample, and creates a new point on the segments between the chosen random point and the nearest point. The new point is located far from the nearest point by a distance equals to the incremental step. If no collision is detected, then the algorithm adds the new point as a vertex to the tree and the segment between the new point and the nearest vertex is added as an edge to the tree. These steps are repeated until a path between the initial and the goal locations is found, or a termination condition is satisfied.

RRT algorithm attracts the attentions due to its simplicity and its success in solving the complex navigation problems, including the problems that have dynamic and kinematic constraints. In the next paragraphs, some of RRT developments and improvements are reviewed.

The basic RRT planner grows one tree and tries to find the goal point. A development of this approach proposed the use of bi-directional trees or multi-trees. These trees bias toward each other in order to merge and form united structure. This strategy enhances the possibility to find a route more quickly because instead of searching for one point, the goal one, any connection with the others trees' nodes can lead to a solution [6, 7].

The second category of RRT improvements based on the changing of sampling strategies; some studies introduce the bias toward the goal configuration, which means choosing the goal location by a specific value of probability instead of taking a random sample. Other researchers suggest making the bias toward hull around the goal [5], or to previous configurations of the success plans [8, 9]. A survey of RRT variations and developments were reviewed and published in [10].

The main drawbacks of RRT algorithm appear when it operates in small and narrow area, due to the random sampling strategy. The basic RRT uses a pseudorandom sample generator. This uniform distribution takes a sample from the space in equal probability, which means, the small regions have a lower probability to sample within them. As a result, the RRT efficiency is decreased when the workspace contains narrow areas.

3   Cell Decomposition

The key idea behind the Cell decomposition algorithms (CDs) is to divide the workspace into manageable regions. These regions are classified into two categories, the areas located in the obstacles space (The obstacle cells) and the areas in the free space (The free calls).

In navigation application, the CDs are utilized to find a path through the free cells. In order to simplify the navigation problem, these algorithms build a graph of the adjacent free cells to represent the free workspace. The graph's nodes represent the free cells, while the graph's edges represent the adjacency relation between the cells; two adjacent cells, which share a common barrier, create an edge in the graph.

The CDs approaches are classified as exact methods and approximation ones. In the exact cell decomposition cases, the free workspace is equal to the union of all generated cells exactly, while in approximation methods the free workspace is approximated by set of adjacent free cells.

An example of exact cell decomposition methods in 2D is the trapezoidal cell decomposition as shown in Fig. 3-a. It creates striped trapezoidal or triangular cells by means of sweeping line technique. Figure 4, shows the graph of adjacency to the example in Fig. 3-a, the shaded boxes represent the route of free cells between the initial and the goal locations.

The other examples of exact cell decomposition methods and its application are proposed and discussed in [1, 3, 11, 12].

The quad-tree approximation algorithm is an example of approximation cell decomposition (ACD) in 2D [2, 13]. It divides the workspace into four quarters. If a quarter locates in the free areas completely, it is marked as a free cell; otherwise, it is marked as an obstacle cell if it locates in obstacles areas completely. The other case when this quarter contains parts of both free and obstacles regions, in this case, the algorithm divides it into four quarters. This process is repeated until all cells are located completely either in free areas or obstacle regions, or a specific resolution is reached. The resolution in this case represents the smallest cell's edge. Figure 3-b shows the quad-tree cell

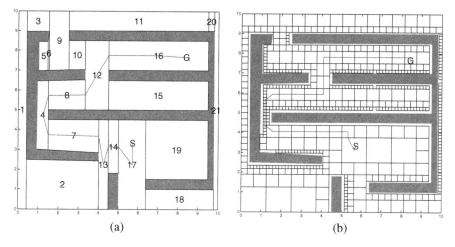

Fig. 3. The free space representation using, a: an exact CD method, b: an approximation CD method

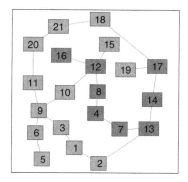

Fig. 4. Cell decomposition's adjacency graph. The dark boxes represent the free route in the workspace between the initial's cell and the goal's cell

decomposition methods. Another example of the approximation cell decomposition in navigation problem is discussed in [14–17].

The main drawback of CDs methods is the sensitivity to the environment changes. Where any small changes require re-executes the algorithm again and generates another adjacency graph.

4   Proposed Methods

In this work, RRT and ACD algorithms are combined together in order to exploit the advantages of each of them. The new planners try to overcome the drawbacks, which affect the performance of the navigation process significantly, by complementing these two approaches. The RRT planner has relatively high tolerance to obstacles shapes and workspace changes. This feature is missing in ACD planner. In addition, The RRT is

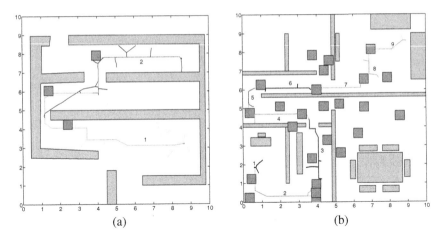

(a)   (b)

Fig. 5. The Proposed methods. The dotted line represents the ACD's path on stationary workspace. a: The RRT validator method creates two RRT trees from the initial and the goal locations. b: The local RRTs method creates nine local RRT trees

not effective in small areas or narrow passage, while ACD planner does not face this problem. Based on that, the efficient spatial planner, ACD, is used to plan a primary path on stationary workspace. Then, this path is used to guide the RRT growth. The RRT planner validates the ACD's path when a query is established in the actual workspace. If a collision is detected due to the change in the workspace, the planner re-plans the path locally through the changed regions.

Two approaches have been proposed to benefit from this combination. The planners focus on the enhancement of navigation problem for omnidirectional robots in partial dynamic workspace. In next sections these two proposed methods are discussed in more detail.

4.1 RRTs Validator Planner

The RRT validator uses ACD's path as guidance to RRT tree's growth. It considers the path's points as an ordered set, and directs the bias of the tree toward these vertices. The RRT trees branch toward these set in the same order, point by point. In the initial state, the probability of choosing the next point of the path is set to the value of 100 %. If a collision is detected, then the probability is reduced in order to allow the RRT explores the free space and attempts to reconnect to original path's point. If it reconnects, then the probability to choose the next point is set again to the value of 100 % to force the planner follows the original ACD's path once again.

This strategy forces the planner to follow the guiding path when it is possible, and at the same time, it gives the planner a freedom to find an alternative local path to the collided segments.

In this paper, two RRT validators are used to validate the path. The first one rooted at the initial position and the second one rooted at the goal position. They try to follow the ACD path, or find an alternative local path. The RRT trees are shown in Fig. 5-a, where they try to follow the ACD' path (the dotted line).

4.2   Local RRTs Planners

The second proposed planner uses simple straight-line planner to connect the ACD path's points and to test the collision. The planner tracks the valid points of the path and creates sequences of these points. In case that all points are valid, then the planner returns these points as a solution for the planning problem. In the other case when the workspace is changed, and a collision happened, the planner breaks the original path sequence on the collided locations and creates multi-sequences of the continuance valid points. It also excludes the points that are located in obstacle areas.

Each of these sequences is associated with RRT tree. The trees explore the space freely with small bias toward the other tree's nodes. When two nodes are connected, the corresponding trees are merged. When all trees are merged, they form a single tree contains the initial and goal locations.

In this planner, our strategy is to generate augmented local RRTs, in order to navigate around the new obstacles locally. Figure 5-b shows the local RRTs method in simulation. In this example, it creates nine local RRT trees based on the ACD path, which generated in the stationary workspace.

5   Tests and Results

The proposed approaches are tested in two different workspaces as shown in Fig. 6. The first workspace represents an office with one route between the rooms, and the second one represents offices, which have two possible routes between them.

The robot in this work is considered a holonomic point moves in the workspace. The results of the proposed methods are compared to the other methods, i.e. the basic RRT algorithm, Goal Bias RRT, and the bias toward the other trees. Figure 7 shows an example of RRT path generated by the proposed methods in the testing workspaces, where in (a) the local RRTs method is used, and in (b) the RRTs validator method is

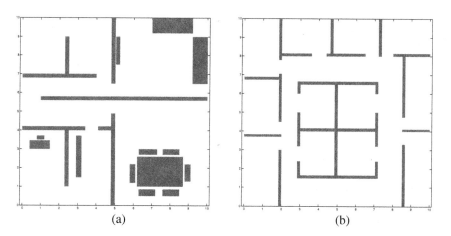

(a)   (b)

Fig. 6. Testing workspace, a: office has one route between the rooms (WS1); b: two routes between offices (WS2)

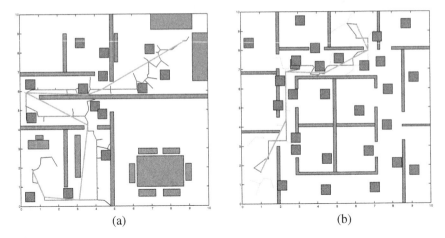

(a)   (b)

Fig. 7. Example of RRT path using a: Local RRTs method; b: RRTs validator method, on partially changed workspaces. The bold lines represent the RRT path and the shorten one in both tested workspaces. The boxes represent the new obstacles

used. The bold line represent the shorten path to RRT's one. Where the algorithm which generates the shortened path is proposed in [18].

5.1   Testing Parameters

The bias values, which are given to the compared methods, are set as shown in Table 1, where the basic RRT chooses a random point without any bias. The goal-bias RRT directs the growth of the tree toward the goal location by selecting this location in probability of 10 %. In the tree's nodes bias, the RRT chooses a point of the others trees by the probability of 30 %, which force the trees to merge more quickly.

Table 1. The probability of choosing next points (The bias value).

Method	Bias value
RRT	0
Goal bias	0.1
Tree node bias	0.3
RRTs validator (valid point)	1
RRTs validator (Collison)	[0.2,0.1,0.7]
Local RRTs	0.3

In our proposed methods, the bias value of the validator RRTs is set to 100 % when no collision is occurred. Otherwise, it has the value of 20 % of the bias toward the next valid point in the ordered set. In addition, the value of 10 % to bias toward any other points in those points set. The planner in this case has the probability of 70 % to explore the workspace freely and biases the growth toward randomly chosen samples. The last method, local RRTs approach, uses the bias toward the other trees by the value of 30 %.

The simulation is repeated 100 times and the average of successful tries are considered when comparing the results. The results include the execution time; the number of RRT iterations which corresponding to the number of RRT's branching attempts; and the number of successful attempts to find a path.

The probabilistically completeness value is estimated using the number of successful attempts. While the efficiency value is estimated using the time of execution and iterations results. The time of execution could vary significantly, based on the hardware and code optimization, while RRT iteration is independent of HW and the programmers skillful.

The ACD resolution is set to be 0.2 unit. The ACD's path points are generated in ordered form, from the initial to the goal locations. They are constructed using the initial and the goal points, the free cells' centers, and the barriers' midpoint between the consequence cells.

We use the Dijkstra algorithm to search in the ACD's graph. The RRT parameters are set as follow; the extension step is equal to 0.3 unit. And, the bias value is fixed at the probability of 100 % for next path' points in case of no collision is detected, and it is reduced when the path is collided within obstacles. The reduced value is divided into three parts. 1- The bias toward the next valid point is set to the value of 20 %. 2- The bias toward other path's points is given the value of 10 %. 3- The rest of bias is relaxed to allow the planner chooses random samples freely. The RRT result is considered as failed, if it cannot find a path after 2000 tries of branching.

5.2   Results and Discussions

In the first workspace, new obstacles are scattered on the original workspace. They are positioned to collide the ACD's path and add more difficulty to navigate through the changed workspace. The workspace's changes are shown in Fig. 8-b, where the boxes represent the new obstacles. The ACD's path is shown as a solid line between the initial and the goal locations. The cycle markers represent the bias points. ACD algorithm approximates the free cells as shown graphically in Fig. 8-a, the path in this case is produced using the Dijkstra searching method in the ACD's adjacency graph.

The numerical results are shown in Table 2, where the proposed methods show a probabilistically completeness. The local RRT method gives the best results in term of efficiency; it has the lowest execution time, and the lowest iteration to find a path. Moreover, the RRT validator method gives a better result comparing to the other competitors. Figure 10-a sums up the iteration results for the first workspace WS1 using the boxplot representation.

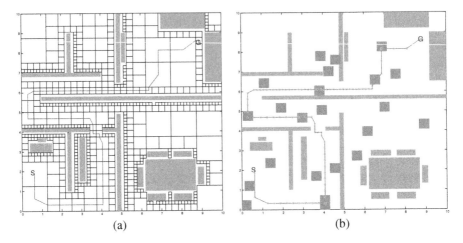

(a)   (b)

Fig. 8. Offices-like workspace (WS1), a: The approximation decomposition of the free region; b: the new obstacles are represented as boxes. ACD' path is represented by the solid line, and the cycle markers represents the bias points

Table 2. The result of the tested methods on WS1.

Method	Mean time [Sec]	Mean iteration	Success [%]
RRT	1.03	1137.11	96
Goal bias	1.12	1180.57	87
Tree node bias	1.23	1365.34	80
RRTs validator	0.45	270.19	**100**
Local RRTs	**0.19**	**95.20**	**100**

In the second workspace, the changes are introduced by scattering new obstacles in the stationary workspace. The new obstacles are collided within the ACD's path, and they produce more narrow passages. Figure 9-b shows the changes in the workspace, where the new obstacles are represented by boxes. The ACD's path is shown in the figure as solid line between the initial and the goal locations. The bias points, which are generated based on this path, are shown in the figure as cycle markers. Figure 9-a, shows the approximation of the free workspace using ACD algorithm.

The numerical results are shown in Table 3, where the proposed methods give the best results; they are probabilistically complete as we infer from the success rate result. Moreover, the local RRT method gives the best results in term of efficiency; it has the lowest execution time, and the lowest iteration average. Figure 10-b condenses the iteration results for WS2 using the boxplot representation.

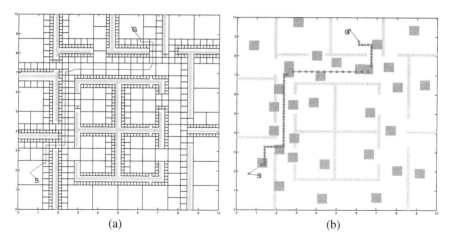

(a)   (b)

Fig. 9. Offices-like workspace (WS2), a: a graphical representation of approximation cell decomposition; b: the new obstacles (boxes). ACD path represented by the solid line, and the bias points represented by cycle markers

Table 3. The result of the tested methods on WS2.

Method	Mean time [Sec.]	Mean iteration	Success [%]
RRT	0.92	817.13	96
Goal bias	0.98	871.06	94
Tree node bias	1.076	1005.10	86
RRTs validator	0.62	332.07	**100**
Local RRTs	**0.24**	**117.17**	**100**

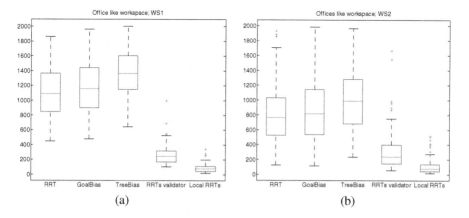

(a)   (b)

Fig. 10. RRT's iteration boxplot for WS1 (a) and WS2 (b)

6   Conclusion

In this work, the approximation cell-decomposition algorithm is combined with the RRT planner in order to enhance the omnidirectional robot's navigation on partially changed workspace. The ACD finds a spatial path on preliminary and stationary workspaces, and then the RRT is used to validate this path on the actual workspace.

Two methods have been proposed in this paper. First, the planner creates instances of RRT, which bias toward the ACD path's points in order form. It updates its bias value based on the collision detection information.

The Second method uses a straight-line planner to connect path's points and creates local RRT trees on both sides of collided segment of the path. The proposed methods compared with the other approaches. The simulation results shows that the suggested methods give the best results in terms of completeness, in addition, the local RRTs method gives the best result in terms of efficiency in the both workspaces.

References

1. Choset, H., Lynch, K.M., Hutchinson, S.: Principles of Robot Motion: Theory, Algorithms, and Implementation. MIT Press, Cambridge (2005)
2. De Berg, M., Cheong, O., van Kreveld, M., Overmars, M.: Computational Geometry. Springer, Heidelberg (2008)
3. LaValle, S.M.: Planning Algorithms. Cambridge University Press, Cambridge (2006)
4. LaValle, S.M.: Rapidly-Exploring Random Trees: A New Tool for Path Planning (1998)
5. LaValle, S.M., Kuffner, J.J.: Rapidly-exploring random trees: progress and prospects. In: 4th Workshop on Algorithmic and Computational Robotics: New Directions, pp. 293–308 (2000)
6. Kuffner, J.J.J., LaValle, S.M.: RRT-connect: an efficient approach to single-query path planning. In: Proceedings of 2000 ICRA Millennium Conference IEEE International Conference Robotic Automation Symposium Proceeding 2, vol. 2, pp. 995–1001 (2000)
7. Strandberg, M.: Augmenting RRT-planners with local trees. In: 2004 IEEE International Conference on Robotics and Automation, Proceedings of ICRA 2004, vol. 4, pp. 3258–3262 (2004)
8. Bruce, J., Veloso, M.: Real-time randomized path planning for robot navigation. In: IEEE/RSJ International Conference on Intelligent Robots and Systems, vol. 3, pp. 2383–2388 (2002)
9. Bruce, J., Bowling, M., Browning, B., Veloso, M.: Multi-robot team response to a multi-robot opponent team (2003)
10. Abbadi, A., Matousek, R.: RRTs review and statistical analysis. Int. J. Math. Comput. Simul. 6, 1–8 (2012)
11. Sleumer, N.H., Tschichold-Gürman, N.: Exact Cell Decomposition of Arrangements used for Path Planning in Robotics (1999)
12. Abbadi, A., Matousek, R., Osmera, P., Knispel, L.: Spatial guidance to RRT planner using cell-decomposition algorithm. In: 20th International Conference on Soft Computing MENDEL (2014)
13. Van den Berg, J.P., Overmars, M.H.: Using workspace information as a guide to non-uniform sampling in probabilistic roadmap planners. Int. J. Robot. Res. 24, 1055–1071 (2005)

14. Katevas, N.I., Tzafestas, S.G., Pnevmatikatos, C.G.: The approximate cell decomposition with local node refinement global path planning method : path nodes refinement and curve parametric interpolation. J. Intell. Robot. Syst. **22**, 289–314 (1998)
15. Lingelbach, F.: Path planning using probabilistic cell decomposition. In: Proceedings of IEEE International Conference on Robotics and Automation ICRA 2004, vol. 1, pp. 467–472 (2004)
16. Cai, C., Ferrari, S.: Information-driven sensor path planning by approximate cell decomposition. IEEE Trans. Syst. Man Cybern. Part B Cybern. **39**, 672–689 (2009)
17. Abbadi, A., Prenosil, V.: Safe path planning using cell decomposition approximation. In: International Conference Distance Learning, Simulation and Communication, Brno (2015)
18. Abbadi, A., Matousek, R., Jancik, S., Roupec, J.: Rapidly-exploring random trees: 3D planning. In: 18th International Conference on Soft Computing MENDEL 2012, pp. 594–599. Brno University of Technology, Brno (2012)

Virtual Operator Station for Teleoperated Mobile Robots

Tomáš Kot[(✉)], Ján Babjak, and Petr Novák

Faculty of Mechanical Engineering, Department of Robotics, VŠB-Technical University Ostrava,
17. listopadu 15, 708 33 Ostrava, Czech Republic
{tomas.kot,jan.babjak,petr.novak}@vsb.cz

Abstract. This paper deals with utilization of a head-mounted display (HMD) for remote control of mobile robots by a human operator. The main goal is to make control of the robot and navigation in unknown terrain easier for the operator by providing stereoscopic images and using virtual reality. Considered is specifically the new HMD device called Oculus Rift, which is a very interesting device because of its great parameters and low price. The device is described in the beginning, together with some of the specific principles of the Oculus 3D display. Then follows the design of a new graphical user interface for teleoperation – virtual operator station, with main focus on visualization of stereoscopic images from robot cameras. Demonstrated is also a way how to display additional data and information to the operator. The resulting interface is a comfortable and highly effective system suitable both for exploration and manipulation tasks in mobile robotics.

Keywords: Operator · Teleoperation · Mobile robot · Head-mounted display · HMD · Virtual reality · Oculus Rift

1 Introduction

Mobile robots controlled remotely by a human operator (teleoperated robots) are preferred over autonomous mobile robots in many fields, for example the very crucial applications related to safety of people during chemical accidents, fires, terrorist attacks or natural disasters. Especially manipulation with dangerous objects (explosives, barrels or containers with dangerous chemical substances etc.) must be done by trained human professionals with their extraordinary decision-making abilities and cannot be accomplished by generalized algorithms.

Mobile robots in these situations are often controlled from a longer distance and may be completely out of direct sight of the operator so he must fully rely on the information provided him by the control system. The most common primary source of feedback is the visual subsystem of the mobile robot containing one or more cameras. Pictures from the cameras are typically displayed on a flat screen, together with additional data [1–3].

Improved feedback can be achieved using stereovision, which provides additional information about depths of individual objects in the camera picture. There however emerges a question how to display the stereoscopic image to the operator. A common way is to use a *head-mounted display* (HMD) [4, 5] that displays different images for

© Springer International Publishing Switzerland 2015
J. Hodicky (Ed.): MESAS 2015, LNCS 9055, pp. 144–153, 2015.
DOI: 10.1007/978-3-319-22383-4_10

each eye. Various HMD devices for *virtual reality* (VR) have been available for few decades already both in military applications and commercially. However, big prices of the HMD devices (reaching even tens of thousands USD) and mediocre parameters, especially of the cheaper ones [6], were the reasons why VR was a marginal, albeit popular and often mentioned concern.

The upcoming HMD device Oculus Rift offers great parameters together with extremely low price and already caused a big wave of new interest in VR, primarily in the gaming industry. We decided to try to utilize it also for teleoperation of mobile robots, together with stereovision. As a testing mobile robot we chose Hercules [7], a four-wheeled mobile robot with a 3-degrees-of-freedom arm fully designed and developed on the Department of Robotics at VŠB-TU Ostrava.

The existing version of control system on the operator's side uses advanced graphical user interface rendered using Direct3D, which assists the operator in multiple ways [8], but is not able to provide a stereoscopic display of the stereovision cameras mounted on the robot arm.

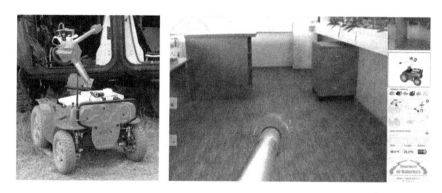

Fig. 1. Mobile robot Hercules and a screenshot of its existing graphical 2D user interface

2   Oculus Rift HMD

Oculus Rift is still in development, but two preliminary Development Kit (DK) versions were already made available for purchase – DK1 in 2012 and DK2 in 2014. Both versions offer some major advantages over other similar devices:

- low price: 350 USD for SD2,
- large field of view (FOV): 110° nominal,
- low weight, good comfort for user,
- ultra-low latency 360° head-tracking in all 6 axes.

Especially FOV is very important for a good sense of virtual reality. Typical commercial HMD devices use two small displays placed in front of each eye and have a very limited FOV between 30 and 45 degrees. There are few professional devices with larger FOV, but they are very expensive, for example the Sensics xSight with 123° FOV and price around 40,000 USD [10]. Oculus Rift contains a single 7-inch screen and two plastic lenses projecting each half of the screen to the corresponding eye.

We had DK1 available for this research project, so the following text will mention only parameters specific for DK1. We are however currently starting experiments with the new improved version (Fig. 2).

Fig. 2. Oculus Rift DK1

2.1 Principle of the 3D Display

Due to the fact that Oculus Rift contains only one LCD screen, it requires different method of rendering than most other HMD devices. The device displays pictures from two cameras, either real-world or virtual (VR), with the distance between them corresponding to the inter-pupillary distance (IPD) of the user and with parallel optical exes. Image for the left eye is displayed on the left half of the screen and image for the right eye on the right half.

Besides having the correct resolution (640 × 800) and aspect ratio (4:5), each camera also must have the correct vertical FOV, which is given by the physical height of the LCD screen and distance of the screen from user's eyes (Fig. 3).

In VR it is quite simple to meet all the requirements, because optical parameters of a virtual camera (aspect ratio and FOV) are given by perspective projection transformation done by a projection matrix.

The lenses are placed in a fixed distance L_{IPD} which does not correspond to the width w_{lcd} of the LCD screen, so each image must be shifted towards the center of the display by h_m (Fig. 3).

$$h_m = \frac{w_{lcd}}{4} - \frac{L_{lcd}}{2} \tag{1}$$

The lenses in Oculus Rift create a significant *pincushion distortion* of the image and the visual defect called *chromatic aberration*. Both these unwanted effects can be removed by an appropriate pre-transformation in a post-processing *pixel shader*, at the

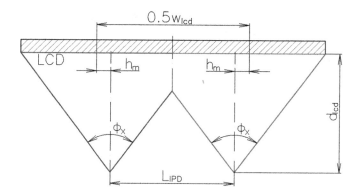

Fig. 3. Physical relation between the eye view cones on the LCD display

cost of some additional GPU processing time. The code for the pixel shader is available in the Oculus SDK documentation and samples [11].

2.2 Convergence

As was already mentioned, the cameras are required to have parallel axes with the convergence point in infinity. They should not be angled towards each other (so-called "toe-in") and also *Horizontal Image Translation* (HIT) should not be performed. Because of how the HMD optics works, the user does not have the sense of watching the LCD screen of the device, his eyes are naturally focusing on individual objects in a virtual world in front of him. If an object is very far away (almost infinitely) in reality or in the rendered 3D virtual world, it appears at the same position on both half-screens and thus both eyes look parallel to focus on it.

3 Stereovision Display

3.1 Direct Rendering of Camera Images

The main goal of this project is to use Oculus Rift to display stereovision images to the operator of a mobile robot, so this is the first problem that must be solved.

The first obvious solution is to directly display the images from real-world cameras onto the screen of the HMD device – left camera on the left half and vice versa. This makes the HMD wearer to feel like if he was standing at the position of the mobile robot. There are however multiple complications in this case.

First, the physical cameras need to have very specific lenses to exactly or at least very closely match the quite big FOV of the device, which can be achieved by using ultra-wide angle or fish-eye lenses [12]. Another complication is the aspect ratio of the Oculus half-screens (4:5), where height is larger than width. Pictures from the cameras would need to be cropped and the operator would be able to see less of the world around the robot than with the current flat screen without stereovision.

It is still possible to use cameras with normal lenses, if the pictures are scaled down to occupy only the middle portion of each half-screen. Practical testing proved that this solution works quite well and a good 3D illusion is achieved, but only a part of the whole FOV is used, which denies one of the main advantages of Oculus Rift.

3.2 Nausea Problems

The biggest problem with direct display of camera images is that it caused nausea to most testing subjects. The reason behind this is that Oculus Rift makes the user feel really immersed in the VR and so his brain expects all input information from eyes and the vestibular system in his inner ear to match. A possible way how to reduce this source of nausea is to use the head-tracking sensors of Oculus and rotate the physical cameras exactly the same way, with as low latency as possible. The Oculus Rift documentation recommends the maximal latency to be around 40 ms [11], but this is almost impossible to achieve, because during this time we need to process the head tracking data, send a command to the robot, wait for physical rotation, read and transmit new camera images and finally display them in the HMD device. In the case of Hercules the mechanical rotation is the biggest source of lag, because cameras are fixed on the manipulator arm to look around the whole arm must move.

There is even a bigger problem if the robot moves, because in this case the cameras are moving in a way completely unrelated to the head movement of the operator. And especially on uneven terrain when the images shake, it is extremely inconvenient to look through the robot cameras using a HMD.

4   Virtual Operator Station

Because of the described problems, a new system was developed – a *virtual operator station*. The operator wearing HMD is put to a virtual space ("room") created completely in a computer and can freely look around by head movements. This virtual room contains several 3D objects, primarily a big rectangular plane with images from the stereovision cameras displayed on it. The room itself is fully black, to provide as little distraction as possible.

Watching the video from the cameras this way feels for the operator as naturally as watching a television or cinema screen with a 3D technology in real life. The biggest source of nausea is removed for most testing subjects, because the brain feels to be part of the virtual room and thus expects the virtual screen to be fixed in space, or to move naturally with head movements, which can easily be accomplished.

4.1 Contents of the Virtual Station

The virtual room is watched from a pair of imaginary stereovision cameras configured according to the Oculus requirements. This pair of cameras is fixed in one point in the room (see the camera symbols on Fig. 4) and can rotate (look around) in all three axes (yaw, pitch, roll) based on user's head movements.

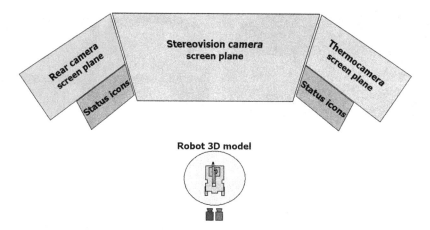

Fig. 4. Schema of the virtual operator station

The biggest rectangle is a virtual screen plane with images of the stereovision cameras. This rectangle is rendered differently for the left and right eye – each time with the appropriate camera image. The screens on left and right sides display pictures from a secondary (rear) camera and from a thermovision camera. Rendered is also a real-time 3D model of the mobile robot with the arm, which helps the operator a lot to during manipulation tasks. Additional necessary information about the robot is displayed below the smaller camera images. After some testing of usability, we decided to display the control elements twice – once on each side, so that they are in the operator's sight most of the time. Important icons can be also displayed over the camera image, as for example the gripper icon on Fig. 5.

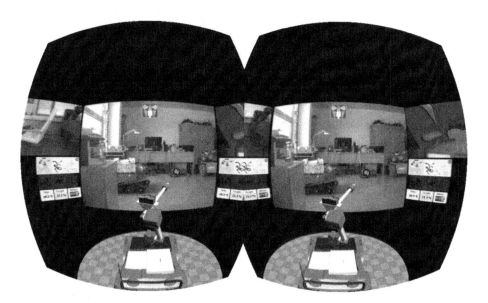

Fig. 5. Image displayed on the Oculus Rift screen (operator is looking ahead)

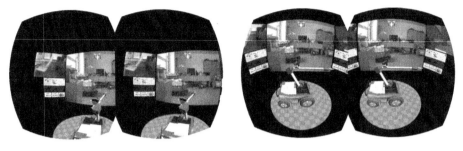

Fig. 6. Images displayed on the Oculus Rift screen (operator is looking to the left/down)

All rectangular planes with camera images or control elements are oriented vertically in the virtual world and rotated towards the virtual head position (Fig. 4). Figures 5 and 6 show the actual view of the virtual world with applied distortion and chromatic aberration, as it is sent to the HMD device LCD.

4.2 Visibility

Only a part of the Oculus LCD can be easily seen through the lenses. The visible part of Fig. 6 is highlighted on Fig. 7. Content of the virtual room was carefully configured based on testing, to show comfortably the whole plane with the main camera image and the robot arm in front of it, in a very convenient location. The operator can look just slightly to the left or right and will be able to see also most of the secondary camera image and all additional information about the robot.

Fig. 7. Physically visible section of the rendered image

The virtual operator station also provides a "zoom-out" mode, in which all screen planes move away from the user so that they all are visible at the same time without having to look around, at the cost of being smaller and thus less detailed.

4.3   Stereovision Cameras

As already mentioned, the images from stereovision cameras are displayed on the biggest virtual screen plane. Attention however must be paid to convergence.

In the virtual scene, the screen plane is rendered in a certain distance from the user. The stereovision image displayed on the screen creates the illusion of additional depth and objects on the picture appear at different distances than the screen itself. An object on the image is placed exactly at the distance of the virtual screen if it is at the same pixel position on both images. For physical cameras with parallel axes, this is valid only for objects in infinity, or very far away. This in fact means that the whole scene "thrusts out" of the screen into the space in front of it.

This is not very good for immersion, because the 3D model of the robot appears to collide with the image, although it is located in front of the screen, and there is also unmatching depth information near the side edges of the virtual screen, where the edge seems to be at two different depths at the same time.

A possible partial solution is to apply HIT before placing the images on the virtual screen plane, to change the convergence point. This does not violate the rule mentioned earlier, because now the camera images are not displayed directly in the HMD.

The images must be shifted outwards (the left one to the left and vice versa), to put the convergence point further away. There is one very important limitation to the translation, because if the images are shifted too much, the convergence point of a particular pixel on the image could be "behind infinity" in the HMD virtual world and the eyes would have to rotate outwards to focus on such a point, which is physically not possible. This creates a lot of eye strain, because the brain is not used to this situation and ineffectually keeps trying to focus.

The maximum allowed translation is equal to the parallax p_{max} of the screen plane in VR, so that objects infinitely far on the camera image appear at infinite distance in the HMD:

$$d' = \frac{W}{4.tg\frac{\phi_x}{2}}, \tag{2}$$

$$P_{max} = \frac{L_{IPD} \cdot d'}{2 \cdot d_s}, \tag{3}$$

where ϕ_x is the horizontal FOV and d' is distance of the projection plane. The p_{max} value is in LCD pixels, but because the camera image pixels do not map 1:1 to LCD pixels, the images must be shifted by p'_{max}:

$$W'_s = \frac{w_s \cdot d'}{d_s}, \tag{4}$$

$$p'_{max} = \frac{p_{max} \cdot W_c}{w'_s}, \tag{5}$$

where w_s represents the width of the virtual screen plane, w'_s is the width of the plane in pixels as it is displayed on the LCD and W_c is horizontal resolution of the camera images.

Shifting the images by this fixed amount does not fully solve the problem with closer objects thrusting out of the screen plane, but at least improves it by placing some objects behind the plane. A better solution would be to analyze the camera images, detect the furthest objects and shift according to them. If the furthest detected objects are not very (infinitely) far way, the HIT may be larger than p_{max}. The value can also be increased without image analysis if the robot is for example designed only for indoor environment, where the maximal possible depth is limited to few meters.

5   Conclusion

The new graphical user interface of the Hercules operator's control system was practically implemented and tested. The application was programmed in MS Visual C ++ and uses Direct3D for graphics rendering. The first reaction of most users was that the system is very impressive, but besides this it is also practical together with stereovision cameras, because the operator can perceive relative depths of obstacles or important objects around the mobile robot.

The idea of a virtual operator station rendered in the HMD device instead of a direct display of the camera images proved to be convenient – while keeping a way how to visualize 3D view of the stereovision cameras, it also reduces possible sources of nausea. The approach also gives additional very interesting possibilities as far as display of other information is concerned. There can be multiple smaller floating screens around the user with images from secondary cameras, an interactive 3D model of the robot showing illustratively its current physical state and also all necessary control elements, information and warning or error icons. Good locations for these additional objects turned out to be on the sides of the main screen or below it, rather than above, because it is less comfortable to look up with the head. Depth in the VR can also be used as a way how to signalize importance of same information, by putting some icons closer to the user than others.

One of the possible problems is that with Oculus HMD on his head, the operator completely loses perception of his surroundings and sees only the VR. This could be improved by mounting two additional cameras directly on the HMD device and rendering their images directly in Oculus instead of the black background of the virtual room to create augmented reality. The cameras however need to have precisely chosen optical lenses to match the Oculus requirements, but this already has been done [13].

Another important discovery was that the stereovision cameras on the mobile robot Hercules (Fig. 1a) are not placed in a very good location, because both cameras see the last link of the arm from a very close distance (Fig. 1b) and produce extremely different views of it that are almost impossible for the brain to fuse together into a single stereo view. The arm occupies a significant portion of the pictures and thus it breaks the overall depth impression.

Acknowledgement. This article has been supported by specific research project SP2015/152 and financed by the state budget of the Czech Republic.

References

1. Cybernet. Operator Control Unit. http://www.cybernet.com/products/robotics.html
2. Orpheus Robotic System Project. http://www.orpheus-project.cz/
3. Fong, T., Thorpe, C.: Vehicle teleoperation interfaces. Auton. Robots **11**, 9–18 (2001). ISSN 0929-5593
4. Amanatiadis, A., Gasteratos, A.: Stereo vision system for remotely operated robots. In: Mollet, N. (ed.) Remote and Telerobotics. InTech, Vienna (2010). ISBN 978-953-307-081-0
5. Wikipedia. Head-mounted display. http://en.wikipedia.org/wiki/Head-mounted_display
6. Virtual Realities, Ltd. Stereoscopic 3D. http://www.vrealities.com/products/stereoscopic-3d
7. Department of Robotics. Hercules. http://robot.vsb.cz/mobile-robots/hercules/
8. Kot, T., Krys, V., Mostýn, V., Novák, P.: Control system of a mobile robot manipulator. In: Proceedings of International Carpathian Control Conference (ICCC) (2014). ISBN: 978-1-4577-1867-0
9. Oculus, V.R.: Oculus Rift. http://www.oculusvr.com/rift/
10. Sensics. xSight HMD. http://sensics.com/head-mounted-displays/technology/xsight-panoramic-hmds/
11. Oculus, V.R.: Oculus Rift SDK Overview https://developer.oculusvr.com/
12. Wikipedia. Angle of view. http://en.wikipedia.org/wiki/Angle_of_view
13. Steptoe, W.: AR-Rift (Part 1). http://willsteptoe.com/post/66968953089/ar-rift-part-1

A State-of-the-Art SWIL (Software in the Loop) Electronic Warfare System Simulator for Performance Prediction and Validation

Timothy Battisti[✉], Gerardina Faruolo, and Lorenzo Magliocchetti

Product Innovation and Advanced EW Systems, Elettronica (ELT) S.p.A., Rome, Italy
{timothy.battisti,gerardina.faruolo,
lorenzo.magliocchetti}@elt.it

Abstract. The main aim of an EW system is to monitor the ElectroMagnetic (EM) spectrum in order to detect, intercept, locate and analyze all the possible threats. When dealing with the complexity of an Electronic Warfare (EW) system and the electromagnetic scenarios inside which it must operate it is necessary to simulate the system performances before making any design decision. To this end, we have appositely developed a SWIL (Software In the Loop) Electronic Warfare system simulator allowing us to define and execute any kind of electromagnetic scenarios aimed at testing and validating the operative EW system characteristics.

Keywords: Electronic Warfare (EW) · Software in the Loop (SWIL) · Simulator · Radar Track File · Electromagnetic (EM) · Pulse Descriptor Word (PDW) · Signal Processing · Data Processing · Event –Driven Methodology

1 Introduction

An EW system has the main goal of detecting, intercepting, identifying, locating, recording and analyzing the electromagnetic transmissions in the environment for the purposes of immediate threats recognition [2, 3]. The design of Electronic Warfare (EW) systems is undoubtedly a challenging task, due to the extreme complexity of overall EW systems architecture, as well as the multitude of ElectroMagnetic (EM) scenarios that usually have to be dealt with. On the other hand, the reaction time required to those systems, of the order of 100 ms, well below the human reaction time requires simulation and validation environment that cannot be implemented by using standard workstations. Since an EW scenario is very complex (given the myriad of signal/data processing events corresponding to just few seconds) and not easily reproducible even in a controlled environment, the Simulator is a useful and fundamental tool to simulate, test and hence validate EW systems in spite of the possible EW scenario. Within this framework, we propose a state-of-the-art simulation environment with system SWIL, through which any desired EM environmental setting can be reproduced, so as to efficiently test and validate the EW system under design. To fully describe an EW scenario, it is necessary to identify the involved electromagnetic emitters, each of which is characterized by its

© Springer International Publishing Switzerland 2015
J. Hodicky (Ed.): MESAS 2015, LNCS 9055, pp. 154–164, 2015.
DOI: 10.1007/978-3-319-22383-4_11

own kinematic and transmitted waveforms. From the simulation point of view, a complete and yet synthetic description is given by a set of Pulse Descriptor Words (PDWs), associated to the transmitted radar pulses. Specifically, once the PDWs have been given in input and converted in a flow of RF signal samples, the proposed simulation environment performs all the elaborations of a real EW system. In particular, the Simulator is partitionable in several conceptual blocks that model the Signal and Data Processing elaboration necessary to receive and discriminate the pulses with respect to the associated radar emitters and produce the Radar Track File (a description of the scenario "reconstruction" provided by the EW system). The Simulator implements also all the algorithms that are used by the EW Manager to define Signal and Data Processing settings as a function of the Radar Track File. Beside the validation and test phase, the Simulator represents a viable mean to properly addressing the design choices, and driving the design toward the finalization of the EW architecture. The importance of the proposed simulation environment is twofold. Firstly, the Data Processing and the EW Manager are essentially "emulation" blocks, therefore their SW algorithmic is in common with the final system. Furthermore, the HW/FW receiving chain (implementing the Signal Processing on the final EW system) can be SW simulated before any physical implementation, minimizing the risks associated to developments or upgrades of an EW architecture. Given the aforementioned considerations, the overall EW architecture can be tested and validated in a more simple and efficient way exploiting the so called SWIL technique. Moreover, starting from the Simulator architecture, the integration of the final EW system can be gradually implemented increasing progressively the number of "emulated" blocks. This allows to integrate and test boards with their algorithmic FW one after the other, thus reducing the complexity of each integration step. The developed Simulator represents a tool able to speed up as much as possible the process of finding innovative architectural solutions for EW systems. In order to achieve this aim, the Simulator has been realized to be fast; more specifically, the simulation time is about only ten times slower than real time (an optimal result taking into account the simulation of HW/FW parts of the EW system). It is important to remark that the last generation integrated EW system designed and developed by ELETTRONICA, named VIRGILIUS, is object of the work presented in this paper. The reminder of the paper is organized as follows. Next section is devoted to the description of the Simulator architecture and the implementation methodology. In Sect. 3 is reported an example of obtainable results and available outputs, for the considered real case study. Finally, some considerations and concluding remarks are given in Sect. 4.

2   System Under Test (SUT) and Simulator

This paragraph is divided in two different sub-sections. In the first sub-section, the functional architecture of the proposed Simulator is described and analyzed. More specifically, we report the organization of the Simulator in terms of functional blocks; each block models a part of the elaboration performed by the EW System under test (in this case the last generation ELETTRONICA integrated system VIRGILIUS). All the elaboration is necessary to generate the Radar Track File containing all the information on the EM scenario collected by the EW system. In the second sub-section, the SW methodology adopted to develop the proposed Simulator is introduced. Taking into account the two important constraints of extreme modularity and speed, the Simulator has been developed adopting the C++ programming language [1]. The object-oriented programming guarantees the great advantage of implementing the models of FW/SW modules by means of an organization in methods and classes. In the final part of the second sub-section, some of the main classes and methods are investigated.

2.1   Simulator Architecture

In the Simulator architecture, it is possible to individuate the functional blocks illustrated in Fig. 1; all the functional blocks are SW and developed in C++ programming language.

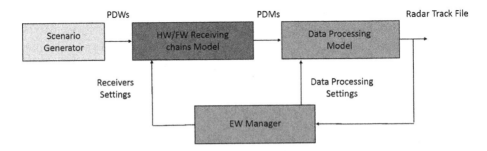

Fig. 1. Simulator architecture

It is important to remark that the Data Processing and the EW Manager are "emulation" blocks (reported in orange inside Fig. 1); more specifically, the associated C++ code is the same as the one on the target EW system. The HW/FW Receiving Chains Model is a "simulated" block that reproduces without modifications all the FW algorithms and models the HW behaviour. Therefore, the proposed Simulator provides a tool able to emulate the whole EW system without physical implementation of the HW/FW receiving chains. In particular, we have developed a so-called SW In Loop Simulator for performance prediction and validation of the EW system under test. The Scenario Generator (green block in Fig. 1) is external to the simulator and its aim is to generate the input required by the Simulator. This input is composed by a set of Pulse Descriptor Words (PDWs), each of which contains all the information associated to a transmitted radar pulse in terms of emitter characteristic parameters (Radio Frequency, Pulse Width, Modulation on Pulse, Time of Arrival, etc.) and kinematic of the platform. The PDWs are stored "off-line" in a data file that is provided in input to the Simulator; the HW/FW Receiving Chains Model elaborates these PDWs in order to generate the corresponding Pulse Descriptor Measures (PDMs). Each PDM represents a translation of a PDW in a format Data Processing compatible with pulse parameters properly degraded as a function of the estimation processes performed in the HW/FW Receiving Chains Model. In the following, we describe the main elaborations and sub-blocks associated to each functional block internal to the proposed Simulator:

1. The EW Manager block models and implements all the algorithms used to define Signal and Data Processing settings as a function of the EM scenario and the current Radar Track File. For instance, the EW Manager sets the receivers tuning in frequency and amplitude dynamic or the filtering on the emitter characteristic parameters needed to discriminate and separate radar pulses. The HW/FW receiving chains are properly set to achieve optimal performance (high probability of radar threat interception is a possible goal) depending on the EM scenario and the generated Radar Track File. The Simulator implements also the management of the Tracking Channels that represent the possibility of allocating HW/FW resources in an optimal way in correspondence of the specific emitter pulses reception. The EW Manager settings are managed by the Task Programmer whose aim is to store them inside the Programming Memory. Other than Task Programmer and Programming Memory, inside the EW Manager we have the Actuator and Arbiter sub-blocks. According to the winning request among the different managed by the Arbiter (on the base of the set of operations required by the EW Manager), the Actuator takes the data in the Programming Memory and properly sets the EW system receiver;

2. The hardware/firmware (HW/FW) receiving chain block models the Signal Processing elaboration whose aim is to convert the RF samples derived from the PDWs in Pulse Descriptor Messages (PDMs). The HW/FW receiving chain block includes the modelling of the whole receiving RF chains and the digital receivers of the EW system under test. The Simulator takes into account all the effects on the received signals due to the microwave components present in the receiving chains (antennas, amplifiers, filters, down-converters, etc.). Both frequency channelized (Super Heterodyne) and not (Wide Open) receivers are modeled in the proposed Simulator. The number and kind of digital receivers and the characteristics of the RF receiving chains to be simulated can be properly set in a simple and rapid way. Therefore, the Simulator represents a useful tool in order to investigate different configurations of the HW/FW receiving chain that can be adopt for the target EW system;

3. The Data Processing block models all the operations on the PDMs necessary to discriminate the pulses with respect to the associated radar emitters, reconstruct their temporal sequence and produce the Radar Track File. The Radar Track File contains all the discovered radar threats with the main characteristics describing their EM transmissions.

2.2 SW Implementation Methodology

The Simulator developed and presented in this paper has the aim of speeding up as much as possible the process of finding innovative architectural solutions. For this reason, and given the complexity of the system to be simulated, the Simulator has been thought in terms of extreme modularity. This approach has allowed us to make it easy to forecast the performance of the system from the initial stages of the project, when it is generally necessary to explore many architectural solutions simultaneously. At the same time and for the same reason as before, the Simulator has been realized to be fast. It is not necessary to respect the constraint of real-time for our purposes (in a simulation sense), but the results have to be available within a reasonable time. Considering the accuracy required in the simulation as well as the domain of simulated entities (SW, FW) the choice of the programming language fell to C++, considered a good compromise between the drivers previously expressed. The object-oriented programming allows to implement the models of FW/SW modules organized in classes. By means of certain design patterns it is possible to specify standard interfaces through which comparisons of alternative modules are simple and quick. A good interface management allows an easy decoupling among the classes and code compilation makes execution fast; moreover, it also allows you to run multiple simulations simultaneously on different processors on the same machine, and an automated framework can be used to speed up the tests. A simulation strategy based upon asynchronous events is used (Event – Driven Methodology). In our sense, an event is an occurrence within the simulation that requires re-evaluation of the internal state of the system. Each event in general can be due to:

- Evaluations within the modules;
- Actions taken between modules or within the same module;
- The overall time of the simulation is evaluated, assuming that the state of the system, between an event and the following, remains unchanged and therefore it is not necessary to observe it.

The events managed by the Simulator can be of two types:

- Cyclic (with a constant or variable period): they are used to simulate periodic events, such as the time update of the FW modules;
- Not cyclic: they are triggered within the modules and used to simulate computing latencies and other delay effects

Within the Simulator, events are modeled as objects and instantiated from the modules that generate them. Each type of event is implemented by a specific class containing:

- References to the modules on which the occurrence of the event generates actions;
- The reference to the module that instantiates the event;
- The actions to be carried out at the event occurrence;
- The absolute time of the event.

In the worst possible case (maximum number of events to be managed by the Simulator), the overall simulation time is about only ten times slower than real time (an optimal result taking into account the simulation of HW/FW parts of the EW system). The class that instantiates the event has the task to enter all the information about the event itself and to communicate the existence of the event (i.e. to 'post' it) to a specific entity whose name is EventPlayer. The EventPlayer is in fact an object that does not have a counterpart in the system but is the 'engine' of the simulation. His job is to keep track of global simulation time and to order and trigger the execution of the events according to their execution time. The execution of the event is atomic from the simulation point of view and consists in running the method EventName::Execute(), compulsory in every event class. The execution of this method triggers one or more of the so-called 'actuation' methods within the modules affected by the event in execution. For example, an event might consider transferring new settings from one source module to two destination modules; in this case, the method `EventApplySettings::Execute()` is composed of two calls

- `destModule1->setSettings(srcModule->getSettings());`
- `destModule2->setSettings(srcModule->getSettings()).`

The event object shall have the references to `srcModule`, `destModule1` and `destModule2` as well as the event time that, for the atomicity of the event itself, shall have already taken into account the delay due to the data transfer. Sometimes it could be necessary to remove from the queue an event that no longer has reason to occur (for example, a future pre-programmed tune within a receiver and no longer required). The event classes provide a disabling capability so that, once a disabled event is selected by the `EventPlayer`, the method `EventName::Execute` is not executed. Once the event is closed, its object is destroyed. For the reasons above expressed, the EventPlayer is an object whose reference must be present in all objects:

- That need to know the global time of the simulation by calling the method `Event Player::GetCurrentTime`;
- They need to 'post' events on the `EventPlayer`.

A particular use of the `EventPlayer` allows breaking actions requiring recursive calls on objects that, without the existence of the `EventPlayer`, would make stack indefinitely grow. Where a complex action can be broken into two elementary subsequent segments, say A and B, it is sufficient to prepare two events, `E(A)` and `E(B)` where the execution time of `E(B)` is equal to the current simulation time plus the execution time of `E(A)` (known a priori), and post them on the `EventPlayer` at the same time. After the execution of `E(A)`, the control then returns to the `EventPlayer` – so the portion of the stack containing the data of `E(A)` methods is unloaded. The `EventPlayer` then calls `E(B)`. From the simulation point of view the end of `E(A)` and the beginning of `E(B)` are contemporary. With the exception of the `EventPlayer` class that, as said before, does not have a counterpart in the simulated system, the other classes in the Simulator represent real entities of the system, either physical, such as FW modules, or intangible as tables of parameters and general settings structure. With regard to the classes that implement physical parts of the system, they are organize in a standardized way in order to make the code more learnable and easily navigable. The attributes of these types of class can be of three kinds:

- Parameter Attributes: contain the necessary parameters to run the algorithms that the class implements (e.g. thresholds tables, control parameters)
- Architecture Attributes: contain references to objects with which interaction is required (e.g. external method calls). It is not necessary that all attributes contain a value. For example, a module may rely on an auxiliary module to perform additional operations. If the auxiliary module is not available, the function related to it is automatically disabled.
- Status Attributes: contain information on the current status of the module (e.g. operative state)

The methods of these types of class generally fall into five categories:

- `GetSettings`/`setSettings`: methods allow to write and read parameter attributes of the class. The methods are called several times during the simulation, for example at each new requested tune of the receivers. These methods are public.
- Link: acting on the architecture attributes, these methods allow to connect objects to other objects. These methods are called at the beginning of the simulation and define the system architecture. These methods are public.
- Execute: is the entry point of the main activity carried out by each module. It typically contains calls to private methods of the same class. This method is public.
- `PostEvent`: this kind of methods deal with the instantiation of the events and they are responsible for setting all the necessary attributes as well as for communicating their references to the `EventPlayer` by calling the method `Event Player::postEvent()`. These methods are private.
- Actuation events: these public methods are called by the `EventPlayer` when an event is executed (calls to them are contained in the method `Event Name::Execute()`).

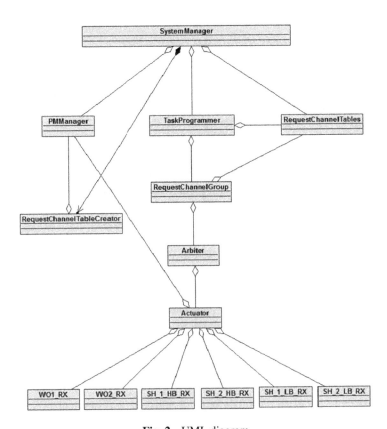

Fig. 2. UML diagram

The classes are organized hierarchically, complying (as much as possible) with the same hierarchy of the system to be simulated. This makes the code quickly adaptable to the demands of the system architects. The definition of the architecture is done:

- Instantiating objects;
- Calling the methods of type 'Link' to establish a connection between the different modules.

Each object has a reference to the objects with which it must interface during the simulation. As said before, some references are optional and their presence (or absence) decides the behavior of the object during the simulation (the algorithms are automatically modified depending on the resources available to the object itself). An UML Diagram representing the C++ classes implemented in order to link the output of the EW Manager to the input of the EW receivers is reported in Fig. 2.

3   Results and Output

For each simulation run, the proposed SW Simulator produces in output the following items:

- The "Log" is a text file that reports the sequence of the main performed operations with the relative results and the corresponding timestamp. This output is fundamental

	Type	Id Rx	FCode	AntT	AntM	TOA [s]	DTOA [µs]
46204	State	SH HB 2	ESM TRK5	PAU	02	82.1183591000	0.0000
46205	StateDrx	SH HB 2	ESM TRK5	--	--	82.1183591000	0.0000
46206	Measure	SH HB 1	ESM TRK5	PAU	03	82.1183600500	0.9500
46207	Measure	WO 2	ESM SEQ	PAU	2A	82.1183600500	0.0000
46208	Measure	WO 1	ESM SEQ	PAU	15	82.1183600500	0.0000
46209	State	SH HB 1	ESM SEQ	PAU	15	82.1183632000	3.1500
46210	StateDrx	SH HB 1	ESM SEQ	--	--	82.1183632000	0.0000
46211	State	SH HB 1	ESM TRK5	PAU	01	82.1190593000	696.1000
46212	StateDrx	SH HB 1	ESM TRK5	--	--	82.1190593000	0.0000
46213	State	SH HB 2	ESM TRK5	PAU	20	82.1190593000	0.0000
46214	StateDrx	SH HB 2	ESM TRK5	--	--	82.1190593000	0.0000
46215	Measure	SH HB 1	ESM TRK5	PAU	21	82.1190600000	0.7000
46216	Measure	WO 2	ESM SEQ	PAU	2A	82.1190600000	0.0000
46217	Measure	WO 1	ESM SEQ	PAU	15	82.1190600000	0.0000
46218	State	SH HB 1	ESM SEQ	PAU	15	82.1190631000	3.1000
46219	StateDrx	SH HB 1	ESM SEQ	--	--	82.1190631000	0.0000
46220	State	SH HB 1	ESM TRK5	PAU	01	82.1195243000	461.2000
46221	StateDrx	SH HB 1	ESM TRK5	--	--	82.1195243000	0.0000
46222	State	SH HB 2	ESM TRK5	PAU	02	82.1195243000	0.0000
46223	StateDrx	SH HB 2	ESM TRK5	--	--	82.1195243000	0.0000
46224	Measure	SH HB 1	ESM TRK5	PAU	03	82.1195250250	0.7250
46225	Measure	WO 2	ESM SEQ	PAU	2A	82.1195250125	-0.0125
46226	Measure	WO 1	ESM SEQ	PAU	15	82.1195250125	0.0000
46227	State	SH HB 1	ESM SEQ	PAU	15	82.1195281000	3.0875
46228	StateDrx	SH HB 1	ESM SEQ	--	--	82.1195281000	0.0000

Fig. 3. An example of "Tagging" file

to check the correctness of the Signal and Data Processing settings coming from the EW Manager;

- The "Tagging" file is a complete list of all the PDMs generated during the simulation; it is important to remark that there exist two different types of PDMs. The first one is the measure PDM that contains all the information estimated by the EW system about a specific radar pulse, for example: Radio Frequency, Pulse Width, Amplitude, Modulation on Pulse, Direction of Arrival etc. The second kind of PDM is represented by the state one that reports all the settings associated to a specific EW receiver, for example: frequency tune, instantaneous dynamic, connected antennas, etc. Both state and measure PDMs have the information of Time of Arrival (TOA), i.e. the time instant of their generation. Measure PDMs include both flags needed to validate radar pulse parameters estimated and the corresponding estimates. For instance, considering the DOA value (fundamental for the EM scenario reconstruction), we have the flag *vDOA* (if equal to one it confirms the validity of the DOA estimation) and a field indicating the algorithm used for its estimation. Moreover, all PDMs report the fields relative to the receiver identification (required to indicate which receiver has generated the measure or to which receiver corresponds the settings decided by the EW Manager) and to the type of activity (the two possibilities are emitter Tracking Channel or search). In Fig. 3 we report an example of "Tagging" file; on almost all

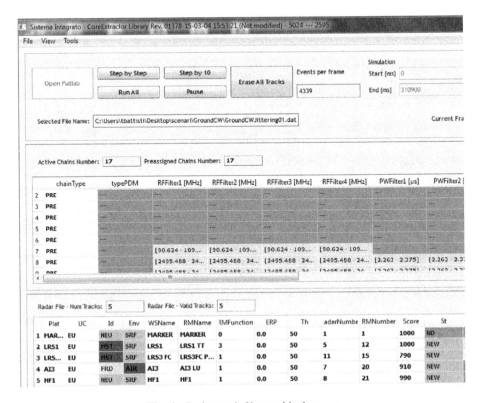

Fig. 4. Radar track file graphical output

PDMs fields it is possible to activate filters in order to select only the PDMs of interest (for example it could be useful to take in consideration only PDMs with RF in a specific sub-band of the monitored EM spectrum). The PDMs in the "Tagging" file represents the input of the Data Processing block whose aim is to discriminate radar threats. Radars discrimination consists in reconstructing the temporal sequence of the PDMs that can be associated to pulses transmitting by the same threat.

- The Radar Track File is the main output of the proposed Simulator; it contains the list of all the intercepted radar emitters with their characteristic parameters. These parameters are clearly derived on the basis of the measure PDMs reported in the "Tagging" file. The Radar Track File is available both in a text file and in an impressive graphical output as illustrated in Fig. 4. The graphical output presents the same fields as the ones shown to an operator of the EW system; other than the characterizing parameters deriving from the measure PDMs, we have a radar emitter identification in terms of Platform and Radar Mode names. Moreover, by means of the graphical output in Fig. 4 it is possible to start simulation, stop simulation and select specific temporal frames to be analyses.

4 Conclusions

Since an EW scenario is very complex (a few seconds correspond to a huge amount of Signal and Data Processing events) and not easily reproducible even in a controlled environment, the SW Simulator is a useful and fundamental tool to test and validate any EW system architecture on any possible scenario. Other than in the final validation phase, the Simulator is especially important in the design and development of an EW system; the Simulator represents a tool able to address properly the design choices driving in an incremental way towards the final EW system implementation. In order to explain this concept, it is important to remark two fundamental characteristics directly deriving from the SW Simulator architecture. The first one is that part of the Data Processing and all the EW Manager implemented in the Simulator are "emulated" blocks, in other words their SW algorithmic is common with the ones on the final target. The second one is that the HW/FW receiving chain can be SW simulated before any physical implementation or modification reducing at least the risks associated to the development or to an upgrade of an EW architecture. On the base of the two considerations above reported, we have that the overall EW architecture can be tested and validated without using the real HW/FW receiving chain but in a more simple and efficient way exploiting the so called "SW-in the loop" technique. Moreover, starting from the Simulator architecture the integration of the final EW system can be gradually implemented increasing progressively the number of "emulated" blocks. In this way, it is possible to integrate and test boards with their algorithmic FW one after the other reducing the complexity with respect to a single step integration. The Simulator has been realized to be fast; more specifically, the simulation time is about only ten times slower than real time (an optimal result taking into account the simulation of HW/FW parts of the EW system).

References

1. Capper, D.M.: Introduction to C++, 1st edn. McGraw-Hill, New York (1997)
2. Meikle, H.: Modern Radar Systems. Artech House, Boston (2001)
3. Vaccaro, D.D.: EW Receiving Systems. Artech House, Boston (1993)

Employing Observation Angles in Pose Recognition; Application for Teach-and-Repeat Robot Navigation

Martin Dörfler$^{(\boxtimes)}$ and Libor Přeučil

Faculty of Electrical Engineering, Department of Cybernetics,
Czech Technical University, Technicka 2, 166 27 Prague 6, Czech Republic
{martin.dorfler,libor.preucil}@ciirc.cvut.cz

Abstract. In this paper, a method is presented which uses landmark bearings to support navigation. The herein introduced approach expands on previous method that uses robust image features in conjunction with dead-reckoning to correct robot bearing. In the presented approach, a combination of omnidirectional camera, and exploiting the observation angles are used to address adjustment of positioning errors of the robot on the fly, without a need for dead-reckoning. This keeps the positioning deviation within specific bounds and thus avoids accumulative nature of dead-reckoning error.

Although this information is insufficient for absolute triangulation, under certain constraints it proves satisfactory for direction estimation. Detecting the arrival at the previously learned location or comparing relative distance of the landmarks for each observation point is also possible.

The presented approach was verified in simulation and on the real robot. Obtained results indicate the feasibility of the approach.

Keywords: Pose recognition · Vision-based · Robust image features · Monocular localization and navigation

1 Introduction

In the context of monocular navigation of mobile robots, robust image features are a convenient tool to recognize landmarks in the camera image. While bearing towards landmarks can be measured precisely and reliably, calculating the absolute position of the robot would require knowing the landmark position. Nevertheless, even relying on bearings only can yield actionable information.

In this paper, a method is presented which uses such information to support navigation. The herein introduced approach expands on previous method that uses robust image features in conjunction with dead-reckoning to correct robot bearing. In the presented approach, the same features are used to address adjustment of positioning errors of the robot on the fly, without a need for dead-reckoning. This keeps the positioning deviation within specific bounds and thus avoids accumulative nature of dead-reckoning error.

© Springer International Publishing Switzerland 2015
J. Hodicky (Ed.): MESAS 2015, LNCS 9055, pp. 165–172, 2015.
DOI: 10.1007/978-3-319-22383-4_12

These improvements are enabled by a combination of employing an omnidirectional camera, and exploiting the observation angles. Multiple landmarks are detected in the image, angles between observed locations of such landmarks are measured. Such angles are partial information that is readily available through most scenes. Although this information is insufficient for absolute triangulation, under certain constraints it proves satisfactory for direction estimation. Detecting the arrival at the prelearned location or comparing relative distance of the landmarks for each observation point is also possible.

Experimental verification of the presented approach was performed with a real robot. Obtained results indicate the feasibility of the approach.

The paper is structured as follows: Sect. 3 presents the method of direction estimation and improvements realised on that method to increase robustness. Following Sect. 4 describes how to apply this method to improve a specific method of teach-and-repeat navigation. Later sections detail the tests performed to verify feasibility of the method. Section 5 shows simulated results and Sect. 6 contains description and results of a real-world experiment.

2   Teach-and-Repeat Method: SURFnav

In [1] and later [2], a method of teach-and-repeat navigation was presented under the name SURFnav. The method utilises SURF features [3] in the monocular camera to detect landmarks, measure bearings to these landmarks, and from this information computes direction correction. This is proven to be sufficient for following a recorded trajectory and for limiting the positioning error of the robot.

The navigation is performed in discrete linear segments. During the teaching phase, the robot is driven along a piecewise linear trajectory and the position of landmarks in the camera image is recorded. In the replay phase, the robot bearing is continuously changed to minimize the distance between the recorded landmark position in the camera image and the measured value.

Assuming the landmarks in finite distance, this causes the trajectory to gradually converge to the recorded path. Lateral displacement of the robot from the expected position is lessened over time. The longitudinal displacement relies on the accuracy of the dead-reckoning.

For the trajectory consisting of multiple direction changes, it is proven that the total diplacement is constrained. This proof holds only under a condition that the trajectory contains enough changes in direction. In the case of long sequence of segments with little change in overall direction only, the longitudinal displacement may grow unrestrained by accumulating dead-reckoning errors.

Some further improvements were made by different authors. Nietche et al. [4] uses computationally efficient Monte Carlo localization to estimate the robot position within a segment relative to the segment start. Dead-reckoning is used as one of the inputs here.

In this paper, another kind of enhancement to the SURFnav method is proposed. Instead of dead-reckoning, a pure visual approach is used to detect end of trajectory segments. Following section describes a method based on measuring angles in camera image to estimate a location. Subsequently, it is used to detect situations of "passing through" or "nearby" previously recorded location.

3   Direction Estimation Method

In [5], we presented a method that enables estimation of direction between two nearby locations from sparse correspondences in the camera image. It was shown to be feasible, despite having problems with landmark misidentification and subsequent outliers causing instability. Here, a short summary of the method is given and improvements are proposed to enable its' use as a support to the SURFnav navigation.

The core idea of the method is based on a simple geometric intuition. If observing a pair of landmarks, the difference of observation angles between these appears larger from closer distance and smaller, if these are more distant. Therefore by comparing views to the same landmarks from two diverse positions, it can be determined which one is located closer to the pair of landmarks. Considering a convex region from which the observations are done, while preserving their ordering in the view, the afore rule can be applied. If starting at a distant position and moving towards a landmark pair, the distance will decrease and the observations will turn more similar to a closer view case.

Expanding this idea to account for mutiple landmarks, it becomes possible to state whether the motion direction is forwards or backwards with respect to each landmark pair. The original method used a simple weighted sum to fuse these partial decisions into a global direction estimation. Simulation results were satisfactory, but the method was easily perturbed by outliers in the landmark detection process. To alleviate this problem, a voting process was employed.

For an arbitrary direction r, we can calculate how many partial decisions point in the similar direction. Since each such information comes with accuracy estimate, we can additionaly weight the votes by our confidence in them. Equation 1 describes the process with more precission. Each partial direction d contributes to voting with the magnitude equal to the difference between the angle axis a and r. The contribution is weighted by maximum error β_d.

$$C = \sum_d \frac{\frac{\pi}{2} - |d - r|}{\max(\beta_d, 1)} \tag{1}$$

If the sum is positive, the target is considered to lie in the half-plane determined by the direction d, thus moving in such direction brings us closer to the target. Negative value of the sum signifies the opposite case.

For some use cases, this is sufficient. If more precise direction estimation is necessary, such calculation can be performed for greater spread of directions. Target is assumed to be located in the intersection of the calculated half-planes.

The performance of the original method has been dependent on a sufficient field of view. For this reason, omnidirectional camera was employed (details in Sect. 6). This presents a tradeof, as cameras with catadioptric mirror cover greater field of view with the same image resolution, making fine details coarser. However, for this method the advantage of the greater field of view is significant, and small inaccuracies in bearing measurement do not introduce significant error (as shown in the original paper).

4   Application to Teach and Repeat Navigation

The ability to detect closeness and direction to a point can be used to enhance teach-and-repeat navigation. As previously established, SURFnav method performs navigation in segments of known length and performs correction of heading only. Dead-reckoning is employed to detect segment position and it's end-point.

Instead of using the dead-reckoning, the proposed approach employs comparison of the observation angles to detect the end of each segment. The advantage is that such detection is based on the observation of surrounding environment only, not dependent on the previous trajectory of the robot. Propagation of error to the further navigation results is thus limited.

Therein, vicinity of the target location is recognized the same way as in [5], detecting a spike in the observed landmark matches. Passing of the target location is indicated by a sharp change in the estimated direction. To increase the speed of the computation, direction estimation can be simplified for those purposes. We calculate the direction only as a 1D projection onto the direction of the robot movement (as shown in Eq. 1). From this, a simple thresholding can be used to detect a direction change.

5   Simulation

The first step in verifying presented concept investigates simulation results. In this phase, only the algorithm itself is tested, not the whole system. For this reason the simulation abstracts away majority of the hardware implementation details. A 2D environment is employed, with randomly placed landmarks. The simulated robot is equipped with omnidirectional camera, and is able to perceive bearing to each landmark.

A first onlook shows proposed correction as a flow field (Fig. 1). It can observed that the proposed correction mainly identifies direction in a correct way. Figure 2 shows distribution of the error in the estimation.

While the error produced is noticeable, it remains small enough to be useable to improve position. More importantly, the less accurate results point in the direction of better results. Existence of such a flow field makes possible to reach the target point by following the successive directions.

Simulation of this process is displayed in the Fig. 3. In this test, starting position was selected randomly, correction vector computed and position iteratively updated. Final trajectories are displayed in the figure.

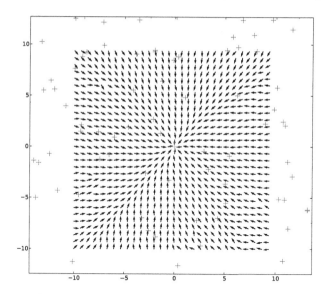

Fig. 1. Estimated direction to target (red), displayed as a flow field and landmarks (blue) (Color figure online)

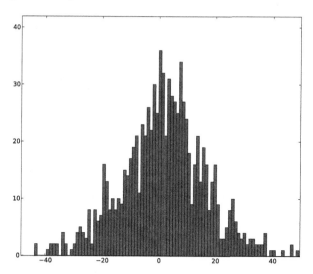

Fig. 2. Histogram of the distribution of the direction error (count vs. direction deviation in degs.)

The full navigation test was performed for the same setup of the environment as in the previous tests. The visibility of landmarks was limited to a certain distance range from the simulated robot, and a multipart trajectory was used. The Fig. 4 shows the test setup. The black line denotes the teached trajectory and the recalled trajectory segments are displayed in color.

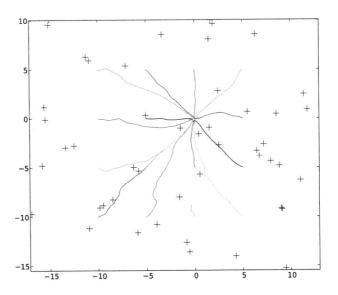

Fig. 3. Trajectories of simulated navigation. Various runs are started from a grid pattern. Trajectories converge into the common target point.

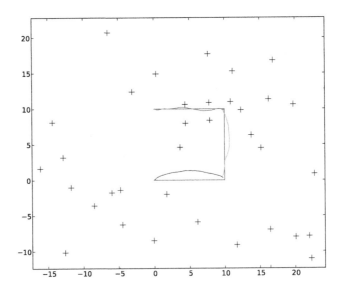

Fig. 4. Navigation along multi-segment trajectory

6   Experiment

As a following up of simulation, the capability to position the robot into vicinity of previously visited locations was tested in a real environment. Following setup was used in the experiment:

A mobile robot was manually driven multiple times along a trajectory consisting of several straight-line segments. The experimental platform used was Evolutionary Robotics' model ER1, fitted with a camera with catadioptric lens. Camera was fitted on top of the robot body, providing a 360° field of view covering the whole surroundings of the robot, without obstruction caused by the robot body. Vertical field of view range is limited, covering approximately 30° interval. The camera records with resolution of 2048 × 1536, and the omni-directional image was unwrapped to 3111 × 241 pixels before processing.

The experiment was performed in the indoor office-type of environment. The experimental scene has primarily been set as static with minor variation in shape and structure. The variations due to presence of the operator and other pedestrians have not been observed as imposing any substantial influence on the experimental results.

During the first run, various locations on the trajectory were recorded. In the following runs, the proposed algorithm was used to detect points on the trajectory closest to the recorded location. The OpenCV [6] implementation of the SURF algorithm was used for landmark detection. The error is calculated as a distance between the closest position to a previously saved target point and the point indicated by the method as the end of a segment (as explained in Fig. 2).

The results are summarized in the Table 1. It displays the statistics of the errors in the closest point recognition.

Table 1. Error in segment termination (five point statistic)

Average difference (cm)	9.1
Median difference (cm)	7.5
Standard deviation	7.1
Maximum difference (cm)	23
Minimum difference (cm)	1.4

As observed herein, the error in finding the segment ending is mostly in the order of centimeters. Although previous exhibits less precision than afforded by a dead-reckoning approach, this error is not accumulative thus it does not grow beyond any limits over the run time of the system. Considering the size of robot and scale of the environment, the precision in average case is fully sufficient for the task of segment ending detection.

7 Conclusion

In this paper, improvements of the original SURFnav methods are discussed. These elaborations consist of replacing monocular forward-facing camera by a top-mounted catadioptric camera, and via recognition of key trajectory points for on-the-fly position recalibration. The recognition is performed by measuring and comparing observation angles of landmarks in the environment. Obtained information is insufficient for absolute triangulation, under certain constraints it proves satisfactory for detecting the arrival at the prelearned locations.

These improvements were aimed at reducing the reliance of the original method on the dead-reckoning, and to expand the conditions under which SURF-nav can be used to cover even previously hostile cases.

Experiments in the simulation and on the real data verify feasibility of the presented approach method.

References

1. Krajník, T., Přeučil, L.: A simple visual navigation system with convergence property. In: Bruyninckx, H., Přeučil, L., Kulich, M. (eds.) European Robotics Symposium 2008. Springer Tracts in Advanced Robotics, vol. 44, pp. 283–292. Springer, Berlin Heidelberg (2008)
2. Krajník, T., Faigl, J., Vonásek, V., Košnar, K., Kulich, M., Přeučil, L.: Simple yet stable bearing-only navigation. J. Field Robot. **27**, 511–533 (2010)
3. Bay, H., Ess, A., Tuytelaars, T., Van Gool, L.: Speeded-up robust features (SURF). Comput. Vis. Image Underst. **110**, 346–359 (2008)
4. Nitsche, M., Pire, T., Krajník, T., Kulich, M., Mejail, M.: Monte carlo localization for teach-and-repeat feature-based navigation. In: Proceedings of Advances in Autonomous Robotics Systems - 15th Annual Conference, TAROS 2014, pp. 13–24, Birmingham, UK, 1–3 September 2014 (2014)
5. Dörfler, M., Přeučil, L.: Position correction using angular differences. In: POSTER 2014–18th International Student Conference on Electrical Engineering. Wiley Subscription Services Inc, A Wiley Company (2014)
6. Bradski, G.: The openCV library. Dr. Dobb's J. Softw. Tools **25**, 120–126 (2000)

Multispectral Stereoscopic Robotic Head Calibration and Evaluation

Petra Kocmanova[1] and Ludek Zalud[2(✉)]

[1] LTR s.r.o., Brno, Czech Republic
`kocmanova.p@fce.vutbr.cz`
[2] CEITEC, Brno University of Technology,
Brno, Czech Republic
`Ludek.zalud@ceitec.vutbr.cz`

Abstract. The aim of the paper is to describe the data-fusion from optical sensors for mobile robotics reconnaissance and mapping. Data are acquired by stereo pair of CCD cameras, stereo pair of thermal imagers, and TOF (time-of-flight) range camera.

The described calibration and data-fusion algorithms may be used for two purposes: visual telepresence (remote control) under extremely wide variety of visual conditions, like fog, smoke, darkness, etc., and for multispectral autonomous digital mapping of the robot's environment.

The fusion is realized by means of spatial data from a TOF camera - the thermal and CCD camera data are comprised in one multispectral 3D model for mapping purposes or stereo image presented to a binocular, head-mounted display. The data acquisition is performed using a sensor head containing the mentioned 5 cameras, which is placed on 3 degrees-of-freedom (DOF) manipulator on Orpheus-X3 reconnaissance robot; both the head and the robot were developed by our working group.

Although the fusion is used for two different tasks – automatic environment mapping and visual telepresence, the utilized calibration and fusion algorithms are, in principle, the same.

Both geometrical calibration of each sensor, and the mutual positions of the sensors in 6-DOFs are calculated from calibration data acquired from newly developed multispectral calibration pattern. For the fusion the corresponding data from the CCD camera and the thermal imager are determined via homogeneous and perspective transformations. The result consists of image containing aligned data from the CCD camera and the thermal imager for each eye or a set of 3D points supplied by color and thermal information. Precision of data-fusion is determined both by calculation from mathematical model and experimental real-scenario evaluation. Precision of data-fusion and subsequently calibration is evaluated by real-environment measurements with help of newly developed multispectral targets.

Keywords: Calibration · Multispectral fusion · Telepresence · Mobile robot

© Springer International Publishing Switzerland 2015
J. Hodicky (Ed.): MESAS 2015, LNCS 9055, pp. 173–184, 2015.
DOI: 10.1007/978-3-319-22383-4_13

1 Introduction

The main aim of the data-fusion described in this article is remote reconnaissance of previously unknown areas under wide variety of visibility conditions including fog, smoke, complete darkness, high illumination dynamics with point light sources, etc. The reconnaissance will be done in real-time through remotely controlled robot called Orpheus-X3 in our case, but in principle the described methods may be used on most remotely controlled UAVs or UGVs, or e.g. on armored vehicles.

The method uses a combination of "classical" tricolor CCD or CMOS cameras working in visible spectrum with thermal imagers working in 7–14 um spectrum. Each of them has certain advantages and disadvantages.

Modern visible-spectrum cameras offer a very good overview of the situation with high resolution for low cost. Their image representation is the most intuitive for the operator. On the other hand the dynamic range of them is much lower than the one of a human eye. They also do not work in complete darkness, cannot see through fog or smoke.

Thermal imagers became widely available during the last couple of years, when their price was reduced significantly. The main advantages - they can percept in fog, at least for short distances, they are also almost unaffected by visible light, so it does not matter how the scene is illuminated (complete darkness, point light sources, ...). The main disadvantages – they typically offer significantly lower pixel resolution comparing to standard cameras, they are still significantly more expensive and the image offered is not so intuitive to the human operator, since it basically corresponds to temperatures of the objects.

So it seems valuable to combine these two imagers into one image. Nowadays several companies provide combined CCD – thermal imagers, but their approach is simplistic – the images are only geometrically aligned, so because of parallax the images do not correspond exactly for most cases. Furthermore the used CCD cameras are typically of low quality and with relatively narrow field of view. So these solutions are not appropriate for telepresence in rescue robotics, where high resolution and wide field of view are necessary.

The technique combining color and thermal imaging was studied by our team in the past [1], but as the sensory prices decreased and TOF (time-of-flight) cameras matured, the technique now may be done more advanced. In this article we introduce a technique for visual spectrum and thermal imager data alignment with help of data from TOF camera. The TOF camera measures a distance of an object, while corresponding pixels are found on color camera and thermal imager. Each of the sensors has to be calibrated for geometrical parameters first. Than mutual position and orientation of all camera focal points in six degrees of freedom is found and used to make the correspondence calibrations.

Since calibration is a vital part of the whole process to achieve good results in terms of fusion precision, great emphasis is laid to it. Two special multispectral calibration patterns were developed and are described.

To assess data-fusion performance in real conditions, we developed novel multi-spectral calibration targets to be placed randomly in the environment. Experiment with these targets is described in this paper.

This is done for two stereo-pairs of cameras, so the resulting image may be presented to head-mounted display with stereovision support, so the operator has a very good spatial representation of the surrounding under any visibility conditions.

It has to be pointed out the sensors on the sensory head will not be used only for this technique; in parallel we also develop SLAM technique with similar texture-mapping algorithms.

2   Hardware

Although the CASSANDRA robotic system is rather complex and contains a several interesting robots, only the Orpheus-X3 is important for the purposes of this paper.

2.1   Orpheus-X3

The Orpheus-X3 is an experimental reconnaissance robot based on the Orpheus-AC2 model made by our team to facilitate the measurement of chemical and biological contamination or radioactivity for military. The Orpheus-X3 offers the same drive configuration as its predecessor, namely the four extremely precise AC motors with harmonic gears directly mechanically coupled to the wheels; this configuration makes the robot very effective in hard terrain and enables it to achieve the maximum speed of 15 km/h. The main difference lies in the chassis, which is not designed as completely waterproof but consists of a series of aluminum plates mounted on a steel frame of welded L-profiles. This modular structural concept makes the robot markedly more versatile, and this is a very important aspect in a robot made primarily for research activities. Furthermore, the device is equipped with a 3DOF manipulator for the sensor head. The manipulator, again, comprises very powerful AC motors combined with extremely precise, low backlash harmonic drive gearboxes made by the Spinea company. The presence of such precise gearboxes can be substantiated by several reasons, mainly by the fact that the robot is used not only for telepresence but also for mobile mapping and SLAM. As currently planned, the robot's only proximity sensor is the TOF camera placed on the sensory head. The Orpheus robots are described in more details in our previous papers, such as [2].

Sensor Head. The sensor head containing five optical sensing elements is shown in Fig. 1. The sensors are as follows:

- Two identical tricolor CCD cameras (see 1 in Fig. 1): TheImagingSource DFK23G445 with the resolution of 1280 × 960 pixels, max. refresh rate of 30 Hz, and GiGe Ethernet protocol. This device is equipped with a Computar 5 mm 1:1.4 lens.

Fig. 1. The sensor head. 1 – tricolor CCD cameras; 2 – thermal imagers; 3 – TOF camera (Color figure online).

- Two identical thermal imagers Flir Tau 640 with the resolution 640 × 480, temperature resolution 0.05 K and Ethernet output.
- One TOF camera (see 3 in Fig. 1): A Mesa Imaging SR4000 with the range of 10 m, resolution of 176 × 144 pixels, and an Ethernet output. The field of view is 56°(h) × 69°(v).

It is obvious from the preceding text that the fields of view (FOVs) of the sensors are similar. The largest FOV captures the TOF camera, which is required for the simultaneous use of stereovision and thermal stereovision. The main disadvantage of the applied TOF camera is its low number of pixels (spatial resolution). Compared to the CCD cameras, it is about 10 times lower in one axis, and in relation to thermal imagers it is twice lower.

3   Sensor Calibration

Calibration of the sensory head comprises the following stages (see Fig. 2): range calibration, temperature calibration, and calibration of intrinsic and extrinsic parameters. SwissRanger manufacturer guarantees absolute accuracy of measured distance ± 15 mm only for 11 × 11central pixels [3] and other image regions don't achieve this accuracy. Range calibration of TOF camera is described in detail in [4].

Temperature calibration is appropriate because of quite poor absolute precision of measured temperatures (2 K according to manufacturer specifications) and is described in [5]. Calibration of intrinsic and extrinsic parameters will be described hereinafter.

3.1   Calibration of Intrinsic and Extrinsic Parameters

We proposed 3 calibration plate based on checkerboard pattern. At first sufficient contrast of the calibration pattern should be achieved only by different materials. This version comprised an aluminum panel (low emissivity; high reflectivity) and a self-adhesive foil (high emissivity; low reflectivity). The main problem related to this initial

Extrinsic parameter calibration

CCD camera - left	CCD camera - right	Thermal imager - left	Thermal imager - right	TOF camera

Intrinsic calibration   **Intrinsic calibration**   **Intrinsic calibration**
                                   Temperature calibration   **Range calibration**

Fig. 2. The calibration diagram for all sensors.

board consisted in the high reflectivity of the aluminum base in cases that images are acquire under non-perpendicular angle (see Fig. 3).

Fig. 3. The initial calibration plate: the left and right CCD cameras (left); the left and right thermal imager cameras (center); the TOF camera intensity image (right).

The second version consisted of an aluminum panel with a laser-cut, anodized pattern and a chipboard covered by a black, matt foil. Anodizing of aluminum panel reduces high reflectivity. Good contrast of checkerboard pattern for thermal imagers was achieved by heating of aluminum part at 50°C.

The final version included a 2 mm laser-cut aluminum plate with active heating. This version is more comfortable and shortens time needed to prepare calibration. (see Fig. 4).

Fig. 4. The final calibration plate: the left and right CCD cameras (left); the left and right thermal imager cameras (center); the TOF camera intensity image (right).

The calibration of the intrinsic and extrinsic parameters comprises the following stages:

- Corner extraction based on automatic corner extraction from Omnidirectional Camera Calibration Toolbox for Matlab [6].

- Homography from extracted corners.
- Intrinsic and extrinsic parameters are computed from homography according to [7].
- Nonlinear optimization that minimizes the sum of the squares of the re-projection errors including the determination of distortion.

Camera calibration model is described in detail in [5]. Table 1 shows values of reprojection errors from calibration used for data fusion evaluation.

Table 1. Reprojection error for each camera from calibration.

	Reprojection error [pixel]
TOF camera	0.36
CCD left camera	0.47
CCD right camera	0.47
Thermal imager left	0.56
Thermal imager right	0.45

4 Data Fusion

Data fusion is performed by means of image transformations. The range measurements of the TOF camera can be displayed into images of the CCD cameras and thermal imagers using spatial coordinates. According to identical points (ID) of the TOF camera transformed into frames of the CCD camera and the thermal imager, the thermal image can be displayed into the CCD image and vice versa (see Fig. 5).

The input data for data fusion include the range measurement, the image coordinates of all sensors, and the results of previous calibration. The procedure comprises the following stages:

- Computation of spatial coordinates measured by TOF camera.
- Homogeneous transformation to determine measured spatial coordinates in frames of other cameras.
- Perspective projection to determine image coordinates in frames of other cameras.
- Correction of recalculated image coordinates to the calibrated position of the principal point.

The spatial coordinates X, Y, and Z are computed according to Eqs. 1 and 2. The homogeneous transformation is determined by Eq. 3, where $R_{[3\times3]}$ is the rotational matrix, $t_{[3\times1]}$ is the translation vector, and X', Y', Z' are the spatial coordinates of the second sensor. The image coordinates of the TOF camera in the next frame $x_{c'}$, $y_{c'}$ are computed using perspective projection (Eq. 4), where f' is the focal length of the second sensor.

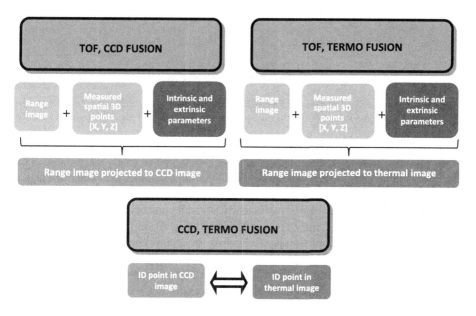

Fig. 5. The data fusion diagram: the TOF and CCD data fusion (up); the TOF and thermal data fusion (center); the CCD and thermal data fusion (down).

$$X = \frac{d_0 x}{f}, Y = \frac{d_0 y}{f} \tag{1}$$

$$Z = d_0 = d \cos \left(\arctan \left(\frac{y}{\sqrt{f^2 + x^2}} \right) \right) \cos \left(\arctan \left(\frac{x}{f} \right) \right) \tag{2}$$

$$\begin{bmatrix} X' \\ Y' \\ Z' \\ 1 \end{bmatrix} = \begin{bmatrix} R & t \\ 0 & 1 \end{bmatrix} \begin{bmatrix} X \\ Y \\ Z \\ 1 \end{bmatrix} \tag{3}$$

$$x'_c = \frac{f' X'}{Z'}, y'_c = \frac{f' Y'}{Z'} \tag{4}$$

5   Independent Evaluation of Data Fusion

The main objective of this paper was evaluating functionality of proposed data fusion. The principle of this evaluation is comparison of identical objects directly extracted from images from CCD cameras and thermal imagers with objects extracted from images from TOF camera and projected to CCD cameras and thermal imagers frames using data fusion algorithm.

Fig. 6. The images of first target for the verification of the data fusion accuracy: the left and right CCD cameras (left); the left and right thermal imager cameras (center); the TOF camera intensity image (right).

For this verification we had to propose objects that may be easily identifiable in the all corresponding images. The first our design of this object was sphere. The main reason for such choice arose from the fact that the robot moves around the objects to be identified, and it is vital that they appear identically from all points of view. The spheres can be recognized without difficulty in a color image (Fig. 6). In the thermal image, the identification was carried out simply via heating the metal spheres to 60°C before the measurement (Fig. 6). We used petanque balls (72 mm in diameter) and a shot put ball (104 mm in diameter). The most difficult problem was to recognize the spheres in the TOF camera images. Although spherical objects are commonly used for terrestrial scan registering [8], metal balls could not be reliably identified mainly due to low spatial resolution of the used TOF camera, range errors, noise, and size of the spheres.

Final design of target clearly identifiable in images of all cameras was aluminum circle covered with black paper in the middle and with 3 M red reflective tape on the edge with active heating. Reflective tape is used for easier identification of targets in images of TOF camera, but significant disadvantages of this reflectivity is missing measured distances, since too big portion of light is returned unidirectionally. The matte paper in the middle of the circle was used to overcome this problem – it is easy-to-be-identified by the TOF camera. We used 3 aluminum circles with 20 cm and 30 cm diameters. The targets are well identifiable on images of all 3 camera types (see Fig. 7).

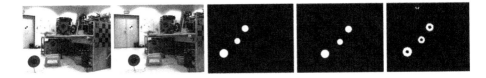

Fig. 7. The images of final target for the verification of the data fusion accuracy: the left and right CCD cameras (left); the left and right thermal imager cameras (center); the TOF camera intensity image (right).

Eighty-seven images were obtained in the experiment under real indoor conditions from the free ride of the robot. 211 extracted objects were used for data fusion evaluation, TOF camera image radial distance for these objects was in range from 1–67 pixels, range for measured distance was from 1.1 to 5.7 m.

Extraction of targets from images comprises the following stages:

- Treasholding.
- Removing small objects (noise) using morphological opening.

- Connection of separated parts using morphological closing.
- Filling closed objects.
- Determining of centroid coordinates.

The differences between the extracted centroid coordinates and those projected from TOF image using data fusion algorithm depending on TOF image radial distances is displayed in Figs. 8–11. Due to the fact that the TOF camera has the lowest resolution, the following figure shown regions that include errors in TOF image centroid extraction in range −0.5 – +0.5 pixel (delimited by the orange horizontal lines). Simulation of the influence of TOF's camera low resolution, distance error and image radial distance on data fusion is described in more details in one of our previous articles [9].

The boundaries of TOF camera distance measurement accuracy regions are displayed in the following figures.

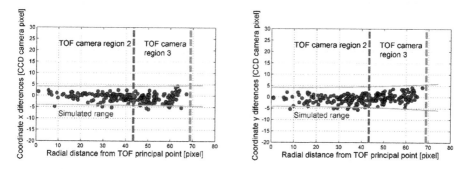

Fig. 8. The coordinate differences determined from the extracted centroids in images of the left CCD camera and from projected TOF image coordinates using the data fusion algorithm: the coordinate x differences (left); the coordinate y differences (right).

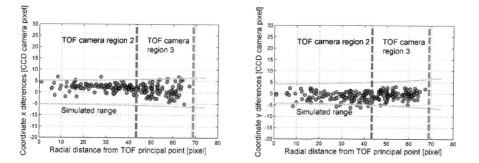

Fig. 9. The coordinate differences determined from the extracted centroids in images of the right CCD camera and from projected TOF image coordinates using the data fusion algorithm: the coordinate x differences (left); the coordinate y differences (right).

Table 2 shows standard deviations $\sigma_{x,}$, σ_y of image coordinates x, y projected by proposed data fusion algorithm. Standard deviation of image position is denoted as σ.

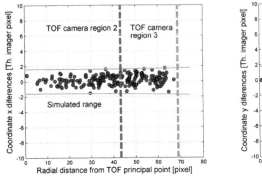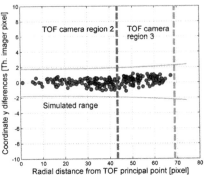

Fig. 10. The coordinate differences determined from the extracted centroids in images of the left thermal imager and from projected TOF image coordinates using the data fusion algorithm: the coordinate x differences (left); the coordinate y differences (right).

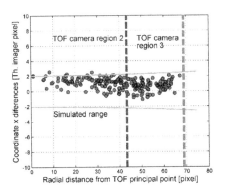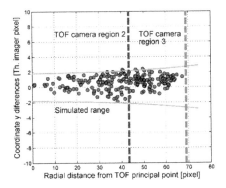

Fig. 11. The coordinate differences determined from the extracted centroids in images of the right thermal imager and from projected TOF image coordinates using the data fusion algorithm: the coordinate x differences (left); the coordinate y differences (right).

Values of standard deviation are given in pixels of CCD cameras and thermal imagers (Figs. 9 and 10).

Table 2. Image coordinates x, y and image position standard deviation of data fusion.

	σ_x [pixel]	σ_y [pixel]	σ[pixel]
CCD left camera	2.6	2.5	3.6
CCD right camera	2.4	2.6	3.5
Thermal imager left	1.4	1.0	1.7
Thermal imager right	0.7	0.8	1.1

6   Conclusion

As it is apparent from experiment described in Sect. 5, the fusion described in Sect. 4 with cameras calibrated according to the procedure described in Sect. 3 is possible, but has its limits. The main problems come from the fact, the cameras have significantly different spatial pixel resolution. It has to be said, the cameras were carefully selected to have parameters appropriate for the main mission of the hereinbefore described sensory head placed on Orpheus-X3 robot – real-time telepresence with augmented reality containing thermal information. So several compromises had to be done during selection – the cameras had to be small enough to be placed on the sensory head and to be moved rapidly during teleoperation as the operator moves with head with speed up to 500°/s, but they had also offer unusually wide field-of-view to make telepresence control intuitive enough for the operator. Furthermore, to make the data-fusion sensible, all the used cameras have to possess similar aspect ratio and field-of view. So the selection of cameras was oriented towards practical usability of the overall system, and resolution compromises arose from this fact.

Considering these facts, we can say the calibration process was successful. Numerical evaluation of data fusion algorithm is as follows: standard deviation for x, y image coordinates is around 2.5 pixels for CCD cameras and around 1 pixel for thermal imagers; standard deviation of image position is around 3.5 pixels for CCD cameras and 1.5 pixels for thermal imagers.

Acknowledgement. This work was supported by VG 2012 2015 096 grant named Cooperative Robotic Exploration of Dangerous Areas by Ministery of Interior, Czech Republic, program BV II/2-VS.

This work was supported by the project CEITEC - Central European Institute of Technology (CZ.1.05/1.1.00/02.0068) from the European Regional Development Fund.

References

1. Zalud, L.: ORPHEUS – reconniaissance teleoperated robotic system. In: 16th IFAC World Congress, Prague, Czech Republic, pp. 1–6 (2005)
2. Zalud, L., Burian, F., Kopecny, L., Kocmanova, P.: Remote robotic exploration of contaminated and dangerous areas. In: International Conference on Military Technologies, Brno, Czech Republic, pp. 525–532 (2013). ISBN 978-80-7231-917-6
3. SR4000 Data Sheet, MESA Imaging AG. Rev. 5.1 (2011)
4. Kocmanova, P., Zalud, L.: Spatial calibration of TOF camera, thermal imager and CCD camera. In: Mendel 2013: 19th International Conference on Soft Computing, pp. s.343–s.348. Brno University of Technology, Fakulty of Mechanical Engineering, Brno (2013). ISBN 978-80-214-4755-4
5. Zalud, L., Kocmanova, P.: Fusion of thermal imaging and CCD camera-based data for stereovision visual telepresence. In: SSRR 2013: 11th IEEE International Symposium on Safety Security and Rescue Robotics, pp. 1–6 (2013)
6. Scaramuzza, D.: OCamCalib: Omnidirectional Camera Calibration Toolbox for Matlab. https://sites.google.com/site/scarabotix/ocamcalib-toolbox

7. Zhang, Z.: Flexible camera calibration by viewing a plane from unknown orientations. In: Proceedings of the Seventh IEEE International Conference on Computer Vision, vol. 1, pp. 666–673. IEEE (1999)
8. El khrachy, I.A.E.H.M.: Towards an automatic registration for terrestrial laser scanner data. Technische Universität Carolo-Wilhelmina, Braunschweig (2007)
9. Kocmanova, P., Zalud, L., Burian, F., Jilek, T.: Multispectral data fusion for robotic reconnaissance and mapping. In: 2014 11th International Conference on Informatics in Control, Automation and Robotics (ICINCO), vol. 02, pp. 459–466, 1–3 September 2014

Marker-Less Augmented Reality for Human Robot Interaction

Karel Košnar[1]([⊠]), Axel Vick[2], Libor Přeučil[1], and Jörg Krüger[2]

[1] Department of Cybernetics Faculty of Electrical Engineering,
Czech Technical University in Prague,
Technicka 2, 166 27 Prague 6, Czech Republic
{kosnar,preucil}@labe.felk.cvut.cz
http://imr.felk.cvut.cz
[2] Insitute for Machine Tools and Factory Management,
Department Industrial Automation Technology, Technische Universität Berlin,
Pascalstr. 8–9, 10587 Berlin, Germany
vick@iwf.tu-berlin.de
https://www.iat.tu-berlin.de

Abstract. This paper presents the marker-less augmented reality system for in-situ visualization of robot's plans to the human operator. The system finds the natural features in the environment and builds the 3D map of the working space during the mapping phase. The stereo from motion method is utilized to compute the 3D position of natural features, while the position of the camera is computed from the artificial markers placed in the working space. Therefore the map is build in the fixed frame of reference frame provided by artificial markers. When the whole working space is mapped, artificial markers are not required for the functionality of the augmented reality system. The actually seen natural features are compared to those stored in the map and camera pose is estimated according found correspondences. The main advantages are that no artificial markers are necessary during regular use of the system, and that method does not rely on the tracking. Even the single frame is sufficient to compute the pose of camera and visualize the robot's plan. As there is a big number of natural features in the environment, the precision of the camera pose estimation is sufficient, when the camera is looking into the mapped working space.

Keywords: Augmented reality · Robotics · Robot-human interaction

1 Introduction

Augmented reality (AR) systems enhance user's perception in order to integrate 3D virtual objects into a 3D real environment in real-time. Due to the adoption of mobile devices with powerful processors, built-in cameras, and fast internet connections, augmented reality is beginning to infiltrate the everyday applications ranging from personal entertainment to industrial deployment.

© Springer International Publishing Switzerland 2015
J. Hodicky (Ed.): MESAS 2015, LNCS 9055, pp. 185–195, 2015.
DOI: 10.1007/978-3-319-22383-4_14

There are two main approaches to AR systems: marker based and marker-less. Basic difference between marker based AR systems and marker-less AR systems is the method used to place virtual objects in the real world. Marker based approach is based on the use of artificial markers that need to be placed in the world to be tracked by the system in order to calculate their position and orientation. The main disadvantage of this approach is necessity to have always at least one artificial marker in the field of view. Utilization of approaches that track simultaneously multiple markers decrease the influence of the occlusions but installation is more complex in this case.

In marker-less AR system any part of the real environment may be used as a marker that can be tracked in order to position virtual objects. Therefore, there are no need for intrusive markers. Nonetheless, tracking and registration techniques become more complex in marker-less AR systems.

This paper presents the marker-less augmented reality system for visualizing robot's plans to the human operator. The considered target application is in-situ plan visualization for industrial manipulators with the possibility of interactive modification of the plan.

As plans for the robot are created in the simulator where degree of conformity of model with reality is limited, there is always need to verify the planned movement of the manipulator before execution. The integration of planned movement into the real environment makes the verification an easy job (Fig. 1).

The paper is further organized as follows:. In next subsection are described related works in field of marker-less augmented reality. Section 2 describes implementation of here proposed marker-less AR system. Experimental results are summarized in Sect. 3. Section 4 concludes the results and gives insight into further development of the system.

Fig. 1. Illustrative image of possible use

1.1 Related Works

Techniques developed for marker-less augmented reality can be classified according to [12] in two main categories: Structure from Motion based and model based.

Structure from Motion (SfM) based techniques are mainly online, since they do not require any previous offline learning phase. Due to this, it is possible to reconstruct a totally unknown environment on the fly. As a drawback, SfM approaches are often very complex. Many efforts have been applied to attach SfM to marker-less AR, but until now only some results were achieved [10].

Simultaneous Localization and Mapping (SLAM) is a well defined and used approach in the robotic community for constructing a representation of the environment on the fly and estimating robot motion. MonoSLAM was created based on the probabilistic SLAM methodology using a single freely-moving wide-angle camera as the only sensor and with a real-time constraint [5]. The MonoSLAM estimates camera pose and creates a sparse map of the environment natural landmarks. It is a very efficient algorithm with a low level of jitter and drift-free, while being robust to handle extreme rotation, occlusion and closed loop. However, it is restricted to indoor environments, smooth camera movement and monochrome camera image.

The advantage of using a model based approach is the possibility of interaction between real and virtual worlds, like occlusion and collision. The 3D model is utilized in the physics simulation and the visibility algorithm, but it is not overlaid onto the image.

Model based techniques can be classified in two categories. The first category methods take only the objects edges into consideration while doing tracking [4,11]. In this category, camera pose is estimated by matching a wireframe 3D model of an object with the real world image edge information. A good initial estimation of the object pose is needed, therefore the initialization is often done manually.

The second one relies on the integration of sequential camera pose estimation. It can makes use of optical flow of the image sequence [1] or uses objects texture information to perform tracking [8,13]. Tracking algorithms based on integration present smoother changes between consecutive poses and the moderate processing load. However, integral techniques tend to accumulate errors produced by sequential pose estimations. all integral techniques are not robust against large camera displacement and optical flow algorithms are also not robust against lighting changes.

2 System Description

Here presented AR system takes advantage of both aforementioned approaches. In the preparation phase, the method utilize robustness of the marker-based AR approaches. During this phase, artificial markers are placed in the working space, providing the fixed frame of reference with known transformation to the frame of reference used with the planning system. Then it builds the 3D map of the working space. The system finds the natural features in the environment and computes 3D position of them making use of the stereo from motion approach, while the position of the camera is computed from localized artificial markers. As the position of the natural landmarks are computed with respect to the frame of reference provided by artificial markers, the whole map is build in this referential frame.

When the whole working space is mapped, artificial markers are not further required for the functionality of the augmented reality. During the regular use, the actually seen natural features are compared to those stored in the map and projection matrix is estimated according found correspondences. The projection matrix is used to project virtual objects into the image of real environment.

Main advantages of proposed approach are robustness to occlusion, as many natural features are used for localization and the probability of occluding all is low. In contrast to other approaches, there is no need to track the position changes, as the camera position is computed separately for each frame.

2.1 Preparation Phase

The preparation phase is dedicated to build the model of the environment, which is further used during the regular use. It is expected, that the mapping of the environment is done only once, before first use of the AR system. At first, artificial markers are placed in the environment before the mapping is started. Without loss of generality, assume that there is one marker placed in the origin of the frame of reference in the further description. When the marker is placed, the camera is moved through the environment to map the whole working space while marker is always in the field of view. The calibrated camera is assumed through the rest of the paper.

Algorithm 1: Mapping

Data: image
Result: map
```
storedPose := computeCameraPosition(image) ;
storedFeatures := computeSURFFeatures(image) ;
while not mapped whole working space do
    actualPosition = computeCameraPosition();
    if ||actualPosition - storedPosition|| > ϑ then
        actualFeatures := computeSURFFeatures();
        actualFeatures3DPositions :=
        triangulate(actualFeatures, storedFeatures,
        actualPosition, storedPosition);
        foreach feature ∈ actualFeatures, 3DPosition ∈
        actualFeatures3DPosition do
            addToMap(feature, 3DPosition);
        storedFeatures := actualFeatures;
        storedPosition := actualPosition;
```

The marker is detected in the image and the position of the camera is computed making use of the ALVAR library [14]. SURF [2] features are detected in the image and stored. Implementation of SURF from OpenCV library [3] is used. Position of the camera is stored as well. For each camera image the marker is detected and position of the camera is computed. Difference of the actual and stored camera position is computed. If the difference is bigger than given threshold, then SURF features are detected in the image, correspondences between stored and actual features are found and 3D position is computed using triangulation. The feature descriptors are stored in the map. This steps are repeated until the whole working space is mapped.

Algorithm 2: Add Feature to the Map

Data: featureDescriptor, 3DPosition, map
Result: updatedMap
```
index, distance :=
findNearestDescriptor(map,featureDescriptor);
if distance < ε then
    insertValue(map,index,3DPosition);
else
    newIndex := insertKey(map, featureDescriptor);
    insertValue(map,newIndex,3DPosition);
```

The features in the map are stored in the associative map, where key is a feature descriptor and value is an array of 3D positions.

Each SURF feature is described by the vector of 64 real numbers. The features with their mutual Euclidean distance smaller than given threshold ϵ is considered similar.

As new feature is added to the map, the associative map is searched for similar features already stored. If the similar feature is presented in the map, only the computed 3D position is added to the associated array otherwise a new key is added to the associative map and 3D position is stored as a value.

The 3D positions of found features are computed by triangulation making use of the Iterative Linear Least Square method [7].

2.2   Regular Use

There is no need for artificial markers during the regular use of here proposed AR system. Camera acquires image of the previously mapped working space. The SURF features are detected and their descriptors are compared to those stored in the map. The 3D position of the camera is then computed and used to place virtual objects into the scene.

Algorithm 3: Compute Transformation Matrix

Data: image, map
Result: transformMatrix
imagePoints := ∅ ;
objectPoints := ∅ ;
detectedFeatures := computeSURFFeatures(image);
foreach feature ∈ detectedFeatures **do**
   index, distance := findNearestDescriptor(map,
   feature.descriptor);
   if distance <ε **then**
      foreach 3Dposition ∈ map[index] **do**
         3Dposition insert into objectPoints;
         feature.position insert into imagePoints;

transformMatrix := solvePnPRansac(imagePoints, objectPoints);

For each detected SURF feature is found the nearest descriptor stored in the map and all 3D positions associated with this nearest descriptor are considered in the perspective-n-point problem. The association of multiple possibly different 3D positions to single SURF descriptor results in big number of outliers, therefore random sample consensus (RANSAC) method is utilized. On other hands, this system of data storage allows very simple and quick retrieval of stored descriptors with associated 3D positions.

The solution makes use of the perspective-n-point problem implementation from OpenCV [3] in the function solvePnPRansac. This function allows to choose the algorithm used inside the Ransac method.

3   Experiments

The test working space was regular office room, where five default ALVAR markers was placed. The default ALVAR multi-marker configuration was used. Those five markers are printed on one A4 paper sheet, one marker of the size 8 cm in the middle of the paper and for markers of size 4 cm, one in each corner. This multi-marker configuration increase robustness of the detection and determination of the camera position. The fixed frame of reference was defined with compliance to the ALVAR system, where origin is set to the big marker and z-axis is perpendicular to the paper sheet.

The test working space was mapped as described in Subsect. 2.1. The resulting map has 862 unique feature descriptors. and 1633 3D positions. The maximum of different 3D positions associated with one descriptor is 16. The memory occupied by the resulting map is 222 kB.

Then the camera was placed into 37 different positions and for each position was taken about 40 images. On these images was measured the precision of the system. The performance was compared to the marker based ALVAR Augmented reality system.

The PnP Ransac algorithm was set as follows: number of iterations was 500, re-projection error was 0.2 and minimal inliers count was 100.

At first the re-projection error was computed. Real position of the marker was manually indicated on each of the test image. The 3D point $[0, 0, 0]$ was projected into the image plane. The projected 2D point should be in the middle of the big marker in the image.

As there is three options for PnP algorithm inside the OpenCV implementation: iterative, P3P and EPnP. P3P is implemented according [6] and utilizes exactly four object and image points. EPnP is implemented according [9].

At first, time consumption of the algorithm is compared. The iterative algorithm can process about 2.9 frames per second, both P3P and EPnP can process 4.4 frames per second. As the iterative algorithm is the most time consuming, it is excluded from further investigation (even the precision is slightly better) (Table 1).

Table 1. Mean and Median of re-projection error [pixels] of the algorithms according the level of occlusion [percent]

Occlusion	Median error		Mean error	
	P3P	EPnP	P3P	EPnP
0	2.2	2.2	5.9	6.0
1	2.4	2.4	6.5	12.7
4	2.5	2.6	8.2	17.5
9	4.2	4.6	23.8	38.9
16	9.0	20.0	45.4	66.5

As the P3P algorithm can better handle the occlusion, it is used in the rest of the experiments. Also the EPnP algorithm has bigger dispersion as can be seen by comparison the median and mean value.

The Fig. 2 depicts the comparison of re-projection error of the marker-based approach (ALVAR library) and here proposed marker-less approach. The boxplot depicts median as a thick horizontal line inside the box generated from first and third quartile and "whiskers" are minimal and maximal value. It means that area covered by the color box contains half of the all measurements.

It can be seen, that the precision of the projection is very similar for both approaches. The 75 percent of measurement with marker-less approach have re-projection error lower than 3.2 pixel.

As the main advantage of the proposed marker-less AR system is robustness to the occlusions, the images was artificially occluded with the rectangle placed in the middle of the image. The size of the rectangle was set to 1, 4, 9 and 16 percent of the image as illustrated on Fig. 3.

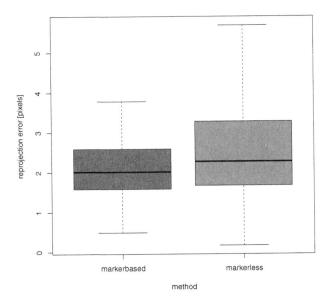

Fig. 2. Re-projection error comparison in pixels

Fig. 3. Example of artificial occlusion (1 %, 4 %, 9 % and 16 % respectively) introduced into the testing images

The resulting re-projection error (in pixels) is depicted on the Fig. 4. As the ALVAR system cannot handle occlusion, results for ALVAR system is not depicted on this graph.

Another performance measure is the camera position error. The real position of the camera was measured for each place and difference between real position and computed position is compared. It is necessary to mention, that there is some systematic error in the computed camera position caused by simplified camera calibration procedure. This systematic error is same for both system in question. Therefore, the absolute value of this error is not testifying and only relative comparison is significant.

The absolute camera position error increases as the distance of camera from the marker increases. It can be seen, that the precision of the marker-less approach is slightly better at bigger distances (Fig. 5).

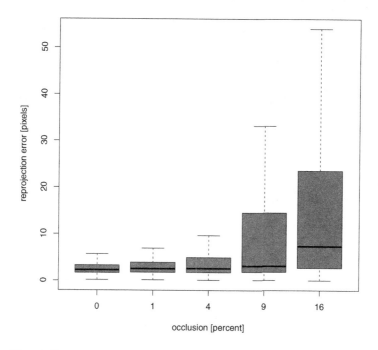

Fig. 4. Re-projection error in pixels for different levels of occlusion

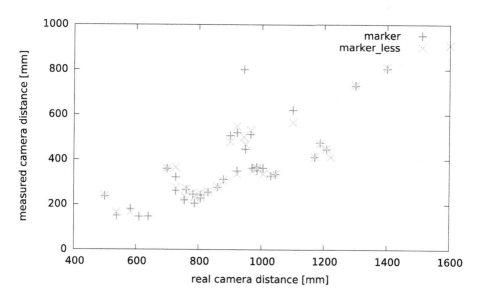

Fig. 5. Camera position error

4   Conclusion

Here presented marker-less augmented reality system is robust to occlusion of 16 percent of the image. The precision is comparable to the marker based augmented reality system ALVAR. In contrast to other marker-less AR systems is able to work on a single image and no tracking system is necessary for function. Therefore, the approach has low computation complexity and memory consumption.

Acknowledgments. This work has been supported by Czech Ministry for Education, Youth and Sport under mobility project number 7AMB14DE004, by German Academic Exchange Service DAAD under mobility project number 57065853 and by Czech Science Foundation under research project No. 13–30155P.

References

1. Basu, S., Essa, I., Pentland, A.: Motion regularization for model-based head tracking. In: Proceedings of 13th International Conference on Pattern Recognition, vol. 3, pp. 611–616. IEEE (1996). http://ieeexplore.ieee.org/lpdocs/epic03/wrapper.htm?arnumber=547019
2. Bay, H., Tuytelaars, T., Gool, L.: SURF: speeded up robust features. In: Proceedings of the Ninth European Conference on Computer Vision. Graz, Austria, May 2006
3. Bradski, G.: The openCV library. Dr Dobbs J. Softw. Tools **25**, 120–125 (2000). http://opencv.willowgarage.com
4. Comport, A.I., Marchand, E., Pressigout, M., Chaumette, F.: Real-time markerless tracking for augmented reality: the virtual visual servoing framework. IEEE Trans. Vis. Comput. Graph. **12**(4), 615–628 (2006)
5. Davison, A.J., Reid, I.D., Molton, N.D., Stasse, O.: MonoSLAM: real-time single camera SLAM. IEEE Trans. Pattern Anal. Mach. Intell. **29**(6), 1052–1067 (2007). http://dl.acm.org/citation.cfm?id=1263144.1263479
6. Gao, X.S., Hou, X.R., Tang, J., Cheng, H.F.: Complete solution classification for the perspective-three-point problem. IEEE Trans. Pattern Anal. Mach. Intell. **25**(8), 930–943 (2003)
7. Hartley, R.I., Sturm, P.: Triangulation. Comput. Vis. Image Underst. **68**(2), 146–157 (1997). http://linkinghub.elsevier.com/retrieve/pii/S1077314297905476
8. Jurie, F., Dhome, M.: A simple and efficient template matching algorithm. In: Proceedings Eighth IEEE International Conference on Computer Vision. ICCV 2001, vol. 2, pp. 544–549. IEEE Computer Soceity (2001). http://ieeexplore.ieee.org/articleDetails.jsp?arnumber=937673
9. Lepetit, V., Moreno-Noguer, F., Fua, P.: EPnP: an accurate O(n) solution to the PnP problem. Int. J. Comput. Vis. **81**(2), 155–166 (2008). http://link.springer.com/10.1007/s11263-008-0152-6
10. Lourakis, M.I.A., Argyros, A.A.: Efficient, causal camera tracking in unprepared environments. Comput. Vis. Image Underst. **99**(2), 259–290 (2005)
11. Roller, D., Daniilidis, K., Nagel, H.H.: Model-based object tracking in monocular image sequences of road traffic scenes. Int. J. Comput. Vis. **10**(3), 257–281 (1993). http://link.springer.com/10.1007/BF01539538

12. Teichrieb, V., Lima, M., Lourenc, E., Bueno, S., Kelner, J., Santos, I.H.F.: A survey of online monocular markerless augmented reality. Int. J. Model. Simul. Petrol. Ind. **1**(1), 1–7 (2007). http://rpcmod.ganer.ex-br.com/revista/articles/1.pdf
13. Uenohara, M., Kanade, T.: Vision-based object registration for real-time image overlay. Comput. Biol. Med. **25**(2), 249–260 (1995). http://www.sciencedirect.com/science/article/pii/001048259400045R
14. VTT Technical Research Centre of Finland: ALVAR: A Library for Virtual and Augmented Reality. http://virtual.vtt.fi/virtual/proj2/multimedia/alvar

Comparison of Local Planning Algorithms for Mobile Robots

Miroslav Kulich$^{(\boxtimes)}$, Viktor Kozák, and Libor Přeučil

Department of Cybernetics, Faculty of Electrical Engineering,
Czech Technical University in Prague, Technicka 2,
166 27 Prague 6, Czech Republic
{kulich,preucil}@ciirc.cvut.cz
viktor-kozak@seznam.cz
http://imr.felk.cvut.cz

Abstract. Local planning algorithms are an essential part of today's mobile robots and autonomous vehicle control. While global planning decides the route of the robot based on initial data given to the planner, local planning is a real-time motion control, based on the feedback from sensors. Its purpose is to keep the robot on an optimal track, following a plan provided by the global planner and to avoid unexpected obstacles. This makes local planning a fundamental part for safe robot navigation. The paper aims to compare three local planning algorithms: the Dynamic Window Approach, Enhanced Vector Field Histogram and Smooth Nearness-Diagram. The comparison was made on various maps in the Player/Stage system and with a real robot in SyRoTek (System for Robotic e-learning). A large set of experiments were made at first to find best configurations for the particular planning algorithms and the robot used. After that, another set of experiments with the found parameters was conducted to gain the results needed for comparison of the algorithms. More than 20,000 simulation runs and 120 hrs of experiments with a real robot were made in total giving the results good statistical credibility.

Keywords: Local planning · Mobile robots · Obstacle avoidance

1 Introduction

When designing an autonomous robotic system, key attention has to be paid to planning functionalities. These functionalities heavily influence behavior of the system and enable it to operate effectively. Planning is typically employed in several layers of a deliberative robotic control architecture [6]. *Mission planning* at the highest level interacts with a human operator and provides consecutive goals to be fulfilled in order to accomplish the whole mission. The intermediate *path planner* generates an obstacle-free path given an actual model of the working environment (either provided by the operator or built autonomously during the mission). This path is then converted into a sequence of control commands to

© Springer International Publishing Switzerland 2015
J. Hodicky (Ed.): MESAS 2015, LNCS 9055, pp. 196–208, 2015.
DOI: 10.1007/978-3-319-22383-4_15

be performed by robot's actuators. This works if the environment is static, its model is precise enough, and movement of the robot is noise-free. In the other case, *local planner/obstacle avoidance module* aims to detect obstacles around the robot with some sensors and modify the path to avoid collisions with obstacles on the fly.

The paper aims to compare performance of three reactive local planning algorithms that are probably mostly used nowadays: the Dynamic Window Approach (DWA) [4], Vector Field Histogram Plus (VFH+) [10] and Smooth Nearness-Diagram (SND) [3]. The comparison was made on various maps in simulation in the Player/Stage system [5] and with a real robot in the SyRoTek system (System for Robotic e-learning) [7].

The rest of the paper is organized as follows. The algorithms to be compared are theoretically described in the next section. Section 3 is devoted description of experiments – the evaluation methodology is introduced and the obtained results are presented and discussed. Finally, concluding remarks are given in Sect. 4.

2   The Compared Methods

2.1   Vector Field Histogram Plus

Vector Field Histogram Plus (some authors call it Enhanced Vector Field Histogram) [10] is an improvement of Borenstein's and Koren's Vector Field Histogram (VFH) [1]. VFH employs a polar histogram grid for representation of robot's surrounding environment. This grid is built from a two-dimensional certainty grid updated from sensor readings taken with a ranging sensor (sonar, laser range-finder). The polar histogram is a vector that moves with the robot. Each element of the histogram corresponds to a circular sector for which information about amount and distance of obstacles in the form of a weighted sum is stored. The histogram after smoothening (by a simple low-pass filtering) has typically *peeks*, i.e. sectors with high values and *valleys*, sectors with low values. Any valley containing sectors with values below a certain threshold can be called a *candidate valley*. If more than one candidate valley is detected, the best one that most closely matches the direction to the current target is selected. Finally, the most suitable sector within the selected valley is chosen as the next goal and the robot is navigated towards it. The whole process is repeated whenever new sensor data are gathered (or in predefined time steps) until the final goal is reached.

VFH+ enhances the original algorithm in several ways. First, threshold hysteresis is used to suppress alternating between several goals in narrow openings that results in robot's movement in the close vicinity of obstacles. Moreover, robot's size is taken into account by enlarging obstacle cells by the robot diameter. Finally, dynamics and kinematics of the robot were not taken into consideration by VFH. Contrary, VFH+ uses a simple approximation of currently possible robot's trajectories by a set of circular arcs with various curvatures assuming that forward and angular velocities are piecewise constant.

2.2 Smooth Nearness Diagram

Another approach was presented by Minguez and Montano [9] as a geometry-based implementation of the reactive navigation method design. The approach called Nearness-Diagram (ND) navigation introduces *gaps* – discontinuities in the nearness of obstacles to the robot which indicate potential paths into occluded areas of the environment. Furthermore, *regions* can defined as the pairs of consecutive gaps, navigable regions are then *valleys*. After assembling all the valleys surrounding the robot, all the gaps are compared against the heading provided by the global planner. The next subgoal and control towards it is determined based on position of two closes obstacles and the width of the valley containing the gap with the heading that best matches the heading to the goal.

Smooth Nearness Diagram (SND) [3] differs from ND in the way the next subgoal is determined. SND measures a threat possessed by each of the obstacles (an obstacle is considered a threat if it lies within the safety distance of the robot) – the treat measure increases as the obstacle gets closer to the robot. Deflection from the desired heading is computed based on threat measurements of each obstacle. The experiment show that oscillatory patterns were suppressed leading to method's performance improvement in narrow corridors.

2.3 Dynamic Window Approach

The Dynamic Window Approach (DWA), introduced by Fox et al. [4], searches control commands directly in the space of velocities and takes limitations of the velocities and accelerations of the robot into account. The approach consists of two parts: a search space is generated at the first, followed by determination of the optimal path in the generated search space.

A two dimensional search space of valid linear and angular velocities is computed directly from the limitations of the velocities and accelerations of the robot. The origin of the space lies in the point representing the current robot's linear and angular velocities. The space is then discretized, i.e. a number of possible pairs of translational and rotational velocities is chosen from the interval between the maximal and minimal velocities. Discretization resolution depends on computational power of the robot and the requested precision. Each velocity pair (v, w) is represented by a circular arc with the starting point in the center of the robot. Its radius is calculated as $r = \frac{v}{w}$ and the length of the arc is set to v. This representation is called the *dynamic window*. All curvatures outside this dynamic window cannot be reached by the robot in the next step, and are thus not considered for obstacle avoidance. Each trajectory is then compared with readings from the laser range finder. The trajectory is considered safe if the robot is able to stop before colliding with any object/obstacle along the path.

Selection of the optimal trajectory is based on three basic attributes, which differ for each velocity pair: angular, velocity, and clearance. The angular attribute favors trajectories with directions close to direction of the global goal position, velocity prefers high linear velocities, while clearance favors trajectories going away from obstacles. The pair from the search space with the highest weighted sum of values of the attributes is chosen as the next control command. Behavior of the algorithm can be easily continuously modified (from safe to fast) by adjusting the weights of the particular attributes.

3   Experimental Evaluation

Performance of the approaches described in the previous sections has been evaluated in several types of environments in simulations using the Player/Stage framework [5], see Sect. 3.1 and with a real robot in the SyRoTek system [7,8], which is described in Sect. 3.2. VFH+ and SND drivers from Player/Stage and our own implementation of DWA (due to its unavailability in Player/Stage) were used for comparison.

3.1   Simulation

The experiments in Player/Stage were performed in five environments differing in a width of passages (see Fig. 1), so performance of the algorithms in narrow corridors, wide passages, open spaces and combination of these can be evaluated. Size of all maps is 3.5×3.8 m and a model of the SyRoTek S1R robot equipped with Hokuyo laser range finder was used [2]. The robot's model was restricted to the maximum speed 0.3 ms/s, the maximum turn-rate 1 rad/s, the maximum acceleration 0.05 m/s, and the maximum turn-rate acceleration 0.05 rad/s. Dimensions of the robot and thus the model are (length × width × height): $174 \times 162 \times 180$ mm.

To ensure a fair comparison, the best settings of the particular methods was determined first, see Sect. 3.1, results in the simulator are described in Sect. 3.1, while Sect. 3.2 is devoted to experiments in the SyRoTek system.

Parameters Settings. Best settings of the VFH+ and DWA algorithms was done in several steps. The algorithms were tested manually at first, with the aim to find configurations with satisfactory results. After that, a broad range of parameter configurations was created in the neighborhood of the parameter values found by hand. These configurations are shown in Table 1.

The SND algorithm has been heavily used at CTU for several years and therefore configuration that is currently used and has been determined as the most reliable was chosen for further evaluation.

The configurations for the DWA and VFH+ algorithms in Table 1 were tested in the *Arena 0* map (Fig. 1a). 10 test runs were made for each configuration and best 60 configurations for DWA and 9 for VFH+, which achieved 100 % success rate, were taken for the final round of experiments described in Sect. 3.1. Note that search for optimal parameter configurations for the DWA algorithm is made on a larger scale than for the VFH+ algorithm. This is because the DWA algorithm was developed as a part of the described work and it is desirable to promptly test its full functionality.

Table 1. Tested parameters. 320 configurations were tested for DWA and 108 configurations for VFH+.

<table>
<tr><td colspan="4" align="center">(a) DWA</td></tr>
<tr><td>Parameter</td><td>Min</td><td>Max</td><td>Step</td></tr>
<tr><td>robot_radius</td><td>0.10</td><td>0.13</td><td>0.01</td></tr>
<tr><td>ValAngle</td><td>5</td><td>20</td><td>5</td></tr>
<tr><td>ValVelocity</td><td>5</td><td>20</td><td>5</td></tr>
<tr><td>ValObstacle</td><td>0</td><td>20</td><td>5</td></tr>
</table>

(b) VFH+

Parameter	Min	Max	Step
cell_size	0.01	0.02	0.01
window_diameter	10	20	10
safety_dist_0ms	0.05	0.09	0.02
weight_desired_dir	5	9	2
free_space_cutoff_0ms	$2 \cdot 10^6$	$4 \cdot 10^6$	10^6

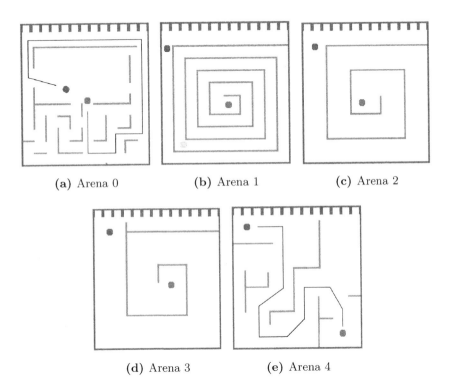

(a) Arena 0   (b) Arena 1   (c) Arena 2

(d) Arena 3   (e) Arena 4

Fig. 1. The testing environments. The narrowest passage of *Arena 0* and *Arena 1* is 28 cm, *Arena 2* and *Arena 4* have the narrowest passage 60 cm, whole *Arena 3* 85.5 cm. The starting position is represented by the blue icon of the robot, and the goal position is represented by the red dot. Some of the maps contain a secondary starting point represented by a yellow icon or a black line representing the desired trajectory of the robot.

Results. In the final evaluation, 50 test runs were made for each configuration of every algorithm (DWA, VFH+, SND) on every map (Fig. 1).

Tables 2, 3, 4, 5, 6 and 7 display resulting statistics from the experiments. The values presented in the tables are: t_{exp}, t_{min}, t_{max}, v_{exp} and the success rate.

Table 2. Results for Arena 0.

Algorithm	t_{exp}	t_{min}	t_{max}	v_{exp}	Success rate
DWA	80.842	77.364	91.326	0.1263	100 %
SND	80.621	78.812	81.654	0.1247	100 %
VFH+	153.701	145.762	164.423	0.0775	32 %
DWA$_{best}$	82.693	77.629	108.207	0.1247	100 %
VFH+$_{best}$	168.896	155.660	182.886	0.0709	22 %

Table 3. Results for Arena 1 when using the first starting point.

Algorithm	t_{exp}	t_{min}	t_{max}	v_{exp}	Success rate
DWA	268.092	239.299	305.973	0.1153	18 %
SND	211.084	208.311	213.881	0.1429	66 %
VFH+	305.431	289.636	322.115	0.1042	20 %
DWA$_{best}$	253.711	233.581	304.169	0.1228	10 %
VFH+$_{best}$	303.762	286.719	324.883	0.1057	14 %

Table 4. Results for Arena 1 when using the second starting point.

Algorithm	t_{exp}	t_{min}	t_{max}	v_{exp}	Success rate
DWA	146.402	143.614	150.819	0.116	56 %
SND	131.035	127.802	133.538	0.127	92 %
VFH+	191.199	177.542	212.584	0.095	60 %
DWA$_{best}$	146.402	143.614	150.819	0.116	56 %
VFH+$_{best}$	189.953	175.381	209.555	0.095	58 %

Table 5. Results for Arena 2

Algorithm	t_{exp}	t_{min}	t_{max}	v_{exp}	Success rate
DWA	84.189	80.400	88.307	0.1715	100 %
SND	85.318	84.542	85.982	0.1656	100 %
VFH+	115.864	108.242	121.508	0.1425	100 %
DWA$_{best}$	86.129	83.206	89.810	0.1691	100 %
VFH+$_{best}$	115.864	108.242	121.508	0.1425	100 %

The t_{exp} is the average time in which the robot reached the goal, t_{min} is the minimal time and t_{max} is the maximal time over all runs. The v_{exp} is the average speed of the robot and the success rate is a percentage value of successful runs.

The tables present the results for the best configuration of each algorithm on the particular map (*DWA* and *VFH+*) and the results for the best configuration

Table 6. Results for Arena 3

Algorithm	t_{exp}	t_{min}	t_{max}	v_{exp}	Success rate
DWA	56.485	54.863	59.866	0.1761	100 %
SND	57.641	56.442	58.428	0.1688	100 %
VFH+	56.976	50.263	67.827	0.2201	100 %
DWA$_{best}$	56.949	55.276	60.168	0.1756	100 %
VFH+$_{best}$	56.976	50.263	67.827	0.2202	100 %

Table 7. Results for Arena 4

Algorithm	t_{exp}	t_{min}	t_{max}	v_{exp}	Success rate
DWA	48.548	46.269	51.362	0.1628	100 %
SND	65.310	64.239	66.157	0.1106	100 %
VFH+	77.051	65.769	120.463	0.1352	80 %
DWA$_{best}$	51.523	47.455	78.900	0.1572	100 %
VFH+$_{best}$	73.684	66.366	112.436	0.1382	66 %

of the DWA and VFH+ algorithms overall (DWA_{best} and $VFH+_{best}$). The best results are chosen at first by the success rate and then by the average time.

Arena 1 simulates a passage through a very narrow corridor (the width of the corridor is less than twice the diameter of the robot). Due to the fact that the algorithms have considerably lower success rate in this map than in other maps, it was possible to push the navigation algorithms to their limits and see differences in their reliability. In order to achieve a higher success rate and thus more statistically relevant data, additional experiments were made with this map, using a different starting point as shown in Fig. 1. Computed data are thus split into two sets of results.

The SND algorithm proved to be the most reliable amongst the three algorithms tested. The results from the *Arena 1* show a big difference between the success rate of the SND algorithm and the success rate of the other two algorithms. This algorithm has time results similar to the other algorithms for most of the maps. The DWA algorithm proved to be less reliable, when used in long narrow passages in *Arena 1*, aside from this map, its performance was mostly equal or superior to the performance of the SND algorithm. The VFH+ algorithm proved to be less reliable than the other two and its time results were worse than the results of the other two algorithms.

A particular situation occurred with the VFH+ driver whenever the robot got stuck close to an obstacle and couldn't go as planned, it seemed to start its "escape function". The escape function appears to have a simple system, the robot keeps turning counter-clockwise, looking for an open space in which it could continue its motion. This function deals with the problem of a robot getting stuck near an obstacle, but has one weakness, the robot always starts turning counter-clockwise regardless of the position of the target. This behavior sometime causes the robot to loose a lot of time just by turning in the opposite direction than the direction of the target. This function makes it unfavorable for the algorithm to be used in environments containing narrow turns in the clockwise direction. If this function would be fixed to select the turning direction accordingly to the position of the target, it could significantly improve the performance of the VFH+ controller.

3.2 Experiments with a Real Robot

Evaluation with a real robot in the SyRoTek system was performed in a similar way as in simulation. SyRoTek is a platform for e-learning and distant experimentation in robotics and related areas consisting of thirteen robots equipped with standard robot sensors (laser range-finders, sonars, odometry, etc.). The robots operate in the Arena of size 3.5×3.8 m and are fully programmable and remotely controlled. Provided global localization system, on-line visualization, interfaces to Player/Stage and ROS enable to perform long-term experiments and experiments with a huge number of trials without human assistance.

The SyRoTek S1R robot equipped with Hokuyo laser range finder was employed. Robot's maximal speed was restricted to $0.45\,\mathrm{ms}^{-1}$ and its maximal turn-rate to $1\,\mathrm{rad\,s}^{-1}$.

A huge set of configurations for all three algorithms was tested first. Based on this, several most promising configurations were chosen for which a detailed evaluation was make.

Parameter Settings. While several simulations could be performed at the same time, the experiments with a real robot could only be made one at the time that made the experiments quite time consuming. Therefore the initial experiments to determine the best configurations were made on a smaller scale than during the simulations. After that 20 test runs were made for three final configurations and for the best configuration from the simulations.

Initial experiments were made on two maps, see Fig. 2: (1) a small set of experiments made on the *Map 1*, with a passage through an environment containing a narrow corridor and (2) a larger set of experiments on *Map 2* containing a passage through an environment with a lot of narrow corridors. Two test runs were made in *Map 1* for each configuration from Table 8 for every algorithm and the best three configurations were chosen accordingly to the success rate and the average speed. Two test runs in *Map 2* were made for each configuration from Table 9 for every algorithm and the best 10 configurations were chosen for the second round of experiments with the best success rate and average speed. 10 runs were made for each configuration in the second round and the three best configurations with the highest success rate and average speed were chosen.

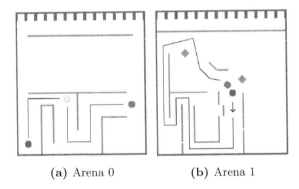

(a) Arena 0   (b) Arena 1

Fig. 2. The real environments in the SyRoTek Arena. The narrowest passage of *Map 1* is 28 cm (and 60 cm when using the second starting point). The narrowest passage of *Map 2* is also 28 cm.

Table 8. Tested parameters for map 1.

Driver	Number of combinations	Parameter	Min	Max	Step
DWA	36	robot_radius	0.08	0.12	0.02
		ValAngle	10	20	10
		ValVelocity	10	20	10
		ValObstacle	0	20	10
VFH+	32	cell_size	0.01	0.02	0.01
		window_diameter	10	20	10
		safety_dist_0ms	0.05	0.09	0.04
		weight_desired_dir	5	9	4
		free_space_cutoff_0ms	$2 \cdot 10^6$	$3 \cdot 10^6$	$1 \cdot 10^6$
SND	27	robot_radius	0.04	0.08	0.02
		min_gap_width	0.12	0.16	0.02
		obstacle_avoid_dist	0.04	0.08	0.02

Table 9. Tested parameters for map 2.

Driver	Number of combinations	Parameter	Min	Max	Step
DWA	48	robot_radius	0.07	0.10	0.01
		ValAngle	10	20	10
		ValVelocity	10	20	10
		ValObstacle	0	20	10
SND	27	robot_radius	0.04	0.08	0.02
		min_gap_width	0.12	0.16	0.02
		obstacle_avoid_dist	0.04	0.08	0.02

Results. The three most suitable configurations of each algorithm from the initial testing were chosen for further experiments together with the best configuration gained from the simulation data. 20 runs were made then for each of these configurations and for both maps.

Tables 10, 11 and 12 present the results for the best configurations of each algorithm in the particular map and the results for the configuration gained from simulation data. Moreover, five-point summaries are depicted in Fig. 3.

Since the VFH+ algorithm wasn't able to complete the whole *Map 1*, an additional starting point has been placed after the narrow part of the passage (see Fig. 2a). The data are thus split into two sets of results. Table 10 presents

Table 10. *Map 1*. Results for the real robot, when using the first starting point. A, B, C are the best configurations from the initial testing, sim stands for the best configuration from simulation evaluation.

Algorithm	Configuration	t_{exp}	t_{min}	t_{max}	Success rate
DWA	**A**	53.478	52.171	54.896	100 %
	B	53.860	51.830	56.792	100 %
	C	58.337	55.530	60.868	95 %
	sim	57.833	55.928	60.781	100 %
SND	A	61.441	59.680	67.977	100 %
	B	60.937	56.670	65.888	100 %
	C	63.321	61.117	68.186	100 %
	sim	63.055	57.268	67.715	100 %

Table 11. *Map 1*. Results for the real robot, when using the second starting point. A, B, C are the best configurations from the initial testing, sim stands for the best configuration from simulation evaluation.

Algorithm	Configuration	t_{exp}	t_{min}	t_{max}	Success rate
DWA	A	33.058	30.561	34.543	95 %
	B	33.456	30.418	35.402	100 %
	C	32.340	30.939	34.405	100 %
	sim	32.321	30.972	33.907	100 %
SND	A	37.602	35.856	39.933	95 %
	B	37.690	36.370	39.404	100 %
	C	37.071	35.358	37.884	100 %
	sim	37.249	35.557	39.390	100 %
VFH+	A	37.707	34.508	41.228	100 %
	B	37.502	34.106	40.962	100 %
	C	36.469	25.398	40.708	100 %
	sim	46.867	34.561	182.435	90 %

Table 12. *Map 2.* Results for the real robot. A, G, B are the best configurations from the initial testing, sim stands for the best configuration from simulation evaluation.

Algorithm	Configuration	t_{exp}	t_{min}	t_{max}	Success rate
DWA	**A**	143.153	124.298	156.942	95 %
	G	144.866	111.429	197.131	95 %
	B	153.975	131.620	167.875	90 %
	sim	174.318	141.168	206.722	80 %
SND	**A**	119.462	116.555	123.733	100 %
	G	120.788	117.771	129.183	100 %
	D	119.949	117.774	126.956	100 %
	sim	140.640	133.426	147.559	95 %

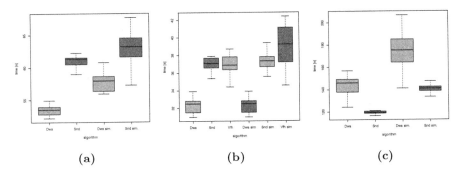

(a)	(b)	(c)

Fig. 3. Graphic comparison of times achieved by each algorithm. (a) *Map 1*, the first starting point, (b) *Map 1*, the second starting point, (c) *Map 2*.

values when the first starting point was chosen and it contains only the results of the DWA and SND algorithms. Table 11 then contains results for all three algorithms traversing the trajectory starting from the second starting point.

The SND algorithm is more reliable and faster in narrow passages than the DWA driver. On the contrary, the DWA driver is faster than the other two approaches when used in open areas. The VFH+ controller was successfully used only in environments, which don't contain narrow passages. In wider environments VFH+ achieved results similar to the other two controllers.

3.3 Discussion

In general, the SND driver has proved to be the most reliable both in simulations and experiments. The DWA algorithm had equal results only when used in environments wider than twice the diameter of the robot.

The choice of the algorithm with best achieved times depends on the environment. The SND controller would be the best choice in narrow environments while the DWA algorithm could be recommended for environments with wider passages.

Both the SND and DWA algorithms should be easy to use. They have only a few parameters tu be tuned and since these parameters are related to the robot radius, it is easy to determine how to set particular parameters, even for an unskilled user.

The VFH+ algorithm is inferior to other two controllers in both reliability and speed. Its parameters in Player/Stage were originally set for a different robot and the description of the parameters is insufficient for a proper recalibration by someone unfamiliar to the driver.

4 Conclusion

The paper presents a comparison of three obstacle avoidance algorithms in a simulated environment and with a real robot in the SyRotek system. Over 20.000 simulations in a simulator and 120 hrs of experiments with a real robot of the SyRoTek system were made to find the best configurations for the drivers implementing the algorithms and to compare the algorithms.

After the best parameter configurations were found, a set of experiments was made to gain the results needed for the comparison of the controllers. The comparison proved the SND driver to be the most reliable one. The SND algorithm also achieved the best time results in narrow environments. The DWA controller was slightly inferior to SND in narrow environments, but in wider environments it proved to have equal results in reliability and equal or superior time results. The VFH+ controller was shown to be insufficient for the use in narrow environments. It doesn't offer any advantages over the other two controllers and its use was accompanied with several difficulties.

Acknowledgments. This work has been supported by the Technology Agency of the Czech Republic under the project no. TE01020197 "Centre for Applied Cybernetics".

References

1. Borenstein, J., Koren, Y.: The vector field histogram - fast obstacle avoidance for mobile robots. IEEE Trans. Robot. Autom. **7**(3), 278–288 (1991)
2. Chudoba, J., Faigl, J., Kulich, M., Košnar, K., Krajník, T., Přeučil, L.: A technical solution of a robotic e-learning system in the SyRoTek project. In: International Conference Compututer Supported Education, pp. 412–417. INSTICC Press (2011)
3. Durham, J., Bullo, F.: Smooth nearness-diagram navigation. In: IEEE/RSJ International Conference on Intelligent Robots and Systems, pp. 690–695, September 2008
4. Fox, D., Burgard, W., Thrun, S.: The dynamic window approach to collision avoidance. IEEE Robot. Autom. Mag. **4**(1), 23–33 (1997)
5. Gerkey, B.P., Vaughan, R.T., Howard, A.: The player/stage project: tools for multi-robot and distributed sensor systems. In: Proceedings of the 11th International Conference on Advanced Robotics, pp. 317–323 (2003)

6. Ingrand, F., Ghallab, M.: Robotics and artificial intelligence: a perspective on deliberation functions. AI Commun. **27**(1), 63–80 (2014). http://dl.acm.org/citation.cfm?id=2594611.2594619

7. Kulich, M., Chudoba, J., Kosnar, K., Krajnik, T., Faigl, J., Preucil, L.: SyRoTek - distance teaching of mobile robotics. IEEE Trans. Educ. **56**(1), 18–23 (2013)

8. Kulich, M., Chudoba, J., Přeučil, L.: Practical applications and experiments with the SyRoTek platform. In: Modelling and Simulation for Autonomous Systems (2015 to appear)

9. Minguez, J., Montano, L.: Nearness diagram (ND) navigation: collision avoidance in troublesome scenarios. IEEE Trans. Robot. Autom. **20**(1), 45–59 (2004)

10. Ulrich, I., Borenstein, J.: VFH+: reliable obstacle avoidance for fast mobile robots. In: Proceedings of IEEE International Conference on Robotics and Automation, vol. 2, pp. 1572–1577, May 1998

Exploration Mobile Robot for Coal Mines

Petr Novák[1(✉)], Ján Babjak[1], Tomáš Kot[1], Petr Olivka[1], and Wojciech Moczulski[2]

[1] Department of Robotics, Faculty of Mechanical Engineering,
VŠB-Technical University Ostrava, 17. listopadu 15, Ostrava, Czech Republic
petr.novak@vsb.cz
[2] Institute of Fundamentals of Machine Design, Silesian University of Technology,
Gliwice, Poland

Abstract. This paper describes a Main Control System (MCS) and 3D map subsystem of the mobile robot TELERESCUER for inspecting coal mine areas affected by catastrophic events. It is carried out in a framework of a EU programme of the Research Fund for Coal and Steel under the grant agreement No. RFCR-CT-2014-00002. The interesting problem is to applicate the very demanding safe requirements of ATEX on the design of the control system including its communication with other robot subsystems. Due to a very innovative and advanced HMI the system allows the rescuer to operate the robot as if he were at the very center point of the scene of the robot's operation.6 This project is solved by consortium of: Silesian University of Technology (Poland), VSB – Technical University of Ostrava (Czech Republic), AITEMIN (Spain), SIMMERSION GMBH (Austria) and SKYTECH RESEARCH (Poland).

Keywords: Robot · TELERESCUER · Coal mine · ATEX · Intrinsic safety

1 Introduction

Despite constant improvement of mining technology and ever more comprehensive knowledge of the geological composition of coal resources, there are still, although rare, catastrophes that happen to coal mines. Among them explosions of methane and coal dust, as well as endogenous fires are encountered. Once such a disaster occurs, teams of very high rained and well-equipped rescuers start to operate in order to save people trapped or injured by the accident, and then to cope with the fire itself. Human rescuers are allowed to enter the restricted area only if several values of critical parameters are achieved, including methane content and temperature. It is easy to imagine how dangerous such missions are.

By the middle 2014 the project titled "System for virtual TELEportation of RESCUER for inspecting coal mine areas affected by catastrophic events (TELERESCUER)" is carried out in a framework of an EU programme of the Research Fund for Coal and Steel under the grant agreement No. RFCR-CT-2014-00002. This project is solved by consortium of: Silesian University of Technology (Poland), VSB – Technical University of Ostrava (Czech Republic), AITEMIN/Carlos III University of Madrid (Spain), SIMMERSION GMBH (Austria) and SKYTECH RESEARCH (Poland) [4, 5, 12, 13].

© Springer International Publishing Switzerland 2015
J. Hodicky (Ed.): MESAS 2015, LNCS 9055, pp. 209–215, 2015.
DOI: 10.1007/978-3-319-22383-4_16

2   Telerescuer

The goal of this project is to develop a system for the virtual teleportation (or virtual immersion) of rescuers to the subterranean areas of a coal mine that have been closed due to a catastrophic event within them. Next application can be exploration and 3D map building of the old mining entries without actual maps and abandoned mines.

The UV TELERESCUER will be equipped with sensors and video cameras (standard and IR) with respect to special conditions of working surroundings. A breakthrough in the operation of such UVs will depend on the real possibility of the virtual immersion – or virtual teleportation – of the rescuer to the area of operation, which will be achieved by combining of the R&D topics:

- An optimized mechanical structure of the mechatronic carrier of the UV for loco-motion in environments with a variety of obstacles 4
- A broadband communication system with a range of more than 500 m in a closed subterranean space from the dam up to a mining disaster site;
- An effective control system for the UV;
- A sensory system for collecting data and signals from the area affected by the cata-strophic failure;
- A System and methods for building 3D maps of an unknown environment and for autonomous navigation in a known environment;
- A knowledge-based methodology and system for the virtual immersion (teleporta-tion) of the rescuer in a hazardous and inaccessible subterranean space affected by a catastrophic event;
- Methods for the realistic simulation of the operations of a rescuer virtually immersed in an environment to be efficiently implemented by a very realistic simulator 5.

2.1   Explosive Atmospheres

Gases, vapours, mists and dusts can all form explosive atmospheres with air. Hazardous area classification is used to identify places where, because of the potential for an explo-sive atmosphere, special precautions over sources of ignition are needed to prevent fires and explosions 1. Hazardous area classification should be carried out as an integral part of the risk assessment to identify places (or areas) where controls over ignition sources are needed (hazardous places) and also those places where they are not (non-hazardous places).

Hazardous places are classified in terms of Group, Category and Zone on the basis of the frequency and duration of the occurrence of an explosive atmosphere. Here descibed system falls into underground mines - Group I 3.

Category M1 (Very high level of protection) - Equipment in this category is required to remain functional with an explosive atmosphere present, high integrity of protection for mining equipment. Two fault conditions.

Category M2 (High level of protection) - This equipment is intended to be de-ener-gised in the event of an explosive atmosphere forming, reliability concept of protection for mining equipment.

There are three basic methods of protection—explosion containment, segregation and prevention. For detailed information see e.g. [14].

For our purposes the next basic and widely often methods are not suitable for MCS due to:

Flameproof Enclosure "d" IEC 60 079-1 – size, big weight, special connectors.

Pressurized Apparatus "p" IEC 60 079-3 – complexity, necessity of the Pressure cylinder of Inert gas,

(*This solution was used by Australian company CSIRO on the mobile robot Numbat, but newly this protection is not for M1 longer*)

Oil Immersion "o" IEC 60 079-6 – not applicable (size, weight).

Powder Filling "q" IEC 60 079-5 – not applicable.

On the base of study and analysing standards mentioned above and recommendation of the Physical-Technical Testing Institute Ostrava 2 the MCS´s designed protection is combination of intrinsic safety and encapsulation. UV TELERESCUER is designing for strictest M1 Category at all, but some parts will have to work only at M2 - primary subsystem for 3D map building based on 3D scanner. In the case of methane occurs their energising will be automatically switched off.

2.2   Main Control System

Requirements for MCS platform is very complex (manage semi-autonomous navigation, analyses of the 3D scan data acquisition, fusing of the clouds of points; communicate with others subsystem – such as motion or sensor). For this reason we chose PC based platform. On the Fig. 1 the schematic diagram of the main UV subsystems is presented. The basic tasks (simplified) of MCS are:

- Control motion of the UV [11].
- Control positioning (tilt and turn) of cameras of the vision subsystem and control of the auxiliary lights. The video transmission is realized directly by telecommunication subsystem, out of MCS [12, 13].
- Data acquisition of the sensory subsystems and their particular evaluation.
- Data acquisition of the 3D map building subsystem – save data for 3D maps, simplification of the information about UV surroundings – obstacle detection and providing its to subsystem of the autonomous behaviour.
- Autonomous operation – on the base information 3D map, IMU and sensory subsystems [7, 12, 13].

It is evident, that requirements on the MCS are pretty challenging – high computing power and low energy consumption due to requests of the intrinsic safety. For this purposes the Industrial PC based on newest processor family Intel Core-M was chosen. There are some reasons for it: brand new CPU (Q3/2014), Low TPD – 4.5 W (it can by even reduced to 3 W), designed for passive cooling (like tablets), and widely used operating system, sufficient amount and kinds of communication interfaces, affordable design software (MS Visual Studio). The both low energy consumption of the PC based on Core-M processor with only passive cooling are optimal for ATEX standard implementation based on encapsulation and intrinsic safety.

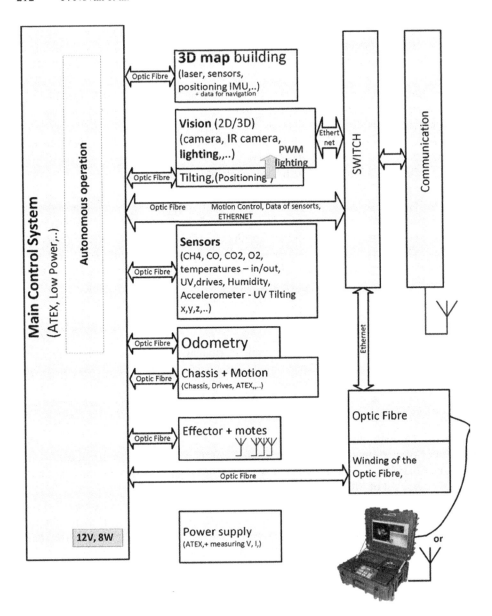

Fig. 1. Schematic diagram of all main TELERESCUER's subsystems

For communication with others subsystem we use optical fibre communication according standard EN 60079-28 Explosive atmospheres - Part 28: Protection of equipment and transmission systems using optical radiation. This is ideal solution for easier implementation of the intrinsically safety connection between subsystems of UV TELE-RESCUER [2]. This way there all electronic subsystems of UV TELERESCUER (3D map, sensory, telecommunication, motion) are separated and can communicate with MCS at 3 Mb/s speed, what is meeting to requirements.

2.3   3D Map Building

The source of data for 3D map building is 3D laser scanner.

The 3D laser scanner is composed from commercial 2D laser scanner. The suitable laser for mining corridor must be able measure black surface with very low reflection of the light. Suitable laser scanner can be selected from the product line of two great producers of laser scanner. One producer is Hokuyo and the second is Sick.

On the base of the real tests in coal mine we chose laser scanner LMS111 for outdoor usage. Its features were founded as satisfactory for measuring even in coal seam.

2D laser scanner is mounted on step motor and rotated in the axis perpendicular to inner axis of the laser rotation. The resulting device measures surroundings in spherical coordinates - two angles and one distance. These measured data can be easily transformed to more usual 3D coordinates. This measuring method was tested on a prototype device.

The result of that measuring is a point cloud. More point clouds have to be connected together. Point cloud can be easy processed by special algorithm called voxelization. This algorithm transforms points to small cubes, reduces and unifies density of point clouds.

The result of voxelization is similar to 2D map represented in grid. This 2D map is composed from three types of small squares. The first type represents free space. The second type of squares is obstacles. The third type is unmeasured space.

The same representation is possible in 3D. But maps are not composed from squares, but they are composed from cubes. All cubes have the same size.

However, 3D map representation by small cubes is very space consuming. Therefore 3D map must be represented in more efficient form. That form is structure octree.

The octree is special form of tree, where the space is dividing to 8 smaller parts - cubes (8 quadrants). All cubes are then repeatedly divided to 8 cubes. This process repeat until required size of smallest cube is achieved.

Octree 3D map is very efficient method of 3D map representation. Nowadays this method is used in many projects for robots navigation.

The octree map representation allows quick search of neighbours, efficient data indexing in data files and division of space to smallest part, where is not necessary to use whole map. This representation gives the possibility to create simpler 2D map for quick navigation. 3D representation can be cut in selected plane and the result will be simple 2D occupancy grid.

Scanning Speed.   The main parameter determining speed of scanning is required resolution. To achieve the same resolution in horizontal and vertical plane, it is necessary to rotate laser scanner in the same size of steps as steps of laser beam, which are 0.5 or $0.25°$ (for actually used scanner Sick LMS111).

The second important factor for 3D scanner speed is frequency of scanning of the laser scanner. This parameter is 25 or 50 Hz.

Now it is possible to compute the required time of scanning for the known angle range $180°$ of scanner rotation and the selected resolution.

$$time = \frac{180}{resolution \cdot frequency} \ [s] \tag{1}$$

The possible combinations are presented in Table 1.

Table 1. 3DScan time for selected resolution (one cloud only!)

Scan time [s]		Resolution [°]	
		0.25	0.5
Scanner frequency [Hz]	25	28.8	14.4
	50	14.4	7.2

The described system of the 3D map building based on the 2D laser scanner SICK LMS111 and controlled by Raspberry Pi was tested in the coal mine Krolowa Luiza in Poland (February 2015). The real scene of the Photo of the turning in the Coal mine and its 3D image, obtained by laser scanner, are presented in the Fig. 2.

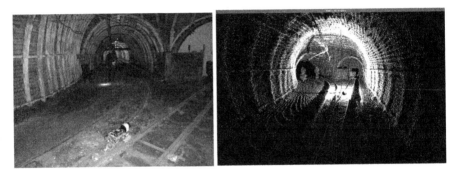

Fig. 2. Photo of the turning in the Coal mine and 3D view on the turning surroundings

3   Conclusion

This paper deals with design of control system of mobile robot for coal mines. In first caption are described working conditions and requirements for this mobile robotic system. In next captions is described restriction from international standards related to coal mines machines design and suggest concept to control. This solution provides safe communication (related to explosive atmospheres). At the close the 3D map building subsystem was described including tests obtained in real mine conditions. This work is related to project "System of the mobile robot TELERESCUER for inspecting coal mine areas affected by catastrophic events", No. RFCR-CT-2014-00002 (ID: 631117, EU, Coal & Steel).

Acknowledgment. The authors thank the European Commission - Research Fund for Coal and Steel for support this project "System of the mobile robot TELERESCUER for inspecting coal mine areas affected by catastrophic events".

References

1. ATEX Directive. http://ec.europa.eu/enterprise/sectors/mechanical/index_en.htm
2. http://ftzu.cz/en/
3. EN 60079-0 Explosive atmospheres - Part 0: Equipment - General requirements
4. Moczulski, W., et al.: System for virtual TELEportation of RESCUER for inspecting coal mine areas affected by catastrophic events. TECHNICAL ANNEX, of the project application (2014)
5. Moczulski, W., Cyran, K., Novak, P., Rodriguez, A., Januszka, M.: TeleRescuer - A Concept of a System for Teleimmersion of a Rescuer to Areas of Coal Mines Affected by Catastrophes. VI Międzynarodowa Konferencja Systemy Mechatroniczne Pojazdów i Maszyn Roboczych (2014)
6. Murphy, R., Kravitz, J., Stover, S., Shoureshi, R.: Mobile robots in mine rescue and recovery. IEEE Robot. Autom. Mag. **16**, 91–103 (2009)
7. Thruny, S., Hahnel, D.: A system for volumetric robotic mapping of abandoned mines. In: Proceedings of ICRA (2003)
8. Rong, X., Song, R., Song, X., Li, Y.: Mechanism and explosion-proof design for a coal mine detection robot. Procedia Eng. **15**, 100–104 (2011)
9. Novák, P., Babjak, J.: Roof support control in longwall technology. In: 14th Coal Operators Conference. University of Wollongong, Australia, 12–14 February 2014, pp. 34–41. ISBN 978 1 925100 02 0
10. Olivka, P.: Sensory Subsystem of the Mobile Robot, doctoral thesis (2014)
11. Babjak, J., Kot, T., Polák, D.: Control System of the Rescue and Fire Extingusihing Robot Hardy. Acta technica corviniensis – Bulletin of engineering (2013). ISSN 2067–3809
12. Novák, P., Babjak, J., Kot, T., Moczulski, W.: Control System of the Mobile Robot TELERESCUER, Applied Mechanics and Materials – to be published (2015)
13. Moczulski, W., Cyran, K., Mostyn, V., Novak, P., Rodriguez, A.: TeleRescuer – A System for Virtual Teleportation of a Rescuer to the Areas of Coal Mines Affected by Catastrophes. MMAR 2015, to be published
14. Gus, H.: Elias Dealing With The ATEX Directive. (Moore Industries International, Inc.) (2008). www.miinet.com

A Generic Testing Framework for Test Driven Development of Robotic Systems

Ali Paikan$^{(\boxtimes)}$, Silvio Traversaro, Francesco Nori, and Lorenzo Natale

Istituto Italiano di Tecnologia (IIT), Genova, Italy
{ali.paikan,silvio.traversaro,francesco.nori,lorenzo.natale}@iit.it

Abstract. This paper proposes a generic framework for test driven development of robotic systems. The framework provides functionalities for developing and running unit tests in a language and middleware independent manner. Tests are developed as independent plug-ins to be loaded and executed by an automated tool. Moreover, a fixture manager prepares the setup (e.g., running robot drivers or simulator) and actively monitors that all the required resources are available before and during the execution of the tests. These functionalities effectively accelerate the development process and cover different levels of robotic system testing. The paper describes the framework and provides realistic examples to show how it has been used to support software development on our robotic platform.

Keywords: Robot testing framework · Unit testing · Test-driven development · Software engineering · Robotics

1 Introduction

Autonomous robots have evolved in complex systems that are increasingly difficult to engineer and develop. A possible approach to tame such complexity is to divide the system into simpler units that are independently developed, tested and integrated at a later stage. Further testing is consequently performed on the whole system; this may trigger re-development or debugging of the individual components in an iterative process. This strategy is known as the test-driven development [3] and it has gained increasing attention as one of the core extreme programming practices. Proper application of this technique requires (i) alternating writing tests and developing functional code in small and rapid iterations and (ii) executing tests automatically to ensure that modifications to existing code (new components, bug fixes or new features) do not disrupt existing functionalities.

Developers have created varieties of tools for supporting test-driven development. These frameworks usually focus on providing support for a specific programming language or for automating unit test execution. For example JUnit [10] is a unit testing framework for Java based on the xUnit [11] test patterns. AUnit [2] is a set of Ada packages based on the xUnit family of unit testing framework which is intended to make it easy to develop and run unit tests.

© Springer International Publishing Switzerland 2015
J. Hodicky (Ed.): MESAS 2015, LNCS 9055, pp. 216–225, 2015.
DOI: 10.1007/978-3-319-22383-4_17

The framework supports easy composition of sets of unit tests to provide flexibility in determining what tests to run for a given purpose. CppUnit [5] is another implementation of the xUnit pattern which supports writing unit tests for C as well as C++ with minimal source modification. It also provides a graphical user interface for monitoring test execution and facilities for generating test results in XML format. Google Test [7] is a multi-platform unit testing library for the C++ programming language, based on the xUnit architecture. It allows for developing different types of tests such as unit tests, integration tests and acceptance tests. The framework also includes a graphical test runner that executes the test binaries.

A unit is the smallest possible testable software component. There is some debate about what exactly constitutes a unit test [9]. For robotic systems a testable unit can be a piece of code, a software component, a driver or even a hardware component such as a sensor or an actuator. A robot testing framework should support different levels of tests, i.e.: component interface tests, integration tests, stress tests and ideally system (application) tests [1]. Tests should be performed on the real robots and on simulation (the latter is a fundamental requisite, it gives more control on the environment and allows to perform fully automated testing). This implies that the framework should be able to setup the required resources (i.e., fixture), like, for example, running drivers to control the motors, executing the simulator and/or possible preparatory routines (e.g. for calibration). Equally importantly, the framework should monitor that these resources remain functional during the execution of the tests, offering hooks to handle failure appropriately (i.e. restarting the robot, performing parking routines, etc.). This is a fundamental requirement for robotics which is not supported by the available testing frameworks. Finally, robotic applications rely on various languages, software libraries and middlewares such as YARP [12], ROS [15] and OROCOS [4]. The testing framework should therefore be designed to offer maximum flexibility to the user in terms of language, dependencies and middleware of choice.

This article proposes the Robot Testing Framework (RTF)[1], a generic testing framework for test driven development of robotic systems. The framework provides functionalities for developing and running unit tests in a language and middleware independent way. Individual tests are developed as independent plug-ins (i.e., using scripting languages or built as dynamically loadable libraries) that are loaded and executed by an automated test runner. A fixture manager prepares the setup (e.g., running the robot drivers or the simulator and its interfaces) and actively monitors that all the dependencies for running the tests remain functional during their execution. These functionalities along with other facilities such as the test result collector, result formatter and remote interface allow for rapid development of tests that cover the various testing levels of robotic systems.

2   Robot Testing Framework

The RTF architecture is based on the well–known xUnit test patterns, which includes a test runner, test result formatters and a test fixtures manager.

---

[1] The source code and documentation of the RTF can be accessed on-line at http://robotology.github.io/robot-testing/index.html.

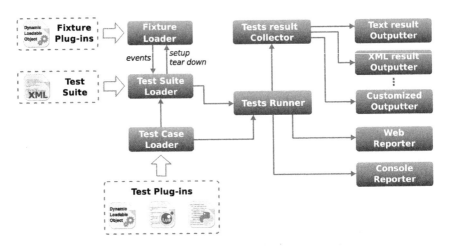

Fig. 1. The architecture of the robot testing framework.

In addition it provides functionalities for defining test cases (i.e. unit tests), suits and assertions. However, to fulfill the requirements of robotic systems, the RTF design provides abstraction levels for the platform (i.e. operating system), the middleware and the programing language. Moreover, RTF provides functionalities for managing complex fixtures which support stress testing at the level of individual components (robot hardware like sensors or actuators) as well as integrated (sub) systems.

Figure 1 demonstrates the main components of the RTF architecture. Test cases can be developed as independent plug-ins using scripting languages or can be built as dynamically loadable libraries. The plug-ins are loaded by the Test Case Loader and are executed by the Test Runner. Test cases can also be grouped in different test suites which are represented using XML. In the latter case, the Test Suite Loader parses the XML file and, using the Test Case Loaders, it loads the corresponding test plug-ins. Each test suit can optionally have a fixture manager which is implemented as a separate plug-in (which is loaded by the Fixture Loader). This fixture plug-in is responsible for setting up the fixture and informing the Test Suite Loader when the fixture fails (e.g. crashes). In this case, the Test Suite Loader restarts the fixture and resumes execution of the remaining test cases. In Sect. 2.3 we describe an example of a fixture plug-in which has been implemented for the YARP middleware. The result of the tests can be monitored from the console (through the Console Reporter) or remotely from a Web browser (through the Web Reporter). The Test Result Collector allows storing data in different formats (for example Fig. 1 shows two components for storing output in text format or XML, Text result Outputter and XML Result Outputter respectively).

2.1 Middleware and Language Abstraction

Within the robotic community, researchers have been developing a large number of software components using different robotic middlewares and varieties of software libraries. Test cases for those components have the same dependencies. To be as generic as possible, an ideal testing framework should allow unit tests to be developed independently and without posing conflicting constraints due to their dependencies.

Middleware independency in RTF is achieved by allowing unit tests to be implemented as independent plug-ins. Each plug-in can be separately compiled and built with the required libraries. This approach separates dependencies between different tests. The test driven development paradigm requires writing automated tests in small and rapid iterations. Therefore, it is important that test development is done easily and with minimal amount of programming. The RTF provides features that allow to easily develop and run the test case plug-ins for different platforms. The following example demonstrates an implementation of a test plug-in that checks a generic sensor using the YARP middleware[2].

An example of implementing a test case plug-in using C++

```
#include <TestCase.h>
// include test-dependent libraries ...
#include <yarp/os/all.h>

// prepare the plugin
PREPARE_PLUGIN(SensorTest)

class SensorTest : public RTF::TestCase {
    yarp::os::BufferedPort<yarp::sig::Vector> port;

public:
    // initialization goes here...
    virtual bool setup(int argc, char** argv) {
        RTF_ASSERT_ERROR_IF(port.open("/sensor"),
                            "Failed to open the port!");
        // intialize the rest ...
        return true;
    }

    // test implementation goes here
    virtual void run() {
        RTF_TEST_REPORT("Reading sensors...");
        yarp::sig::Vector *data = port.read();
        RTF_TEST_CHECK(data, "reading sensor error!");
        RTF_TEST_CHECK(data->size() == 6, "sensor size error!");
    }
}
```

---

[2] In YARP data from generic sensors are published and read from Port objects. BufferedPort is a specialization of Port that support streaming operations.

```
    // finalization goes here...
    virtual void tearDown(){
        port.close();
    }
};
```

As demonstrated in the listing, a test case in RTF requires only to write a few lines of code. This example is written using the C++ language. A test case is an instance of a class that derives from the abstract RTF::TestCase class; the developer is required only to fill the run() method with the test functional code. Optionally the test can specify its own context (i.e. a fixture) which can be prepared in the setup() method. This method is called to initialize the context before executing the test functional code (run()). Similarly the tearDown() method is called to terminate the context after running the test. The PREPARE_PLUGIN macro adds the required code for generating the plug-in. The RTF also provides macros for error assertion and condition checking. During test execution these macros generate detailed information which are uniformly formatted to be stored or reported to the user.

Unlike most of the available unit testing frameworks, RTF does not enforce adoption of a single programming language. Indeed the framework provides a clean and simple abstraction layer for developing test case plug-ins using different scripting languages. The following listing demonstrates an example for testing an encoder using the Lua [8] programing language and the YARP middleware.

An example of implementing a test case plug-in using Lua

```
--import test-dependent libraries ...
require("yarp")

-- initialization goes here...
TestCase.setup = function(parameters)
    TestCase.setName("EncoderTest")
    port = yarp.BufferedPortBottle()
    if port:open("/encoder") ~= true then
        TestCase.assertError("Failed to open the port!")
    end
    -- intialize the rest ...
    return true
end

-- test implementation goes here
TestCase.run = function()
    TestCase.testReport("Reading encoder...")
    local data = port:read()
    TestCase.testCheck(data ~= nil, "reading encoder error.")
end
```

```
-- finalization goes here...
TestCase.tearDown = function()
    port:close()
end
```

This example is similar to the example of implementing a test case using C++. The above script, simply opens a YARP port and checks whether robot encoder data is available or not. The test functional code is implemented in the function `TestCase.run()` whereas initialization and termination of fixtures are done in the functions `TestCase.setup()` and `tearDown()` respectively. Similarly to the C++ example, error assertions and condition checking functions are also available for Lua.

2.2 Test Suites

A test suite is a set of test cases which share the same test fixture [11]. In RTF a set of test cases (plug-ins) can be grouped as a test suite using an XML file and executed using the test runner. This allows the unit tests to be easily organized in different test suites which are easy to maintain and extend. the following listing shows an example of a test suite (called `BasicChecking`) that checks a sensor and an encoder using the test cases described in Sect. 2.1.

An example of a RTF test suite

```
<?xml version="1.0" encoding="UTF-8"?>
<suit name="BasicChecking">
    <description> checking the robot </description>
    <environment> simulator </environment>
    <fixture param="--launch sim.xml"> MyFixtureManager </fixture>

    <!-- add the unit plug-ins -->
    <test type="dll" param=""> SensorTest </test>
    <test type="lua" param=""> EncoderTest </test>
    ...
</suit>
```

Two test cases (`SensorTest` and `EncoderTest`) are added to the test suite using the `<test>` tags; the property `type` specifies the type of the plug-in (e.g., dll or lua for C++ and Lua respectively). Each test case can optionally have parameters (i.e. `param="..."`) which can be accessed inside the test's `setup()` method for its initialization. The `<environment>` tag can specify a set of parameters which form a common *environment* for the test cases in the suite. Using these variables test cases can be quickly adapted and re-used for execution in different situations (i.e. real robot versus simulator). As previously discussed a test suite has a fixture manager (specified by the `<fixture>` tag) which prepares the test contexts for the unit tests. Fixture managers are also plug-ins so that different implementations can exist for different platforms (i.e. operating systems and/or middleware). The following section provides more details about the Fixture Manager.

2.3 Fixture Manager Plug-In

System tests in robotics require execution of a complex fixture which provides the set of basic functionalities for running the tests (i.e. low-level software components for interfacing with the robot or the simulator, etc.). Importantly the fixture should be monitored during the execution of the tests to ensure robustness against failures. We decided to implement the fixture manager as a separate plug-in to avoid reimplementing or simply interfering with the deployment policy of the robotic framework of choice. Middlewares usually have their own policies for configuring and deploying components and executing applications. For example, Orocos components are compiled as dynamic loadable libraries, configured using XML files and launched using the Orocos component deployer (i.e., deployer-corba). ROS components (nodes) are configured using launch files and executed by the roslaunch toolset. In the YARP middleware the yarpmanager [14] that gives users the possibility to execute and monitor the lifecycle of applications from an XML description file[3]. In short an application XML file contains the necessary information for configuring and launching the individual executables (called modules in YARP terminology) using the yarpmanager. The framework provides a rich set of the functionalities such as launching executables on a cluster of computers, monitoring their execution and recovering programs from failure. The following example demonstrates the implementation (pseudo-code) of a fixture manager plug-in which uses the yarpmanager libraries to set up and monitor a test fixture.

An example of implementing the fixture manager plug-in for the YARP middleware

```
#include <FixtureManager.h>
#include <yarp/manager/manager.h>
PREPARE_FIXTURE_PLUGIN(MyFixtureManager) // prepare the plug-in

class MyFixtureManager : public RTF::FixtureManager,
                                 yarp::Manager {
public:
    virtual bool setup(int argc, char** argv) {
        // load the application and run all the modules
        yarp::Manager::loadApplication(...);
        RTF_ASSERT_ERROR_IF(yarp::Manager::run(),
                        "failed to run!");
        // monitor the modules execution
        yarp::Manager::enableWatchDog();
        return true;
    }
```

---

[3] Please refer to http://wiki.icub.org/yarpdoc/yarpmanager.html for the structure and syntax of the YARP application description file.

```
virtual void tearDown() {
    yarp::Manager::stop()   // stop the modules
}

// this is called from the yarp::Manager
// if the execution of the modules fails
virtual void onExecutableFailed(void* which) {
    // inform the test suite/runner
    getDispatcher()->fixtureCollapsed("reason...");
}
};
```

As it is shown in the above example, a fixture manager plug-in is an instance of a class that derives from RTF::FixtureManager and implements the setup() and tearDown() methods. The test runner calls the function setup() before running the test cases in a test suite. In the above example, we use the yarpmanager functionalities (implemented in the yarp::Manager class) to load an XML application file and run the modules that make the corresponding fixture. When terminating the execution of a test suite, the test runner calls tearDown() to tear down the fixture and stop all modules. In the setup() method we also enable the yarpmanager watchdog functionality; this feature monitors the proper execution of all the modules in the fixture. The onExecutableFailed() method is inherited from the yarp::Manager class. The failure of one of these modules (which are monitored in the yarp::Manager) triggers the onExecutableFailed() method; this function notifies the test runner by calling the fixtureCollapsed() function. This event-sender function interrupts the test runner which, in turn, tries to restart the fixture by calling the setup() method. If this operation succeeds the test runner continues execution of the next test case, otherwise, the proper error message is reported.

2.4   Running and Monitoring Unit Tests

As described previously (See also Fig. 1), the test cases (i.e., as shared libraries or scripts) can be uniformly executed using the RTF test runner. The test runner[4] is a multi-platform tool that loads and runs the test cases in various ways. It can run a single test case, multiple test cases from a given path, a full test suite or multiple test suites from a given path. The test runner utility also provides functionalities to monitor the tests execution progress and the results remotely using a Web browser. Moreover, RTF provides web services (via a standard Ajax [6] framework) which can be used for developing any Web-based graphical user interfaces.

Figure 2 shows an example of using the RTF to tests the iCub [13] robot using its simulator. A set of test case plug-ins were developed and grouped in a test suite. The test suite was configured with the YARP fixture manager to

---

[4] Please refer to http://robotology.github.io/robot-testing/documentation/testrunner. html for the documentation of the test runner.

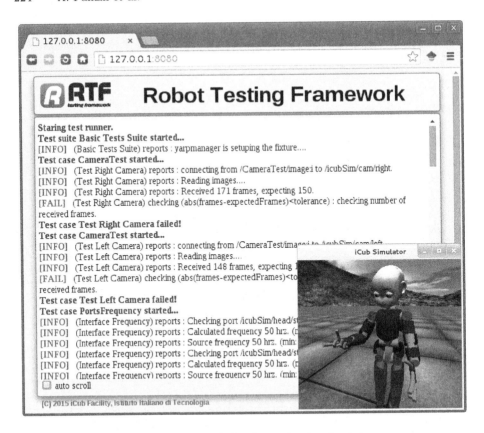

Fig. 2. Testing the iCub robot using its simulator.

run the iCub simulator. The iCub simulator was automatically launched using the YARP fixture manager before executing individual tests. The figure shows the results of the test as they are collected and monitored from a Web browser. The source code of the example and further test units for YARP middleware and iCub robots are available at https://github.com/robotology/icub-tests.

3   Conclusions

In this paper we have described RTF, a generic testing framework for the test driven development of robotic systems. We have discussed the requirements that we consider peculiar to the application and that motivated the development and our design choices, namely: (i) the necessity to separate the dependencies of individual tests to avoid mutual constraints and (ii) the need to deal with different level of testing from individual components to system tests. The latter is particular important because it required to introduce a sophisticated mechanism for dealing with complex test fixtures.

We have described the architecture of RTF by demonstrating different examples. RTF provides functionalities for developing unit tests in a platform, middleware and language independent manner. Middleware and language independency in RTF is achieved by allowing developers to implement and build the unit tests as independent plug-ins using different programming languages. A fixture manager prepares the setup (e.g., running robot interfaces, simulator) and actively monitors that all the requirements for running the tests are satisfied during the execution of the tests. At the moment we are actively developing tests for the iCub humanoid robot and the YARP middleware; using these features we plan to deploy fully automated tests not only for hardware components but also for robot controllers and complex behaviors that rely on the correct execution of different layers of software. These tests are available on the following repository: https://github.com/robotology/icub-tests. The framework has been currently tested with the YARP middleware but it can be used for any test-driven development and other middlewares and robots.

Acknowledgments. The research leading to these results has received funding from the European FP7 ICT project No. 611832 (WALK-MAN) and No. 600716 (CoDyCo).

References

1. Abran, A., Bourque, P., Dupuis, R., Moore, J.W.: Guide to the Software Engineering Body of Knowledge-SWEBOK. IEEE Press, Piscataway (2001)
2. AdaCore: Ada unit testing framework (2012). http://libre.adacore.com/tools/aunit
3. Beck, K.: Test-driven Development: by Example. Addison-Wesley Professional, Boston (2003)
4. Bruyninckx, H.: Open robot control software: the OROCOS project. In: IEEE International Conference on Robotics and Automation. vol. 3, pp. 2523–2528. IEEE (2001)
5. freedesktop: cppUnit test framework (2013). http://freedesktop.org/wiki/Software/cppunit
6. Garrett, J.J., et al.: Ajax: A new approach to web applications (2005)
7. Google: Google C++ Testing Framework (2013). http://code.google.com/p/googletest
8. Ierusalimschy, R., De Figueiredo, L.H., Celes Filho, W.: Lua-an extensible extension language. Softw. Pract. Experience **26**(6), 635–652 (1996)
9. Janzen, D., Saiedian, H.: Test-driven development: concepts, taxonomy, and future direction. Computer **9**, 43–50 (2005)
10. Link, J.: Unit testing in Java: How Tests Drive the Code. Morgan Kaufmann, San Francisco (2003)
11. Meszaros, G.: xUnit Test Patterns: Refactoring Test Code. Pearson Education, Boston (2007)
12. Metta, G., Fitzpatrick, P., Natale, L.: Towards Long-Lived Robot Genes. Elsevier, Amsterdam (2007)
13. Metta, G., Sandini, G., Vernon, D.: The iCub humanoid robot: an open platform for research in embodied cognition. In: Proceedings of the 8th Workshop on Performance Metrics for Intelligent Systems, pp. 50–56 (2008)
14. Paikan, A.: yarpmanager: a way of running and managing multiple programs on a set of machines (2011). http://wiki.icub.org/yarpdoc/yarpmanager.html
15. Quigley, M., Conley, K., Gerkey, B.P., Faust, J., Foote, T., Leibs, J., Wheeler, R., Ng, A.Y.: Ros: an open-source robot operating system. In: ICRA Workshop on Open Source Software (2009)

Multi-objective Aircraft Trajectory Optimization for Weather Avoidance and Emissions Reduction

Gabriella Serafino[⊠]

Selex ES, Ronchi dei Legionari (GO), Gorizia, Italy
gabriella.serafino@selex-es.com

Abstract. In this paper are reported Selex results of the tests, performed in a simulation environment, of multi-object trajectory optimization algorithms, for weather avoidance and emissions reduction. These optimization algorithms, developed under European Clean Sky project, are based on operational research concepts, and they are aimed to calculate optimized trajectory in terms of several emission reduction. The emissions to be simultaneously reduced are CO2, proportional to fuel consumption, NOx and noise. The simultaneous reduction of all these three pollutants is nontrivial as reducing one pollutant can lead to an increase in the others. The chosen approach, to reduce simultaneously the different emissions, is to combine the different pollutant using a linear combination of the weighted emissions. The automatic generation of the optimized trajectories is later validated in realistic flight simulator to verify the results with an easy, safe and economic way.

Keywords: Multi-object trajectory optimization · Emissions reduction · Weather avoidance · Flight simulation

1 Introduction

During the different phase of flight the aircraft engines emit a lot of chemical pollution and Noise.

The most important chemical emissions, connected with greenhouse effect, are carbon dioxide (CO_2), water (H_2O), nitrogen oxides (NOx), and sulfur oxides (SOx) [3].

In accordance to ACARE target [4] and Clean Sky [21] program (that has founded the research reported in the paper), the main emissions to be reduced are NOx, CO2 and Noise.

Inter-dependencies between noise, NOx and CO2 emissions are complex and require careful evaluation prior to regulatory, operational or design decisions [1, 2].

In this paper such emissions are calculated in accordance to the atmospheric and meteorological conditions in climb phase the 3rd April 2013 and it is proposed a method for multi-object trajectory optimization to reduce all the considered emissions.

In the following paragraph, an overview of models and data used to calculate aircraft emissions is provided.

© Springer International Publishing Switzerland 2015
J. Hodicky (Ed.): MESAS 2015, LNCS 9055, pp. 226–239, 2015.
DOI: 10.1007/978-3-319-22383-4_18

2 Aircraft Performances: Model Used and Emission Calculation

To calculate aircraft emissions (CO_2 and NO_x, Noise), EUROCONTROL aircraft BADA model [5], ICAO [6] data and NASA Method2Boeing [7, 20], Doc29 [8], ISA standard and NOAA RAP weather prediction models are used.

2.1 Aircraft Model

The considered aircraft model are based on BADA (Base of Aircraft Data) developed by Eurocontrol [5]. BADA is a collection of ASCII files that specifies aircraft operation performance parameters, airline procedure parameters and aircraft performance summary tables for a huge number of aircraft types.

The most important equations used by the BADA operations performance model is the Total-Energy Model that allows one to compute thrust using the aircraft velocity vector as a function of true airspeed and rate of climb or descent, in addition to other parameters [5]. From thrust computation, BADA model is used to evaluate the fuel flow of the aircraft. For the jet and turboprop engines, the fuel flow is a function of true airspeed and thrust, in addition to other parameters (pressure, humidity, temperature, air density, etc.).

2.2 Emissions Model

The most important emissions, for the greenhouse effect, originate from fuel burned in aircraft engines, are CO_2 and NO_x, but also methane, nitrous oxide and other by-product gases are emitted. The emissions depend on the fuel type, aircraft type, engine type, engine load and flying altitude.

It is common usage to specify the amount of produced emissions of aircraft engines in the form of so-called emission indices (EI). The EI is the mass of a substance in grams per kilogram of fuel burned [9].

The emission model considered is the Boeing method 2 algorithms [7], it is used for the correction of the ICAO [6] engine emission indices in order to take into account weather parameters, such as temperature, pressure and relative humidity at various altitudes.

The Boeing method 2 (BM2) algorithms are used in AEM3 [7] for the adjustment of the ICAO NO_x, CO and HC engine emission indices to consider the changes in temperature, pressure, relative humidity at altitude as well as Mach number. The used methodology to calculate the emissions is reported in [7].

2.3 Noise Model

There are various decibel scales used to define and measure sound in terms that can be related to human perception. An important property of sound is its frequency spectrum - the way that its acoustic energy is distributed across the audible frequency range (from 20 Hz to 20 kHz approximately). Two particular scales are important for aircraft noise - A-weighted sound level and Tone-corrected Perceived Noise Level [8].

The A-weighting is a simple filter applied to sound measurements which applies more or less emphasis to different frequencies to mirror the frequency sensitivity of the human ear at moderate sound energy levels [10]. A-weighted sound level is an almost universally used scale of environmental noise level: it is used for most aircraft noise monitoring applications as well as for the description of road, rail and industrial noise. A-weighted levels are usually denoted as LA. The noise impact assessments that generate the need for noise exposure contours generally rely on A-weighted metrics and these are therefore of primary interest in this guidance; although there are exceptions, Perceived Noise Level applications are confined mostly to aircraft design and certification.

Noise metrics may be thought of as measures of noise 'dose'. There are two main types, describing (1) single noise events (Single Event Noise Metrics) and (2) total noise experienced over longer time periods (Cumulative Noise Metrics).

Noise levels are usually defined at fixed observer locations or mapped as contours (i.e. iso-lines) depicting the area where the specified levels are exceeded. They are used - especially cumulative metrics - in all domains of transportation noise, in our case air-traffic.

These are used to describe the acoustic event caused by a single aircraft movement. Two types are in common usage, both can be determined by measurements as well as by calculations using suitable models (that are the principle subject of this guidance). They are (1) Lmax, based on (1) the maximum sound intensity during the event and (2) LE, based on the total sound energy in the event. The total sound energy can be expressed as the product of the maximum sound intensity and an 'effective duration' of the event.

An aircraft noise event can be described by its observed level-time-history L(t).

These are the maximum (frequency-weighted) sound level Lmax and a duration t. Common definitions of the duration are the effective duration, te, i.e. the duration of a noise event with the constant level Lmax that contains the same sound energy as the noise event described by the level-time-history L(t).

Three corresponding single event metrics of particular importance in aircraft noise [11–13] are (1) Maximum A-weighted Sound level (abbreviation LAmax), (2) Sound Exposure Level (acronym SEL, abbreviation LAE) and (3) Effective Perceived Noise Level (acronym EPNL, abbreviation LEPN).

LAmax is still the favored metric for day to day noise monitoring at airports.

EPNL is the metric for aircraft noise certification limits laid down by ICAO Annex 16 [13], which all new civil aircraft have to meet. Certification gives noise levels at specific points rather than information on the total noise in the general vicinity of the flight path. An indication of the latter is provided by contours of constant single event noise level - so-called "noise footprints". Noise footprints are useful performance indicators for noise abatement flight procedures since they reflect the impact of noise on the ground of the whole flight path (flight altitude, engine power setting and aircraft speed at all points) rather than only from a part of it.

As the decibel scale is logarithmic, long term aircraft noise exposure indices can be logically and conveniently expressed in the form L + K lg N, where L is the average event level (in decibels of some kind), N is the number of events during the time period of interest, and K is a constant which quantifies the relative importance of noise level and number.

2.4   Weather Model

As mentioned before, in order to compute aircraft emissions, it is required the atmospheric distribution, in altitude, of the following meteorological data: density of air, pressure, temperature, relative humidity, wind intensity, speed and direction, and clouds reflectivity. These data, except density of the air, are available through numerical weather models that several weather organizations in the world develop for analysis of current situations and forecasts.

For the tests were used data from USA, available in internet, in particular the Rapid Refresh (RAP) model from NOAA/NCEP operational weather prediction system, running every hour.

The RAP is an atmospheric prediction system that consists primarily of a numerical forecast model and an analysis system to initialize the model. Models run hourly, with analysis and hourly forecasts out to 18 h. RAP files are stored in the GRIB2 file format. GRIB (GRIdded Binary) is a mathematically concise data format commonly used in meteorology to store historical and forecast weather data. The minimum grid spatial resolution is 13 km. In particular, for the tests were used GRIB2 file that uses 37 vertical levels (isobaric levels) with a grid having a horizontal spatial resolution of 20 km with a dimension of 225 × 301 grid cells. From these files were used geo-referred information about pressure, temperature, relative humidity, wind speed and direction, and clouds reflectivity (from on-ground the weather radar data), the other variable needed were taken from ISA standard model.

3   Problem Approach

The approach chosen, to identify better trajectories in terms of emission reduction, to identify the weights to perform multi-object trajectory optimization, to calculate the emissions associated to the selected trajectory, is a graph approach, with algorithms coming from the operational research field (i.e. Djikstra, Pareto Front, etc.).

3.1   Grid of Feasible Trajectories

A graph of a set of feasible trajectories, based on the models considered above (BADA, RAP, ICAO, etc.), for a certain aircraft, in a certain volume of space, in which are available the atmospheric information, is constructed. Such a graph is used to calculated the emissions associated to all the trajectories and to select the better one in terms of emission and noise reduction.

Using aircraft and atmospheric parameters, it is possible to decide whether there is an arc in the graph G. The arch exists if the following four quantities lie within suitable bounds: the distance between 2 adjacent nodes, the bank angle between the 2 adjacent nodes, the speed and the altitude variation. The bounds are determined considering the limitations imposed by the pilot manual [14, 15] of the considered aircraft with the selected engines, so the corresponding maneuvers are safe as they are inside the flight envelope of the selected aircraft for the current meteorological conditions.

The Graph is constructed by means of recursive algorithms: starting from a node, all the nodes that are close to it in the components latitude, longitude and altitude, are checked to see if they can be reached and thus the corresponding arc in the Graph exists [19]. The reachable states are recursively checked against their neighbors, until all the possible arcs of the Graph are created, obtaining a Graph representative, with its arcs, of a set of feasible trajectories under aircraft constraints.

In the proposed Graph it is possible to consider the avoidance of the NO-flight zones, i.e., regions where flights are not permitted due to bad weather conditions, NOTAM or other conflicts. In order to define NO-flight zones, other meteorological data from airborne or ground weather radars, and available forecasts can be used. An arc is removed from the Graph if it intersects the forbidden region on the basis of the corresponding spatial coordinates and a node is removed from the Graph if it's coordinates (latitude, longitude, altitude) are inside the NO-flights zone.

The values of the emissions on the arcs are weighted and linearly combined (the sum of the used weights is equal to 1), the Djikstra algorithm is used to select the optimized trajectory on the graph.

3.2   Pareto Front to Order the Solutions

The optimization of fuel consumption (proportional to $CO2$ emission [1]), NOx and Noise in many cases and phase of flight are concurrent [2, 16], so it is not so easy to find a way to optimize together all the 3 emissions.

In general for a nontrivial multi-objective optimization problem, there does not exist a single solution that simultaneously optimizes each objective. In that case, the objective functions are said to be conflicting, and there exists a (possibly infinite number of) Pareto optimal solutions. A solution is called non-dominated, Pareto optimal, Pareto efficient or non-inferior, if none of the objective functions can be improved in value without impairment in some of the other objective values. Without additional preference information, all Pareto optimal solutions can be considered mathematically equally good (as vectors cannot be ordered completely). The set of Pareto optimal solutions is often called the Pareto front. The methodology proposed in this paper aims at combining the set of emissions computed during a flight phase (the results in climb phase are reported below), considering the aircraft moving from an initial waypoint toward a final waypoint. The emissions, that typically have different units of measurement and different ranges, have been normalized considering the typical range of emissions in that flight phase as described in the ICAO databank for $CO2$ [6, 17], the Boeing model for NOX [7] and the DOC29 [8] for Noise. The aircraft model used in the simulation is derived by BADA database [5] for A320. The optimized trajectory is then used to compute the emissions in climb phase given that set of weights. Changing the set of weights at the input and computing the corresponding optimized trajectories and related emissions, it is possible to determined what set of weights produces non-dominated Pareto solution. Repeating this computation on different flights and different weather condition, it is possible to study what is the best set of weights for that type of aircraft. The main contribution of this paper is to investigate the optimal values for the emissions weights in a specific climb phase. In general more than one solution was obtained and the decision maker, typically the flight company, can choose which pollutant is more important to be reduced in that flight area and determine the cost index.

The Pareto optimal solution method is tested on the climb phase of the trajectory of an A320, NKS724 (from Flightaware), in USA and using the real atmospheric condition contained in a GRIB file downloaded from NOAA database to calculate the emissions. The multi-objective function was computed using a linear combination of the three pollutants: CO_2, NOx and Noise. The weights for each pollutant in the optimization algorithm are chosen between 0.0 and 1.0 and the sum of the three weights is one.

4 Application and Results

In the present paragraph the results obtained applying, the described methods, to an A320, in climb phase in real atmospheric condition, are presented. The considered trajectory is originated from the International Airport of Fort Lauderdale-Hollywood (KFLL) on April 3rd 2013 at about 01 p.m. (UTC): NKS724. It is considered the climb phase, until cruise flight level is reached. The aircraft is A320 and it is supposed that its mass is 64000 kg.

4.1 Meteorological Data

Meteorological data are RAP data of April 3rd 2013 at about 01 p.m (UTC) (available in http://motherlode.ucar.edu:8080/thredds/catalog/fmrc/NCEP/RAP/CONUS_20km/files/catalog.html). Wind speed and direction at altitude equal to about 5000 m are depicted in the following figure (Fig. 1).

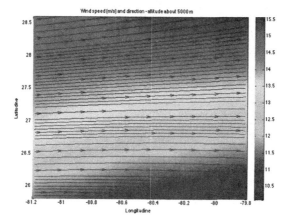

Fig. 1. The wind speed, direction (arrows) and intensity (different colors) at 5000 m (Color figure online).

4.2   Route and Aircraft Emissions

In the following table are reported the starting and ending points of the climb phase of the considered trajectory (Table 1).

Table 1. Initial and final position aircraft position.

	Start Lat (°)	Start Lon (°)	Start Alt (m)	End Lat (°)	End Lon (°)	End Alt (m)
climb	26.08	−80.114	457	28.43	−81.009	11278

In order to compute noise emissions we set two observation points for the climb phase (25.789 N -80.2263E) and (26.0105 N -80.1777E).

The real trajectory is taken from "FlightAware" website (http://flightaware.com).

In the following figure (Fig. 3) the "normal" trajectory (in this case the trajectory of April 3rd 2013 at about 01 p.m.) (blue) and the trajectory of April 4th 2013 (black) are depicted, related to real cloud reflectivity the April 3rd 2013 at about 01 p.m (Fig. 2).

In the following tables, emissions of the aircraft are reported. In Table 2 the estimated emissions of the trajectory in different atmospheric conditions are reported. In particular are calculated the emissions associated to the same trajectory with the real

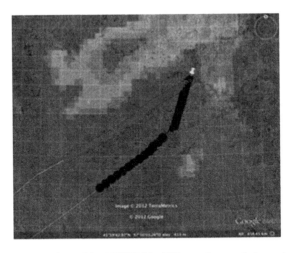

Fig. 2. Two trajectories performed by NKS724 in different days and atmospheric conditions are reported (Color figure online).

Table 2. Estimated emissions of NKS724 in different atmospheric conditions

NKS724	Real meteo	1 h forecast	3 h forecast	6 h forecast
CO2 (kg)	5366	5415	5423	5407
NOx (kg)	62.99	63.76	63.98	63.63
Noise (dB)	53.33	54.18	54.03	54.93

meteorological conditions and the ones forecasted one, three and six hours before, in order to assess the impact of meteorological conditions on the emissions.

The differences in the calculated emissions depend mainly on wind and cloud reflectivity values that are not so reliable for what concern the prediction [18]. On the other side, pressure, temperature and humidity prediction are more reliable in few hour prediction [7].

Then, using the weighted Graph of the feasible trajectories, the emissions associated to different trajectories are calculated. In Table 3 are reported the emissions associated to the real flight (column 2 in Table 3) and the ones associated to optimized trajectories, applying Dijkstra mono or multi-object to select an optimized trajectory in accordance to different criteria (Table 3, in column 3 Dijkstra Mono-objective CO2, 4 Dijkstra Mono-objective NOx, 5 Dijkstra Mono-objective Noise, 6 Dijkstra Multi-objective).

4.3   Comparison of Emissions Associated to Optimized Trajectory Using Pareto

The optimization of more than one objective sets a problem on how to combine the single objectives in order to find a satisfactory solution. In the reported tests the three pollutants (CO2, NOx and Noise) were combined using a linear combination. Varying and combining the different weights it was possible to find a set of solutions "ordered" using the definition of Pareto optimal solutions often called Pareto Front.

This method was tested on the climb phase of the trajectory NKS724. The multi-objective function was computed using a linear combination of the three pollutants: CO2, NOx and Noise. The weights for each pollutant in the objective function used by Dijkstra's algorithm are between 0.0 and 1.0 with a step of 0.1 and the sum of the three weights must be one.

In the following table the solutions found using Dijkstra algorithm are reported. The first three columns report the weights used in the multi-objective function, the

Table 3. NKS724 emissions and emission associated to optimized trajectories.

	FA emit	Dijkstra's algorithm			
		CO2	NOx	Noise	MO2
CO2 (kg)	5366	5364	6249	5365	5365
NOx (kg)	62,99	107	54,41	55	56
Noise (dB)	53.33	53,89	45,21	45,21	51.38

successive three columns report the value of the three pollutants computed. In bold are reported the solutions belonging to the Pareto front.

In the selected case the Minimum Noise emission is connected to the minimum NOx emission (generally both are minimized in case of constant engine regime). On the contrary Fuel consumption (and CO_2 that is proportional by a factor of 3.18) are minimized when NOx and Noise increase.

It is possible to identify some cases (underlined in pink in Table 4) in which there is a limited emission of CO_2 (fuel consumption) in correspondence of low emission of NOx and Noise. Generally, the decision maker (i.e. the flight company) chooses the trajectory emission index and the weights and the criteria to be used to optimize the trajectory.

In case the weather prediction (RAP) are not available, it is possible to use ISA standard model to calculate the emissions associated to the trajectory. In the following paragraph are reported and compared the emissions, associated to the real trajectory of NKS724, calculated with different atmospheric information (RAP, ISA RAP without wind).

4.4   Comparison of Pollutant Emissions Using Different Atmospheric Information RAP (Real Meteorological Data), ISA Data and RAP Without Wind

When real atmospheric data are not available, it is possible to use ISA standard data to calculate trajectory emissions.

Table 4. Emissions associated to multi-object optimized trajectories (underlined in green for the minimum Noise and NOx emission, in cyan for min CO_2; in pink min CO_2 for min NOX and Noise).

Dijkstra's algorithm Pareto Front (climb NKS724)					
CO2 weight	NOx weight	Noise weight	CO2 emission	NOx emission	Noise Emission
0,0	0,0	1,0	10922,48	168,44	39,70
0,0	0,1-1,0	0,9-0,0	6249,07	54,41	45,21
0,1-1,0	0,0-0,4	0,9-0,0	5345,86	107,48	53,89
0,1-0,5	0,1-0,8	0,8-0,0	5364,82	88,10	51,68
0,1	0,6-0,9	0,3-0,0	5425,02	78,24	55,72

In each of the following tables, the values of pollutions emissions for each mono-objective optimized trajectory (Opt CO2, Opt NOx and Opt Noise) are reported with the different percentages respect real atmospheric data. In each table, the third, the fourth and the fifth column identify the optimal trajectory minimizing a specific pollutant (for instance, OptCO2 is the optimal trajectory computed using Q-AI minimizing CO2). In the third, the fourth and the fifth row there are the pollutant emissions for each trajectory computed using RAP data. In the subsequent three rows, there are the emissions computed using ISA formulas and in the last three rows the emissions computed using RAP without wind (Table 5).

Table 5. Emissions associated to mono-object (CO2, NOx, Nose) optimized trajectories calculated with real atmospheric condition (from RAP), ISA standard atmospheric condition and RAP data without wind

NKS 724 Climb phase		Opt CO2	Opt NOx	Opt Noise
RAP	CO2 (Kg)	5345	6249	10922
	NOx (Kg)	107.47	54.4	168.4
	Noise (dB)	53.8	45.2	39.6
ISA	CO2 (Kg)	5219 (−2 %)	6066 (−2 %)	7322 (−32 %)
	NOx (Kg)	87.8 (−18 %)	51.1 (−6 %)	85.7 (−49 %)
	Noise (dB)	72.5 (+25 %)	59.9 (+24 %)	57.9 (+31 %)
RAP without wind	CO2 (Kg)	5234 (−2 %)	6057 (−3 %)	7330 (−32 %)
	NOx (Kg)	105.2 (−2 %)	54 (−0,7 %)	99.4 (−32 %)
	Noise (dB)	72.5 (+25 %)	59.9 (+24 %)	57.9 (+31 %)

From the results, one can note that sometimes the optimal trajectory computed using RAP data is not optimal if emissions are computed using ISA formulas or RAP without wind.

Moreover, the CO2 and NOx emissions computed using ISA formulas are less than the emission computed using RAP data. On the contrary, the noise emissions are greater when computed using ISA formulas. The emissions computed with ISA data and RAP without wind are very similar. This proves that wind has a big impact on pollutant emissions.

4.5   Data Validation in X-plane Flight Simulator

The optimized trajectories have been validated in a X-plane flight simulator (Figs. 3 and 4) in which the correct models of A320 and engines were selected, the trajectories were uploaded in the FMS (flight management system) and the real Grib file contained the considered RAP file was uploaded in the simulation. In this way it was possible to

Fig. 3. X-plane flight simulator in which is visible the selected aircraft (A320) flight along the optimized trajectory (in pink in the picture) uploaded in FMS (Color figure online).

Fig. 4. X-plane flight simulator cockpit view of the selected A320

verify that the aircraft was following the optimized trajectory in the proper way, with little deviations.

The X-plane flight simulator was connected by Ethernet LAN to MARS in weather radar mode simulation (Fig. 5), in which it was uploaded the considered weather situation. In this way it was possible to see the aircraft moving along the trajectory uploaded on the FMS and the weather reflectivity evolving coherently with the aircraft movement. When the weather radar detect the unforeseen weather event (weather reflectivity) it sends this information to the trajectory optimized that automatically updates the graph of feasible trajectories, generates an optimized trajectory and it sends it to the FMS, so the aircraft begins to follow the new updated trajectory.

Fig. 5. MARS weather radar simulator display in which the cloud reflectivity is visualized

5   Conclusion

The tests carried out to define a set of weights for a climb phase of a trajectory have been executed considering the trajectory of NKS724 in climb phase.

In first part of the paper, the models (aircraft, weather, emissions, noise) used to calculate emissions (CO_2, NOx, Noise) associated to the trajectories in different atmospheric conditions were described.

Then the procedure used to perform multi-object trajectory optimization and identify a set of weights, based on operational research concept and Pareto Front was reported.

Later the test results for aircraft NKS724 in climb phase the 3rd April 2013 were provided.

Finally the description of the optimized trajectories validated in a flight simulator connected with a weather radar simulator were reported.

In the chosen case it was possible to notice that NOx and Noise emission were lower with the same choice of emissions weights, and it was possible to identify some set of weights, and so some trajectories, for which CO_2 emission was not so high while NOx and Noise emissions were low.

The choice of the weight of each pollutant remains a strategic decision in standard meteorological conditions; it has to be taken by the decision makers (regulatory agencies, aircraft company, etc.). The choice of the weights could be considered in no-standard meteorological conditions but it is not trivial to define what are no-standard conditions and to find in real cases.

In case the real atmospheric condition are not available, or some parameters are missed, it is possible to use the ISA standard parameters to calculate aircraft emissions. The obtained results seem in percentage similar to the real results for what concern the trajectory optimized for CO2 (and so fuel) and NOx reduction and less accurates for what concern the trajectory optimized for noise reduction, and in general for the Noise emission calculation.

Depending on atmospheric conditions and phase of flight, the emissions associated to the trajectories can be in accordance or concurrent [2], so would be interesting, for future works, to perform a statistic for different flights, in different weather conditions and different phase of flights.

References

1. Jardine, C.N.: Calculating the Environmental Impact of Aviation Emissions. University of Oxford, Oxford (2005)
2. Interdependencies between emissions of CO2, NOx and Noise from aviation, policy discussion paper 9 (2010)
3. Waitz, I., Townsend, J., Cutcher-Gershenfeld, J., Greitzer, E., Kerrebrock, J.: Aviation and the Environment: Report to the United States Congress, Partnership for Air Transp. Noise and Emissions Reduction. MIT, Cambridge (2004)
4. ACARE – Advisory Council for Aeronautics Research in Europe –Strategic Research Agenda 2, vol. 1, October 2004
5. Nuic, A.: User Manual for the base of Aircraft Data (BADA) Revision 3.10, Eurocontrol Experimental Center (2012)
6. International Civil Aviation Organization (ICAO). ICAO Engine Exhaust Emissions Databank, Issue 15-B (2007)
7. The Advanced Emission Model (AEMIII), ver 1.5, Eurocontrol, Validation report (2004)
8. ECAC. CEAC Doc. 29, Report on Standard Method of Computing Noise Contours around Civil Airports, vol. 1: Application guide (2005)
9. Dopelheuer, A.: Aircraft emission parameter modeling. Air Space Europe 2, 34–37 (2000)
10. International Electrotechnical Commission: Sound level meters. IEC 61672-1 (2002)
11. International Organization for Standardization: Acoustics – Procedure for describing aircraft noise heard on the ground. ISO 3891 (1978). (This standard may be replaced or supplemented by a new standard that is currently in draft form as ISO/CD 20906 (2003): Unattended monitoring of aircraft sound in the vicinity of airports)
12. International Organization for Standardization: Acoustics – Description, measurement and assessment of environmental noise – Part 1: Basic quantities and assessment procedures. ISO 1996-1 (2001)
13. International Civil Aviation Organization: International Standards and Recommended Practices, Environmental Protection, Annex 16, vol. I, Aircraft Noise, 4th edn., July 2005
14. Airbus A-320 POH: Pilot's Operating Handbook. http://www.despair.ch/staff/library/thc003.pdf
15. AIRBUS, A318/A319/A320/A321 Flight deck and systems briefing for pilots, Ref . STL 945.7136/97 – Issue 4 (2007)

16. General Aviation Pilot's Guide to preflight Weather Planning, Weather self-briefings, and weather Decision Making; FAA, December 2009

17. Dynamic Cost Indexing, Outline istructions for calculating emissions and associated costs and impacts; C06/1200BE, Imperial College London, 28 August 2008

18. Serafino, G., Bernabò, M., Mininel, S., Stecco, G., Nolich, M., Ukovich, W., Pedroncelli, G., Fanti, M.P.: Effects of weather condition on aircraft emissions in climb phase. In: Digital Avionics Systems Conference (DASC), Williamsburg, VA, USA, pp. 3A6-1–3A6-12, October 2012

19. Fanti, M.P., Mininel, S., Nolich, M., Stecco, G., Ukovich, W., Bernabò, M., Serafino, G.: Flight path optimization for minimizing emissions and avoiding weather hazard. In: ACC, June 2014

20. Baughcum, S.L., Tritz, T.G., Henderson, S.C., Pickett, D.C.: Scheduled Civil Aircraft Emissions Inventories for 1992: Database Development and Analysis, Appendix D: Boeing Method 2 Fuel Flow Methodology Description, Report NASA CR 4700, The Boeing Company (1996)

21. Clean Sky ITD Systems for Green Operations Grant Agreement; MTM

Author Index